Fod
Rio
Janeiro

Fodor's Travel Publications, Inc.
New York and London

ISBN 0-679-01816-6

Fodor's Rio de Janeiro

Editors: Alice Thompson, Denise Nolty
Editorial Contributors: Edwin Taylor, Michael Adams, Dwight V. Gast, David Laskin
Art Director: Fabrizio La Rocca
Cartographer: David Lindroth
Illustrator: Karl Tanner
Cover Photograph: K. Scholz/H. Armstrong Roberts

Design: Vignelli Associates

Special Sales

Fodor's Travel Publications are available at special discounts for bulk purchases (100 copies or more) for sales promotions or premiums. Special editions, including personalized covers, excerpts of existing guides, and corporate imprints, can be created in large quantities for special needs. For more information write to Special Marketing, Fodor's Travel Publications, 201 East 50th St., New York, NY 10022. Inquiries from the United Kingdom should be sent to Fodor's Travel Publications, 30–32 Bedford Square, London WC1B 3SG.

MANUFACTURED IN THE UNITED STATES OF AMERICA
10 9 8 7 6 5 4 3 2 1

Contents

Maps and Plans

Foreword

This is an exciting time for Fodor's, as we continue our program to rewrite, reformat, and redesign all 140 of our guides. Here are just a few of the ambitious new features:

★ Brand-new computer-generated maps locating all the top attractions, hotels, restaurants, and shops

★ A unique system of numbers and legends to help readers move effortlessly between text and maps

★ A new star rating system for hotels and restaurants

★ Restaurant reviews by major food critics around the world

★ Stamped, self-addressed postcards, bound into every guide, give readers a chance to help evaluate hotels and restaurants

★ Complete page redesign for instant retrieval of information

★ FODOR'S CHOICE—Our favorite museums, beaches, cafés, romantic hideaways, festivals, and more

★ HIGHLIGHTS—An insider's look at the most important developments in tourism during the past year

★ TIME OUT—The best and most convenient lunch stops along exploring routes

★ Exclusive background essays create a powerful portrait of each destination

★ A mini-journal for travelers to keep track of their own itineraries and addresses

We wish to express our gratitude to the Brazilian Tourism Board in New York and Rio for their assistance in the preparation of this guidebook, especially to Eliane Freitas and Ana Bravo in New York. We would also like to thank Celina Taylor, Vera Maria Fonseca Rodrigues, and Kristen Christensen for their research work.

While every care has been taken to ensure the accuracy of the information in this guide, the passage of time will always bring change, and consequently, the publisher cannot accept responsibility for errors that may occur.

All prices and opening times quoted here are based on information available to us at press time. Hours and admission fees may change, however, and the prudent traveler will avoid inconvenience by calling ahead.

Fodor's wants to hear about your travel experiences, both pleasant and unpleasant. When a hotel or restaurant fails to live up to its billing, let us know and we will investigate the complaint and revise our entries where the facts warrant it.

Send your letters to the editors of Fodor's Travel Publications, 201 E. 50th Street, New York, NY 10022.

Highlights and Fodor's Choice

Highlights

After reaching a low point in 1987, when Rio barely escaped being put on the U.S. State Department's travel blacklist, the city made a comeback in 1988 and 1989. City officials tackled crime, pollution, and transportation problems, and visitors should see the payoff in 1990.

To combat **street crime** officials have invested in improved security for foreign visitors, including the addition of multilingual staffers to man the police emergency line, 190; the creation of a special 600-man police force to patrol the beach areas; the installation of more telephone-equipped police guard posts along the beaches; and an increased number of plainclothes officers on the beaches, at the airports, and in the port area. In addition, many of the top hotels have hired private security guards to watch over guests.

The nighttime **"string of pearls,"** a trademark of Copacabana Beach for decades, disappeared in 1988, when the city replaced its aging streetlights with a new lighting system along the beachfront drive, Avenida Atlântica. The powerful illumination may have removed some of the surface romance of Copacabana, but it has increased security and brought nightlife back to the beach. Evening soccer and volleyball games now go on beneath the lights, and increasingly cariocas and tourists are rediscovering the pleasure of nighttime promenades on the sand. Speaking of sand, there's good news here, too: At press time an ambitious program is underway to replace Copacabana's dirty sand with 1,350 truckloads of new sand. Officials hope to have the improved beach ready for the start of the 1990 season.

At the end of 1988, work was completed on a long-overdue project on the **Leblon** beachfront that should provide a lasting solution to frequent breakdowns in the area's ocean-outfall sewage system. Pounding waves have broken up the tubes of the system on several occasions, increasing the level of pollution at Leblon and nearby beaches. The tubes have now been placed under the beachfront avenue instead of the beach, thus protecting them from wave action. Expectations at press time were for a marked improvement in the quality of the water.

The city government has finally come up with the funds to proceed with an extension of Rio's **subway system** to the beach neighborhoods of Copacabana and Ipanema. When finished in 1991, the subway will whisk visitors between Ipanema, Copacabana, and downtown in a fraction of the time required today. The subway extension should also improve the city's chaotic traffic situation.

Construction also continues in 1990 on a $250 million second terminal building for Rio's **international airport,** already the largest in South America. The existing terminal, which serves both national and international flights, was designed to handle 7 million passengers annually, a figure that was surpassed in 1986. The new terminal should be in operation by 1992.

After years of neglect, Rio has at last begun to take an interest in preserving its historical past. The city government has created a program called **Cultural Corridor,** which provides fiscal incentives for merchants who restore their buildings. The result has been a remarkable flowering of spick-and-span 19th-century buildings previously lost in the maze of downtown streets and alleys. There are an estimated 1,500 of these structures in the area crisscrossed by Carioca, Uruguaiana, Sete de Setembro, Mercado, and Lapa streets in downtown Rio. Since the program took effect, some 200 of these buildings have been restored, with work under way on another 120. Ornamented facades, delicate iron grillwork, and bright colors are the trademarks of these buildings, most of which are three or four stories tall. The program thus far has been an enormous success, to the extent that the area is now starting to attract tourist groups with the potential of becoming a Rio version of New Orleans's French Quarter. Sadly, however, funding for upkeep of the newly renovated buildings has not been forthcoming, and many are already showing signs of poor maintenance.

Meanwhile, the city's infamous port neighborhood is also undergoing a transformation. Work has started on a major renovation of the **Praça Mauá** area, until now a seedy urban wasteland. The plaza has been expanded and the sidewalks widened to give visitors an enlarged and cleaned-up public square. Next, a nearby port authority building will be converted into a compact shopping area with restaurants. In 1990, a 28-story office building, the **Rio International Business Center,** will be a further complement to the reborn Mauá district. Finally, a few blocks away, the former headquarters of the Bank of Brazil, a six-story building dating from 1880, is being converted into a cultural center with a theater, cinema, and art exhibition halls. When all of this is finished in 1990, downtown Rio will have at last emerged from its own shadows and be able to offer attractive alternatives for the city's tourists.

The year 1989 saw the introduction of a new currency, the ***cruzado novo,*** part of a package aimed at stemming Brazil's relentless inflation. While forecasts of exchange rates through 1990 can't be made with any certainty, indications are that the dollar will remain extremely strong. Great news for travelers in 1989 was the introduction of a new **floating exchange rate** for tourists. This rate, expected to parallel the black market, is an alternative to the artificially low "official" rate and will be available at banks, travel agencies, some hotels, and authorized exchange houses. By presenting their passports, tourists will be able to exchange dollars at this advantageous rate without any of the qualms (or risks) that accompany black market transactions. Visitors should avoid taxi drivers and others offering to buy their dollars.

On the hotel front, the **Rio Sheraton** continues to move ahead with a major $14-million renovation, the latest addition being the smartly revamped **Mirador** restaurant. The restaurant, which boasts magnificent views of Ipanema and Leblon beaches, will feature Italian, German, and seafood buffets on different nights, as well as a traditional Brazilian *feijoada* on Saturday. Scheduled to be concluded shortly is a complete remodeling of the hotel's rooms.

Signs are increasing that Rio is on the verge of a new **hotel construction boom.** The momentum is coming from a new scheme called debt conversion, which permits American, European, and Japanese banks holding Brazilian IOUs to convert these into investments in the Brazilian economy. The program began in 1988, and tourism has been one of the main beneficiaries; as the country's tourism capital, Rio stands to gain the most. Projects under way or on the drawing board include construction of a new $80-million five-star hotel on Copacabana's beachfront drive—Hilton is interested; a luxury hotel-and-resort condominium complex in the Barra da Tijuca, site of Rio's longest and most unspoiled beach; and a $150-million hotel-and-condominium resort near the historical city of Paratí, south of Rio on the Costa Verde.

Tourists visiting Rio can now pick up a diploma in samba dancing. Riotur, the city tourism authority, has launched the **Samba University,** whose "campus" is the Carnival Museum in Rio's Sambadrome, the location of each year's Carnival parade. Classes with 50 participants will be held four afternoons a week, year-round, offering lectures with audiovisuals plus the dance lessons themselves. Offered through travel agents, the university package deal includes a brief show by real samba dancers and a photo of each graduating student in a Carnival costume.

The Tourism Authority's new traveler-assistance line can provide visitors with a variety of information, including activities listings, street directions, and filing complaints with the police. The number is 1516 (outside the city you will need to dial 210 first); the operators are multilingual.

Fodor's Choice

No two people will agree on what makes a perfect vacation, but it's fun and helpful to know what others think. We hope you'll have a chance to experience some of Fodor's Choices yourself while visiting Rio. For detailed information about each entry, refer to the appropriate chapters in this guidebook.

Beaches

Arpoador
Grumari
Ipanema, up the canal that separates it from Leblon
Sugarloaf end of Copacabana, known as Leme
Recreio dos Bandeirantes

Hotels

Inter-Continental Rio *(Very Expensive)*
Rio Palace *(Very Expensive)*
Rio Sheraton *(Very Expensive)*
Leme Palace *(Expensive)*
Ouro Verde *(Expensive)*
Ipanema Inn *(Moderate)*
Miramar Palace *(Moderate)*
Tropical Tourist *(Inexpensive)*

Restaurants

Monseigneur *(Very Expensive)*
Le Saint Honoré *(Very Expensive)*
Valentino's *(Very Expensive)*
Ouro Verde *(Expensive)*
Petronius *(Expensive)*
The Lord Jim Pub *(Moderate)*
Moenda *(Moderate)*
Porcão *(Moderate)*
La Mole *(Inexpensive)*

Romance

Before-dinner drinks at Rio's
Dinner at Le Saint Honoré
Late-afternoon walk on the beach at Ipanema facing Dois
Dois Irmaos Mountain
Drinks at Antonino in the evening or at sunset
Fishermen casting their nets into the sea at Arpoador in the morning
Drinks from the rooftop bar at the Rio Othon Palace

Sunsets

From the rocks at Arpoador
From Sugarloaf
From Corcovado
From anywhere around the lagoon
From São Conrado facing Gávea Mountain
From the bay looking toward the city

Taste Treats

Sunday *cozido* at the Caesar Park Hotel
Saturday *feijoada* at the Rio Sheraton
Crepes suzette at the Ouro Verde
Moqueca at the Quatro Sete Meia
Fresh fruit drinks from fruit-juice bars in Ipanema

Best Viewpoints

Corcovado at any time of day
Lagoon, best in the evening, sunset, or sunrise
Sugarloaf at sunset
Avenida Niemeyer from Leblon to São Conrado
Pedra Bonita from the hang glider platform

After Hours

Late-night supper at Pizzeria Guanabara
Dancing until dawn at Caligola or Hippopotamus
Breakfast at dawn at the Caesar Park or Le Meridien hotels

Metropolitan Rio de Janeiro

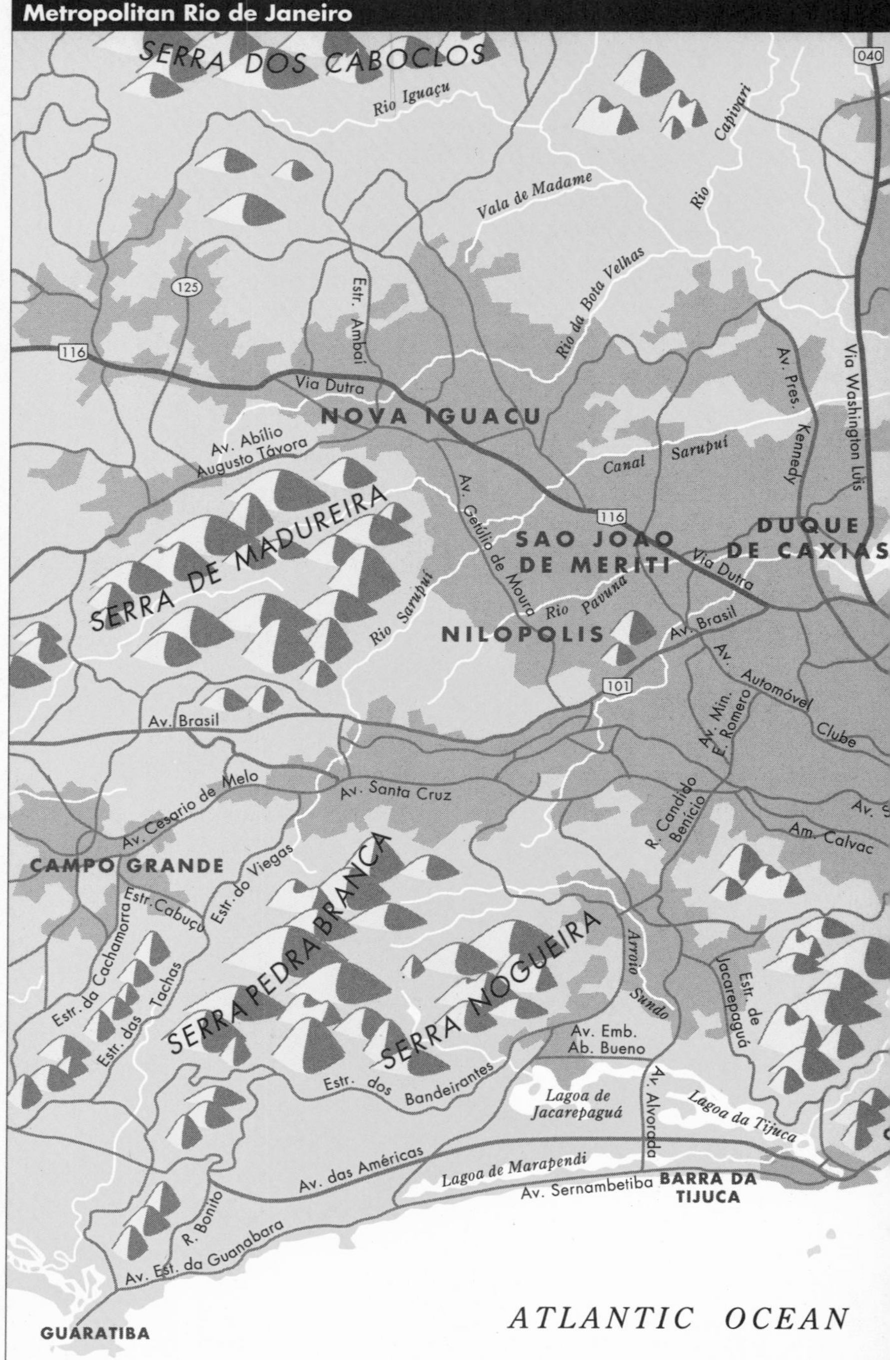

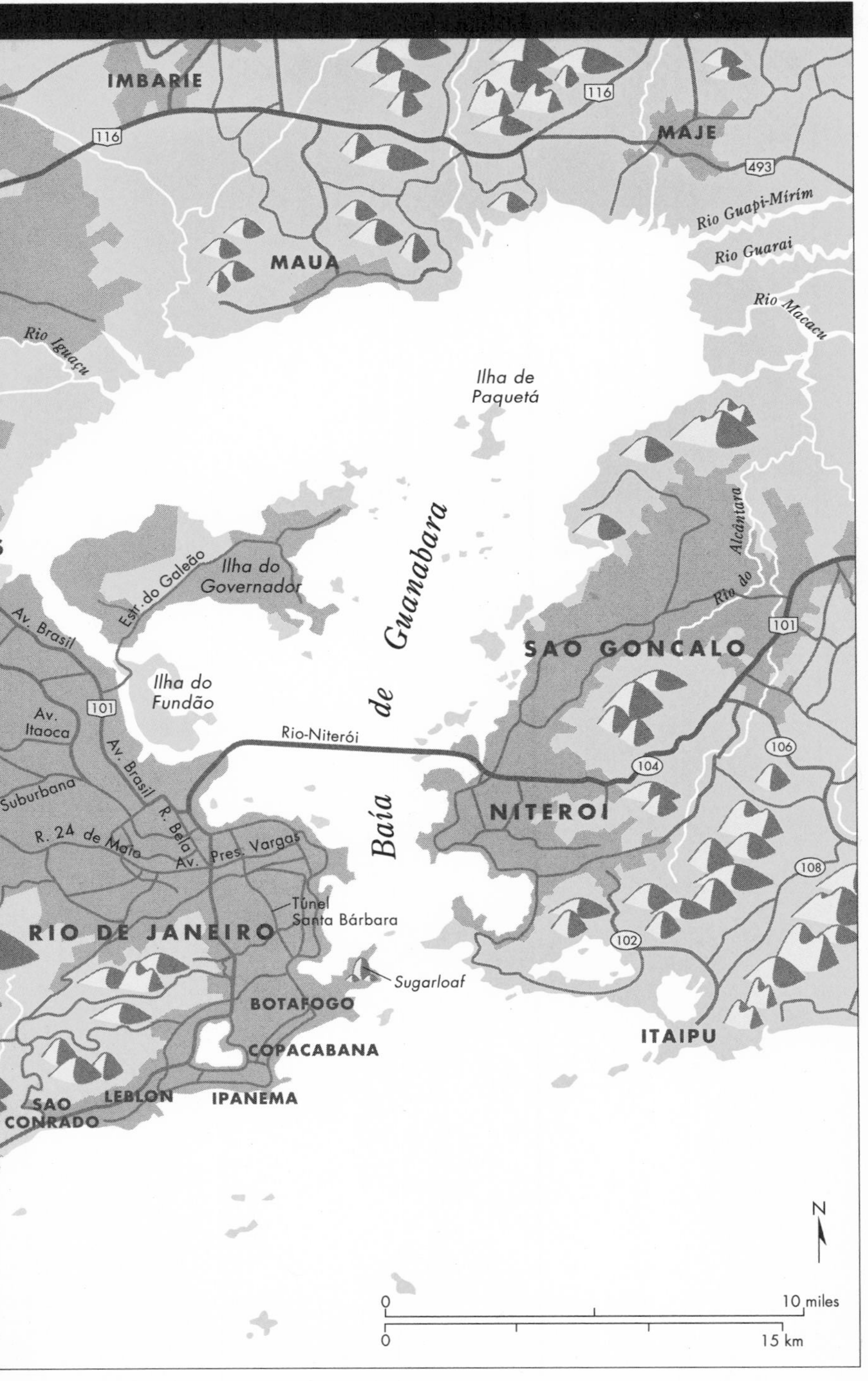

IMBARIE
116
MAJE
493
Rio Guapi-Mirím
Rio Guarai
Rio Macacu
MAUA
Rio Iguaçu
Ilha de Paquetá
Baía de Guanabara
Ilha do Governador
Estr. do Galeão
Alcântara
Rio do
101
SAO GONCALO
Av. Brasil
Ilha do Fundão
Av. Itaoca
Rio-Niterói
106
104
Suburbana
R. Bela
NITEROI
R. 24 de Maio
Av. Pres. Vargas
108
Túnel Santa Bárbara
RIO DE JANEIRO
102
Sugarloaf
BOTAFOGO
ITAIPU
COPACABANA
SAO CONRADO
LEBLON
IPANEMA
N
0
10 miles
0
15 km

Downtown Rio, Ipanema, Copacabana

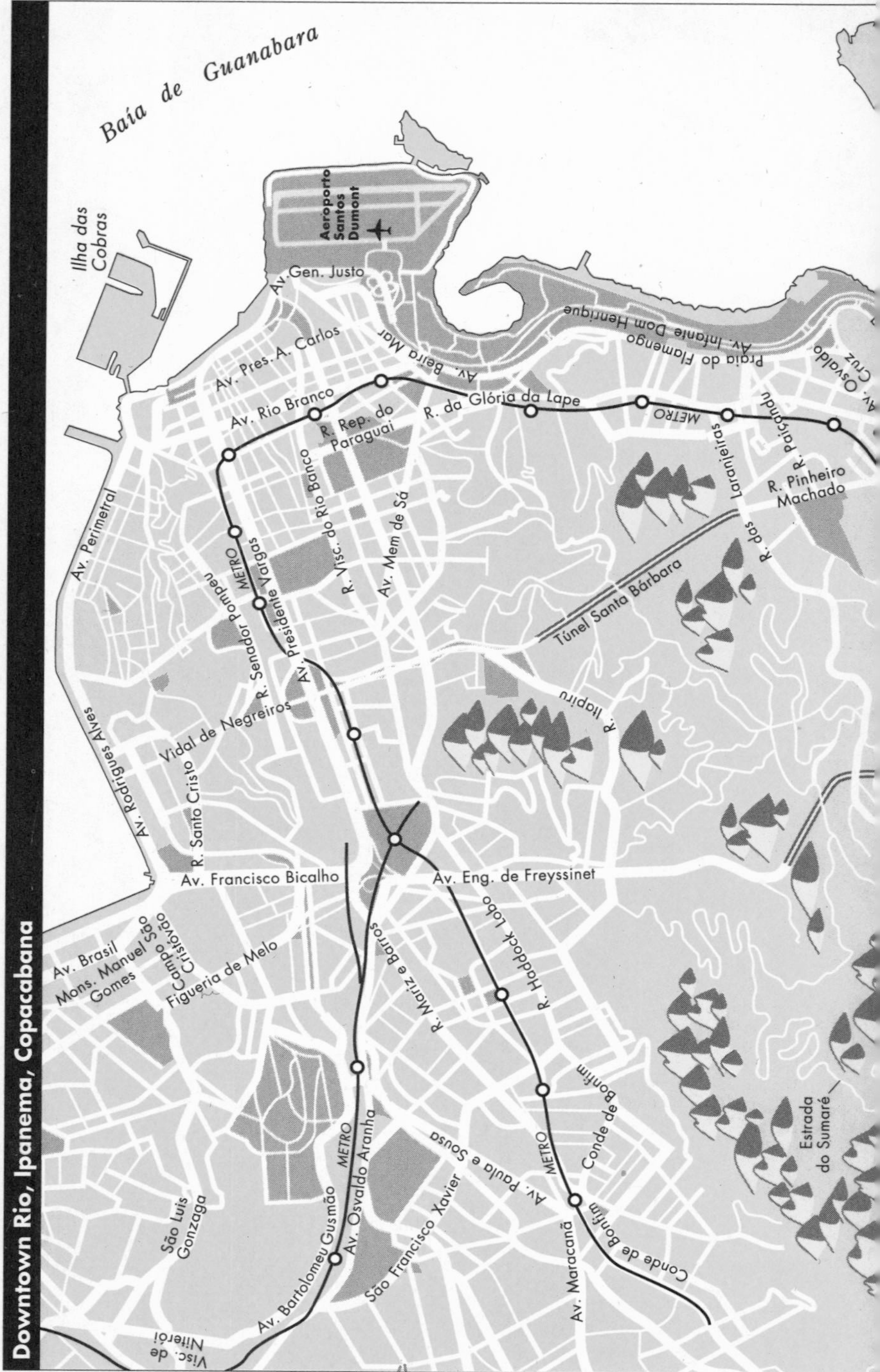

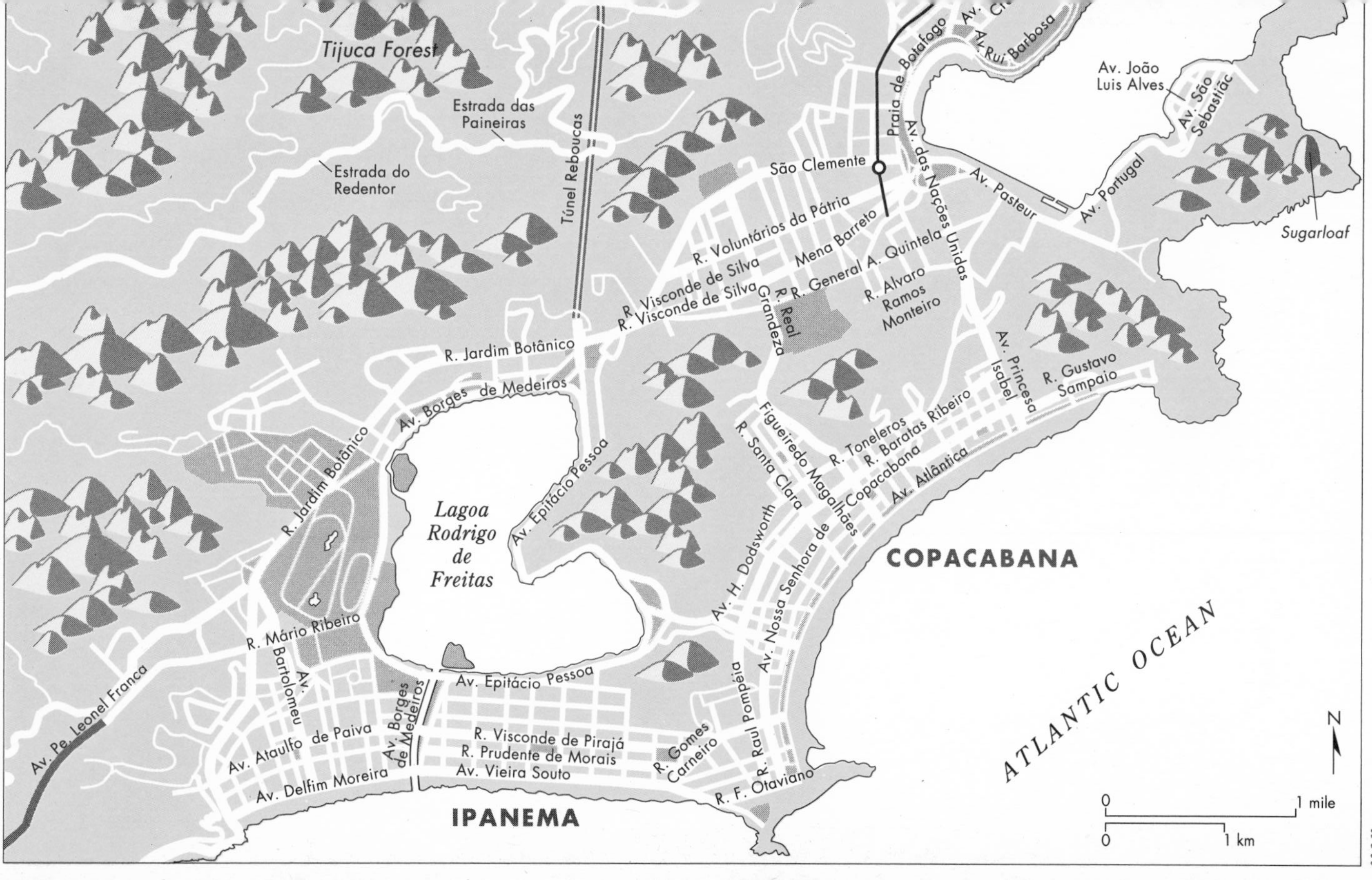
Tijuca Forest
Estrada das Paineiras
Estrada do Redentor
Túnel Rebouças
São Clemente
Praia de Botafogo
Av. Rui Barbosa
Av. João Luis Alves
Av. São Sebastião
Sugarloaf
Av. Portugal
Av. Pasteur
Av. das Nações Unidas
R. Voluntários da Pátria
Mena Barreto
R. General A. Quintela
R. Alvaro Ramos Monteiro
R. Visconde de Silva
R. Visconde de Silva
R. Real Grandeza
R. Jardim Botânico
Av. Borges de Medeiros
Av. Princesa Isabel
R. Gustavo Sampaio
R. Tonelero
R. Barata Ribeiro
R. Copacabana
Av. Atlântica
Figueiredo Magalhães
R. Santa Clara
Av. H. Dodsworth
Av. Nossa Senhora de
Av. Epitácio Pessoa
Lagoa Rodrigo de Freitas
R. Jardim Botânico
R. Mário Ribeiro
Av. Bartolomeu
Av. Epitácio Pessoa
COPACABANA
ATLANTIC OCEAN
Av. Pe. Leonel Franca
Av. Ataulfo de Paiva
Av. Borges de Medeiros
Av. Delfim Moreira
R. Visconde de Pirajá
R. Prudente de Morais
Av. Vieira Souto
R. Gomes Carneiro
R. Raul Pompéia
R. F. Otaviano
IPANEMA
N
0
1 mile
0
1 km

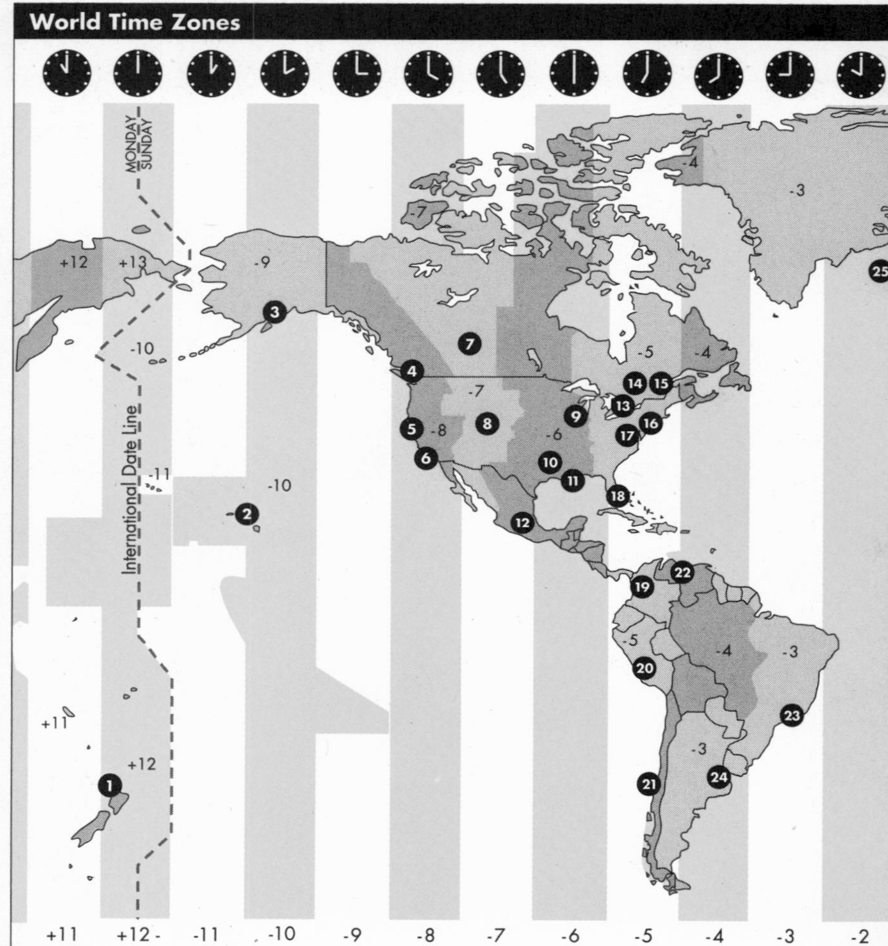

Numbers below vertical bands relate each zone to Greenwich Mean Time (0 hrs.). Local times may differ, as indicated by lightface numbers on the map.

Algiers, **29**
Anchorage, **3**
Athens, **41**
Auckland, **1**
Baghdad, **46**
Bangkok, **50**
Beijing, **54**
Berlin, **34**
Bogotá, **19**
Budapest, **37**
Buenos Aires, **24**
Caracas, **22**
Chicago, **9**
Copenhagen, **33**
Dallas, **10**
Delhi, **48**
Denver, **8**
Djakarta, **53**
Dublin, **26**
Edmonton, **7**
Hong Kong, **56**
Honolulu, **2**
Istanbul, **40**
Jerusalem, **42**
Johannesburg, **44**
Lima, **20**
Lisbon, **28**
London (Greenwich), **27**
Los Angeles, **6**
Madrid, **38**
Manila, **57**

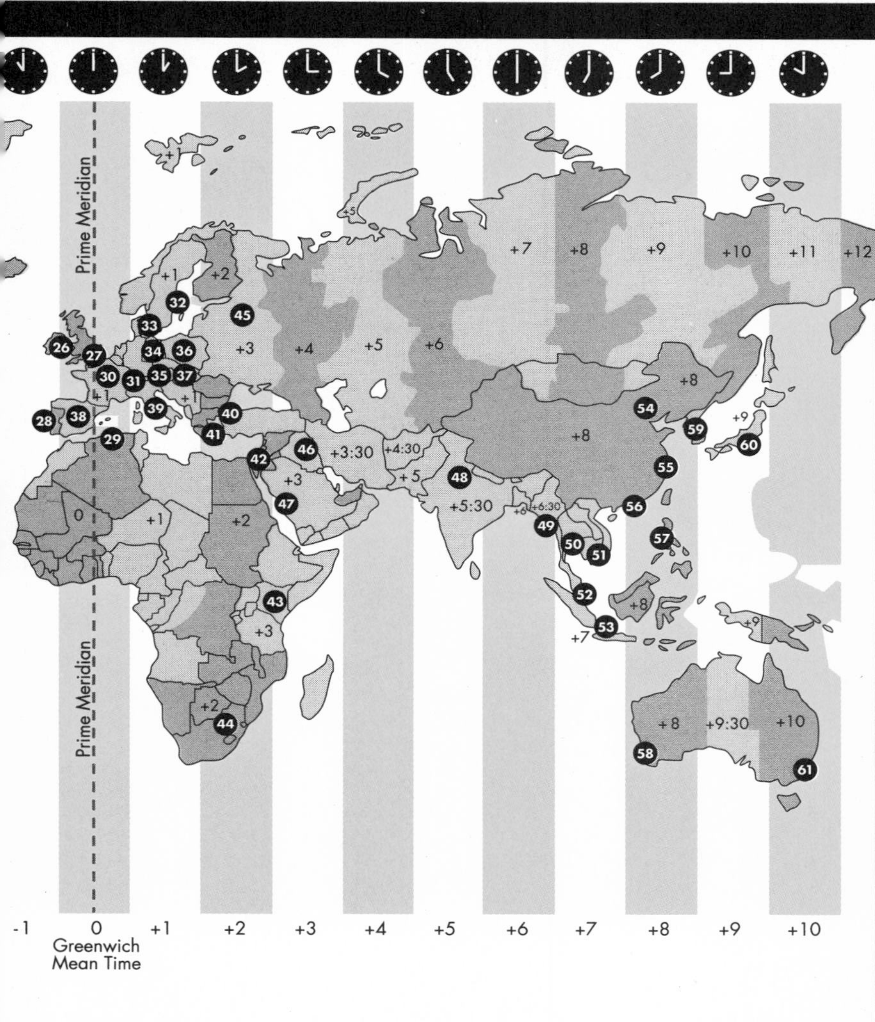

Mecca, **47**
Mexico City, **12**
Miami, **18**
Montreal, **15**
Moscow, **45**
Nairobi, **43**
New Orleans, **11**
New York City, **16**

Ottawa, **14**
Paris, **30**
Perth, **58**
Reykjavík, **25**
Rio de Janeiro, **23**
Rome, **39**
Saigon, **51**

San Francisco, **5**
Santiago, **21**
Seoul, **59**
Shanghai, **55**
Singapore, **52**
Stockholm, **32**
Sydney, **61**
Tokyo, **60**

Toronto, **13**
Vancouver, **4**
Vienna, **35**
Warsaw, **36**
Washington, DC, **17**
Yangon, **49**
Zürich, **31**

Introduction

by Michael Adams

Michael Adams is a New York–based writer whose love of Brazil began several years ago and continues to flourish.

When you first arrive in Rio de Janeiro, think of the journey from airport to hotel as a brief spell of purgatory, minor dues to be paid for entry into what harried Americans will consider heaven. If you've traveled overnight, your tongue can be thick and your eyes bleary, and the initial sights that welcome you—mostly gray, nondescript industrial buildings—are unpromising. But by the time you reach Avenida Atlântica, flanked on one side by white beach and azure sea, and on the other by the pleasure-palace hotels that stand as testimony to the city's eternal lure, your heart will leap with expectation.

Now you're truly in Rio, where the wicked angels and shimmering devils known as cariocas dwell.

While the meaning of "carioca" stretches back into the country's earliest European history (when a Portuguese trading station was known as a "white man's house," or carioca), the word today defines more than birthplace or residence: It represents an ethos of pride and sensuality that is recognized throughout Brazil—if not always kindly. The serious and business-minded Paulistas of São Paulo seem to have a particular aversion to their more pleasure-loving neighbors in Rio. Faced with a typical carioca exhibition of playfulness, braggadocio, or indulgence, the true Paulista is likely to frown and shrug as if to say, "What can you expect?"

But what sparks Paulista exasperation can be a narcotic for the visitor. While in Rio, prepare to have your senses engaged and your inhibitions untied. For the only true way to experience this sun-kissed land is to borrow the carioca spirit. And don't be surprised if you find yourself reluctant to give it back.

What mixture of location, climate, history, and race commingled to create the alchemy that is Rio? Perhaps some mysteries are not meant to be solved. But surely much of the carioca verve comes from the sheer physical splendor of the city: Seemingly endless beaches, sculpted promontories, and the ocean stretching into an infinity that seems to keep the rest of the world very far away.

As if to match nature's own efforts, cariocas strive mightily to be worthy of their surroundings. As descendants of a multitude of ethnic strains—Portuguese, Dutch, African, German, Brazilian Indian—they are a gorgeous, complicated lot, spectacular to behold. And they know it. In Rio, narcissism is a fine art, and for proof, take a walk at any time of day along the ocean. Here both sexes offer lean limbs and tight muscles to the sun and to all appraising eyes, with only a few scraps of brilliant cloth providing a perfunctory nod to modesty. (But nudity? No, no, no. This, you are reminded, is a Catholic country.)

Religious principles do not prevent cariocas from trying to take control over what God has forgotten—or at least allowed to sag. Plastic surgeons in Rio are nearly as common as newsstands in New York, and their handiwork goes a long way in explaining why so many men and women remain beautiful long after nature should have had her due. Youth and beauty are prized as long as time (or money) will allow.

To return to the beaches (as you will, since their draw is magnetic), think of them as an immutable element of carioca life, woven into its fabric like gold in a Chinese tapestry. Choose Copacabana, Ipanema, or Leblon; spread a towel and join the melee. Office workers stretch out on lunch hours, doffing work clothes to reveal bathing suits underneath; strutting, oiled teens carry surfboards and kites; sweating joggers stop to drink sweet fruit juices and gnaw the white flesh of a coconut. Business is conducted here, too, with rolled-up trousers and briefcases shielded from the sand. Bodies are painstakingly molded on parallel bars or in energetic "no hands" volleyball games. If you go to the more remote São Conrado Beach, look up to watch hang gliders float effortlessly from the cliffs, like mythological creatures. Whatever beach you choose, be ready for a turn-on. Sexuality is ever on parade.

For the carioca, a respite from the beach can also mean food and drink, and herein lies an amusing contradiction: They prefer their stomachs flat, but they are also fond of feeding them. The tension between appetite and ego is constant. Lunches can be long, voluble, sybaritic; dinners are late and equally indulgent. On Saturdays, it's *feijoada,* the national dish and a sensualist's dream—great mounds of garlicky pork, black beans, rice, with cool orange slices as a balm for the deliciously spicy assault. Or at a *churrascaria,* a steak house, brisk waiters will bring endless courses of red barbecued meat and sublime side dishes—including hearts of palm almost obscene in their size and texture—until even the most gluttonous will beg for mercy.

The gustatory pleasures of Rio are liquid as well. Take the liquid charge of dynamite known as the *caipirinha,* whose principal ingredient, the potent sugarcane liquor *cachaça,* is wrapped in the silkiness of sugar, lime, and ice. Or *cafèzinho,* bullets of caffeine, each sweetened by what seems half its weight in sugar. Complete a carioca meal and know you're alive.

And, of course, Rio is music. If you think you know Brazilian music from its Stan Getz/João Gilberto onslaught some years back, think again. Oh, you'll hear "The Girl From Ipanema" in Rio, but freed from its elevator-music prison. Strummed poolside by a single guitarist, the song suddenly makes vivid sense, and you'll feel it enter your bones (and you are hereby dared to keep it out of your head as you walk the city or beaches). But make room in your being for all of Rio's music, from the deafening rhythmic samba heard in deliciously tacky nightclubs to the performers creating their own (and more politically oriented) Brazilian musical renaissance.

You'll be seduced by a host of images in Rio: the poetry of hips swaying along sidewalk mosaics; the joyous bustle of vendors at Sunday's Hippie Fair; the tipsy babble of a sidewalk café as latecomers sip their last glass of wine under the stars; the blanket of luminescent lights unfolding beneath Sugarloaf.

Walk through the city at any time and relish the lyrical cascade of the language—difficult to learn but impossible to forget. Conversation is an art here. At its most spirited, it is machine-gun fast, with pitch and emphasis ascending and careening. Yet in its quietest moments, it is a language made for seduction.

Don't worry if you find it difficult to learn the odd nasalities and fricatives of Brazilian Portuguese. The basics—hello, good-bye, thank you—are easy enough, and cariocas get a heavy dose of English via television, movies, and music. Most will delight in sharing their expertise and using some of the most charmingly accented English you'll ever hear.

Perhaps the word most readily applicable to the carioca is intensity, borne of a passionate dedication to life. What else is Carnival but a chance to celebrate the rapture of being alive? Appetites indulged exuberantly throughout the rest of the year become giddy cartoons during Carnival, gross and lively caricatures of gluttony, lust, and colorful exhibitionism. It seems at times that the normal carioca pastimes are merely low-key rehearsals for the carnal glory of Carnival. But no matter what time of year you visit Rio, Carnival is in the air.

Cariocas are pleasure-seekers, without doubt. It may be because they constantly battle the vicissitudes of living in a country where the government is often quirky, inflation runs amok, poverty looms grimly from the hillsides, and natural disaster can wreak destruction in an eye blink. Yet chafing against injustice and strife has turned grit into gemstone. The answer is to glorify life, not despair of it. Ask a Brazilian "How are you?" and the common response is "*Tudo bem.*" Not "I am fine," but "*All* is fine," and nowhere is this attitude more deeply felt than in Rio. The world seen from this vantage point is a beautiful place, despite evidence to the contrary. Here, they seem to say, we are blessed.

And why not? Look up from almost any point in the city, and there, on Corcovado, is Cristo Redentor, Christ the Redeemer. Arms outstretched, the statue of Christ reaches to embrace *o cidade maravilhosa,* offering a gentle benediction to miscreants and scamps, all trespasses and mischief forgiven for the sinners' radiant joy.

1 Essential Information

Before You Go

Government Tourist Offices

For free brochures, an up-to-date calendar of events, and other general information, contact **Embratur, The Brazilian Tourism Office** (551 5th Ave., Suite 421, New York, NY 10176, tel. 212/286–9600). The state of Rio has its own tourism authority, located in downtown Rio. You can pick up several useful publications there once you arrive; if you prefer to call or write ahead, contact **Turisrio** (Rua da Assembléia 10, 7th & 8th Floors, 20011 Rio de Janeiro, RJ, Brazil, tel. 55–021/221–8422).

Tour Groups

Package tours are a good idea if you are willing to trade independence for a guide who knows the language, a fairly solid guarantee that you will see at least the major highlights, and some savings on airfare, hotels, and ground transportation. While there are some fully escorted tours through Rio, Rio-only tours are typically a hybrid of group and independent packages, with transportation between the airport and hotel, some meals, and some sightseeing included, but on a flexible schedule. Listed below is a sampling of tour operators with Rio on their itineraries.

When considering a tour, be sure to find out (1) exactly what expenses are included—particularly tips, taxes, side trips, additional meals, and entertainment; (2) ratings of all hotels on the itinerary and the facilities they offer; (3) cancellation policies for both you and the tour operator; (4) the number of travelers in your group; and (5) if you are traveling alone, the cost of the single supplement. Most tour operators request that bookings be made through a travel agent—in most cases there is no additional charge for this.

General-Interest Tours

Hemphill/Harris Travel (16000 Ventura Blvd., Suite 200, Encino, CA 91436, tel. 800/421–0454 or in CA, 800/252–2103) offers two top-quality escorted tours that include Rio: a 16-day in-depth look at Brazil and a 17-day trip through Brazil, Argentina, Peru, and Ecuador. **American Express** (100 Church St., New York, NY 10007, tel. 800/241–1700 or 212/312–1205), **Abreu Tours** (60 E. 42nd St., New York, NY 10165, tel. 800/223–1580 or 212/661–0555), and **Ladatco Tours** (2220 Coral Way, Miami, FL 33145, tel. 800/327–6162 or in FL, 800/327–9960) all offer escorted tours as well as basically independent packages that include airfare, hotel, ground transportation, half-day sightseeing trips, and breakfasts.

Special-Interest Tours

Adventure

New for 1990 is a lively Brazil tour from **Sobek International** (Box 1089, Angels Camp, CA 95222, tel. 209/736–4524). After taking in Rio's version of wildlife, participants trek, boat, and camp their way through some of the more remote parts of the country.

Carnival

Almost all of the tour operators listed under General-Interest Tours (above) and Package Deals for Independent Travelers (below) put together special Carnival packages. With the demand for accommodations and inflated high-season prices that accompany Carnival, you would do well to book a package, even if you don't usually like to. This is one time tour operator clout particularly pays off—they bring thousands of tourists in year after year, reserve blocks of rooms well in advance, and are much less likely to get bumped by overbooked hotels.

Cruises **Princess Cruises** (2029 Century Park E, Los Angeles, CA 90067, tel. 213/553–1770) and **Sun Line Cruises** (1 Rockefeller Plaza, Suite 315, New York, NY 10020, tel. 800/872–6400 or in NY, 212/397–6400) sail to and from Rio during the spring season. Princess's ship is the big (1,200 passengers), luxurious *Sky Princess;* Sun Line's classy *Stella Solaris* carries about half as many guests.

Cruise lines also offer special Carnival packages that include tickets to special events.

Natural History **Questers Tours and Travel** (257 Park Ave. S, New York, NY 10010, tel. 212/673–3120) contrasts urban Rio with Brazil's unique wilderness areas. Treks to observe such creatures as giant anteaters, hyacinth macaws, and several rare species of monkey in a wide variety of settings precede an exploration of Rio, its famous beaches, and surrounding mountains.

Package Deals for Independent Travelers

American Express, Abreu Tours, and **Ladatco Tours** (*see* General-Interest Tours, above, for addresses) all offer packages including airfare, hotel, transportation to and from your hotel, a half-day sightseeing tour, and some meals (typically breakfasts). **Melia Tours** (450 7th Ave., Suite 1803, New York, NY 10123, tel. 212/967–6565) offers a similar deal, with the option of adding on stops at other Brazilian and South American cities. **Varig Brazilian Airlines** (tel. 800/468–2744 or 212/340–0360) offers airfare/hotel packages through several different tour operators—they can refer you to the one nearest to you.

Tips for British Travelers

Tourist Information Contact the **Brazilian Tourist Office** (32 Green St., London W1, tel. 01/499–0877) for brochures and tourist information.

Insurance We recommend that to cover health and driving mishaps, you insure yourself with **Europ Assistance** (252 High St., Croydon, Surrey CRO INF, tel. 01/680–1234). It is also wise to take out insurance to cover the loss of luggage (although check that such a loss isn't already covered in any existing homeowner's policies you may have). Trip-cancellation insurance is another wise buy. **The Association of British Insurers** (Aldermary House, Queen St., London EC4, tel. 01/248–4477) will give comprehensive advice on all aspects of vacation insurance.

Tour Operators Here is a selection of British companies offering packages to Rio (also contact your travel agent for the latest information):

Bales Tours (Bales House, Barrington Rd., Dorking, Surrey RH4 3EJ, tel. 0306/885–991) offers a 10-day package to Rio, with prices starting at £725.

Kuoni Travel Ltd. (Kuoni House, Dorking, Surrey RH5 3EJ, tel. 0306/740–500) has five-night packages in luxury hotels starting from £666.

South American Experience (c/o Garden Studios, 11 Betterton St., Covent Garden, London WC2H 4BP, tel. 441/379–0344) offers tailor-made holidays in a wide range of price categories.

Sovereign Worldwide (Groundstar House, London Rd., Crawley RH10 2TB, tel. 0293/561–444) has a 14-day "Brazil Roundup" package, with six nights in Rio and stops in Brasília, Manaus, and Salvador. The package price begins at £1,507.

Airlines and Airfares **British Airways** and **Varig Brazilian Airlines** are the only airlines that fly directly from London to Rio; **Canadian Airlines, KLM, British Midland,** and **Air Portugal** are among the other services with indirect flights. At press time (mid-1989), an APEX fare to Rio was £701 in low season, and £734 in high season.

South American Experience (c/o Garden Studios, 11 Betterton St., Covent Garden, London WC2H 4BP, tel. 441/379–0344) offers budget bookings: At press time a flight to Rio on Varig was available for £539.

When to Go

High season in Rio lasts from November to April, December through March being the Brazilian summer. The seasons are conveniently reversed below the equator, so that winter in the Northern Hemisphere corresponds to Brazil's summer. Temperatures at this time are hot, between 85° and 105° F (29°–40° C). Summer is also the rainy season, but the downpours serve to dehumidify the air and give fair-skinned visitors respite from the strong tropical sun. If you need to escape from winter, this time of year is right for you. But remember, the prices, like the temperatures, are highest during this period. Room rates jump, scheduled flights and charter packages increase accordingly, and even prices in restaurants and shops are higher. If you're looking for a bargain, stick to the off-season.

Carnival occurs during the five days preceding Ash Wednesday (February 23–27 in 1990; February 8–12 in 1991). The exact date is variable, depending on the fluctuations of the religious calendar, but the hike in prices (sometimes 200% to 300% for hotel rooms) remains constant. To secure a room in one of the best hotels, independent travelers are advised to book at least a year in advance.

Rio is jammed with tourists and other celebrants during Carnival, so if you don't like crowds consider coming at some other time. Also keep in mind that thousands of *sambistas*, devotees of samba participating in the parade, cannot tend to their regular jobs and stage the show as well. If service isn't up to par, be patient and relax: Most people agree that the pluses of Carnival far outweigh the minuses.

Although not as well-known or widely publicized as Carnival, New Year's Eve in Rio is quite an impressive sight. The major hotels in Copacabana sponsor a massive midnight fireworks display, and many throw elegant parties for their guests. But the most moving experience of the evening takes place on the beach, where African *macumba* (Brazil's version of voodoo) ceremonies take place.

The less frenzied atmosphere of the off-season, combined with cooler temperatures and more economical rates, attracts visitors even more than the galas do. From May to September, the sun still shines, and the 70° F (21° C) temperatures make sightseeing especially pleasant for those not used to tropical heat. In addition, winter initiates Rio's cultural season of art, dance, and music festivals, permitting the off-season traveler to experience Brazil's cultural variety as well as the easygoing pace of the carioca lifestyle. Simply put, during the off-season there is a greater opportunity to experience the Brazilian's rather than the tourist's Rio.

Climate The following are average daily maximum and minimum temperatures for Rio de Janeiro.

Jan.	84F	29C	**May**	77F	25C	**Sept.**	75F	24C
	73	23		66	19		65	18
Feb.	85F	29C	**June**	76F	24C	**Oct.**	77F	25C
	73	23		64	18		66	19
Mar.	83F	28C	**July**	75F	24C	**Nov.**	79F	26C
	72	22		63	17		68	20
Apr.	80F	27C	**Aug.**	76F	24C	**Dec.**	82F	28C
	69	21		64	18		71	22

Updated hourly weather information in 235 cities around the world—180 of them in the United States—is only a phone call away. Telephone numbers for **WeatherTrak** in the 12 cities where the service is available may be obtained by calling 800/247–3282. A taped message will tell you to dial the three-digit access code to any of the 235 destinations. The code is either the area code (in the United States) or the first three letters of the foreign city. For a list of all access codes send a stamped, self-addressed envelope to Cities, Box 7000, Dallas, TX 75209. For further information, phone 214/869–3035 or 800/247–3282.

Festivals and Seasonal Events

Dec. 31/Jan. 1: New Year's Eve festivities include the usual parties and fireworks. The elegant *Reveillon* bashes thrown by many hotels, with traditional gourmet foods and dancing to live music until dawn, offer a distinctly local flavor. Down on Copacabana Beach, ritual music pulses as the priestesses known as *filhas de santo* light candles and set up small shrines to Iemanjá, goddess of the sea. Dressed all in white, they set afloat boats carrying candles, white lilies, perfume, and other gifts; if the waves take a boat out to sea, the sender's wishes for the year will come true.

Jan.: The Rio Fashion Show proves that Rio takes fashion every bit as seriously as New York and Paris. And with Brazilian currency considerably weaker than French francs, this might well be the place to splurge on couture. Even if you're not in Rio to shop, the show provides a glamorous preview of styles to come.

Feb.: Carnival is the biggest party of the year, a no-holds-barred week of singing and dancing in the streets. All work closes down as residents don wild costumes and splashy floats parade through the city carrying samba dancers and musicians. Hotels and clubs sponsor posh Carnival balls. At the end of Carnival, the champion samba schools parade, showing off their moves, at the Sambadrome. Expect the city to be jammed and the hotels to be booked as much as a year in advance.

Mar.–Apr.: Easter is celebrated throughout Brazil with passion plays, processions, and reenactments of significant events in the life of Christ. Most of the major events take place outside of Rio; your travel agent or tour operator should be able to arrange an excursion for you if you are interested.

Apr.: Brazilian Formula I Grand Prix is held at Rio's Jacarepagua racetrack. This is world-class auto racing, a colorful, pulse-quickening, noisy event.

May: Festo do Divino (Festival of the Divine Holy Spirit) was first introduced in Brazil in the 16th century. Held in nearby Paratí—a historic city dedicated as a national monument because of its carefully preserved colonial architecture—the celebration features folk singing and dancing, colorful decorations, and a sizable fair.

June: Festas Juninas (The June Festivals) honor a string of saints (chief among them are St. John, St. Peter, and St. Anthony) with traditional parties and fairs.

June: The Rio Fashion Show this month is the winter version of the popular cause célèbre.

Aug.: Grande Premio Brasil is Brazil's biggest horse race, featuring competitors from several countries. The Grande Premio is traditionally held on the first Sunday in August at the Jockey Club. A big-money sweepstakes is also held, adding to the tense flow of betting money.

Aug.: Rio Marathon has been attracting a growing number of international marathoners. This annual event is set against the lively backdrop of the city's landmarks.

Aug.–Sept.: Free Jazz Festival, a week-long paean to the many styles of jazz, presents an eclectic mix of local, national, and international musicians.

Nov.: FestRio, The International Film, Television, and Video Festival, provides valuable exposure for Brazilian filmmakers, and attempts to balance commercial films with more experimental works. Full-length and short films from around the world—many shown for the first time—are screened and compete for a variety of honors. Screenings are typically open to the public.

Nov.: Feira da Providência, held in the Riocentro convention facility, is a gigantic showcase for regional produce, cooking, and handicrafts. This is a good opportunity to sample foods from different regions of Brazil, pick up gifts, and soak up some native energy.

What to Pack

Pack light: Baggage carts are scarce at airports, and luggage restrictions on international flights are tight. Chances are you'll wish you had come with a half-empty suitcase because you'll find knockout fashions in all the shops. Summer, December through March, can be very hot and humid; winter, May through October, is comfortable, with temperatures rarely dipping below 70° F.

Clothing For summer, take casual, loose-fitting clothes made of natural fabrics to see you through days of heat and high humidity. Walking shorts, T-shirts, slacks, and sundresses are acceptable everywhere. Casual comfort is the only clothing commandment in Rio. In Copacabana, Ipanema, and Leblon, people walk around in bikinis on and off the beach. In the business district and for sightseeing, wear slacks and cotton jerseys or casual dresses in the summer. Bring a jacket or sweater for the air-conditioned restaurants and hotels. In winter, bring lightweight clothes that can be layered. Leave the high heels at home: The sidewalks in Rio are made of small tiles that can catch and ruin high heels and trip you as well. Evening wear is casual; few restaurants require jacket and tie for dinner, although lunch in the downtown area can be more formal.

Miscellaneous It's advisable to wear a hat and sun-block lotion while on the beach and while sightseeing during the summer. Bring a spare pair of eyeglasses and sunglasses and an adequate supply of any prescription drugs you may need. You can probably find what you require in the pharmacies, but you may need a local doctor's prescription. Rain and sun alternate with astounding speed, regardless of the season. You probably won't need a raincoat, but an umbrella is a must for the short, intense tropical rainstorms.

Luggage

Carry-on Luggage Passengers on U.S. airlines are limited to two carry-on bags. For a bag you wish to store under the seat, the maximum dimensions are 9 + 14 + 22 inches. For bags that can be hung in a closet or on a luggage rack, the maximum dimensions are 4 + 23 + 45 inches. For bags you wish to store in an overhead bin, the maximum dimensions are 10 + 14 + 36 inches. Any item that exceeds the specified dimensions may be rejected as a carryon and taken as checked baggage. Keep in mind that an airline can adapt the rules to circumstances, so on an especially crowded flight don't be surprised if you are only allowed one carry-on bag.

In addition to the two carryons, you may bring aboard a handbag (pocketbook or purse); an overcoat or wrap; an umbrella; a camera; a reasonable amount of reading material; an infant bag; crutches, a cane, braces, or a prosthetic device; and an infant/child safety seat.

Foreign airlines have slightly different policies. They generally allow only one piece of carry-on luggage in tourist class, in addition to handbags and bags filled with duty-free goods. Passengers in first and business class are also allowed to carry on one garment bag. It is best to call your airline to find out its current policy.

Checked Luggage U.S. airlines allow passengers to check in two suitcases whose total dimensions (length plus width plus height) do not exceed 60 inches. There are no weight restrictions.

Rules governing foreign airlines can vary, so check with your travel agent or the airline before you go. All airlines allow passengers to check in two bags. In general, expect the weight restriction on them to be a maximum of 70 pounds each, and the size restriction on the first bag to be 62 inches total dimensions, and on the second bag, 55 inches total dimensions.

Taking Money Abroad

Traveler's checks and all major U.S. credit cards are widely accepted in Rio. The large hotels, restaurants, and department stores accept cards readily, but some of the smaller restaurants and shops operate on a cash-only basis. In Rio you are always better off paying cash, because your credit card bill will be calculated and charged to your account at the official exchange rate of the day of purchase, which could represent a loss to you of at least 20%, and up to 35% to 40%.

In January 1989, Brazil introduced a new floating exchange rate for tourists. Previously, tourists carrying dollars were obliged to either exchange at the artificially low official rate at hotels and banks or seek out black market operators who could offer a substantially higher rate. Under the new system, banks, travel agents, brokerage houses, some hotels, and officially authorized currency exchanges (called *casas de câmbio*) will offer the floating rate upon presentation of a passport. The rate should approximate the black market rate with the obvious advantage that it is entirely legal.

To get the most for your dollars, exchange them at the floating rate and then pay for your purchases in cash. When paying your hotel bill, ask for the bill in *cruzados*. Do not pay in dollars, since they will probably calculate it at the official rate.

It is best to bring all the money you will need with you. Transferring money through a Brazilian bank is time-consuming and fraught with bureaucracy; you will not receive dollars, only cruzados computed at the official rate.

It's wise to change a small amount of money into cruzados before you arrive to avoid waiting in long lines at airport currency-exchange booths, but remember that this way you won't get anywhere near the most advantageous rate. Some U.S. banks will change your money into cruzados, but if your local bank doesn't provide this service, you can exchange money through **Deak International.** To find the office nearest you, contact Deak (630 5th Ave., New York, NY 10011, tel. 212/635–0515).

For safety, it's always wise to carry some traveler's checks. The most widely recognized are **American Express, Barclays, Thomas Cook,** and those issued through major commercial banks such as **Citibank** and **Bank of America.** Some banks will issue the checks free to established customers, but most charge a 1% commission fee. Buy some of the traveler's checks in small denominations to cash toward the end of your trip. This will save your having to cash a large check and ending up with more foreign currency than you need. You can also buy the traveler's checks in cruzados, but this is not a good idea since the exchange will be calculated at the official rate. Remember to take the addresses of offices in Rio where you can get refunds for lost or stolen traveler's checks.

At press time, the best place to exchange traveler's checks for cruzados is at branches of the Bank of Brazil; other money changers were offering the low official rate, not the advantageous tourist rate.

Getting Money from Home

There are at least three ways to get money from home:

1) Have it sent through a large commercial bank with a branch in Rio. The only drawback is that you must have an account with the bank; if not, you will have to go through your own bank and the process will be slower and more expensive.

2) Have it sent through **American Express.** If you are a cardholder, you can cash a personal check or a counter check at an American Express office; the amount varies with the type of card you have. If you have an American Express green card, you can cash a check for up to $1,000; $200 will be in cash and $800 in traveler's checks. There is a 1% commission fee on the traveler's checks. You can also get money through **American Express MoneyGram.** Through this service, you can receive up to $5,000 cash. It works this way: You call home and ask someone to go to an American Express office or American Express MoneyGram agent located in a retail outlet and fill out an American Express MoneyGram. It can be paid for with cash or any major credit card. The person making the payment is given a reference number and telephones you with that number. The American Express MoneyGram agent calls an 800 number and authorizes the transfer of funds to an American Express office or participating agency in Rio. In most cases, the money is available immediately on a 24-hour basis. You pick it up by showing identification and giving the reference number. Fees vary according to the amount of money sent. For sending $300, the fee is $22; for $5,000, $150. For the American Express MoneyGram location nearest your home and the location of offices in Rio, call 800/543–4080. You don't have to be a cardholder to use this service.

3) Have it sent through **Western Union.** The U.S. number is 800/325–6000. If you have a MasterCard or Visa, you can have money sent for any amount up to your credit limit. If not, have someone take cash or a certified check to a Western Union office. The money will be delivered in two business days to a bank in Rio. Fees vary with the amount of money sent. For $1,000, the fee is $69; for $500, $59. Add $4 if you pay with a credit card.

Brazilian Currency

In January 1989, the government of President José Sarney launched an economic package designed to stem Brazil's relentless inflation, which was averaging over 400% a year. Prices on all goods were frozen, and a new currency, the *cruzado novo,* abbreviated NCz$, was introduced to replace the *cruzado,* abbreviated Cz$.

Under the new monetary system, 1,000 cruzados became one cruzado novo, with 100 *centavos,* or cents, to each cruzado novo. Circulating together with the new currency are old cruzado notes in the values of 10,000, 5,000, 1,000, and 100, and 10-, 5-, and 1-cruzado coins. The cruzado bills are all stamped cruzado novo. As a further complication, there are also *cruzeiro* notes in circulation, although the cruzeiro, abbreviated Cr$, was replaced as the nation's currency in 1986 during the Sarney government's first currency reform.

As a rule of thumb, look at the notes you receive: If they are marked cruzado novo (NCz$), they are worth face value; if they are marked cruzado (Cz$), remove three zeros; and if they are marked cruzeiro (Cr$), remove six zeros.

What It Will Cost

The meager worth of the cruzado, Brazil's currency, has made Rio a wonderland for tourists carrying dollars. Most prices are extremely low compared to what you would pay in the U.S. or Europe. Among hotels there are styles and categories for all budgets, ranging from $150 for a double room in deluxe beachfront hotels down to $35–$50 for a functional apartment-hotel room with kitchen. Tourists will find the beach neighborhoods, particularly Ipanema and Copacabana, generally the most expensive for lodging and dining.

Taxes Hotels charge a 10% service tax. This tax is levied on the entire bill, including laundry, phone calls, or any other services you may have used. Restaurants also charge a 10% service charge, but this is considered part of the tip (*see* Tipping in Staying in Rio, below). There is no sales tax in Brazil. Airport departure tax on international flights is about U.S. $10.

Sample Costs Cup of coffee, 6¢; bottle of beer or glass of draft, 25¢; soft drink, 15¢; fresh fruit drink, 40¢; hamburger, 30¢–75¢; three-mile taxi ride, $1.50; four-hour sightseeing tour, $13; dinner for one at top restaurant with Brazilian wine, $8–$12.

Passports and Visas

Americans All U.S. citizens entering Brazil must have a passport and a visa. Visas are issued for stays of up to 90 days. Applications for a new passport must be made in person; renewals can be obtained in person or by mail. First-time applicants should apply at least five weeks in advance of their departure date to one of the 13 U.S. Passport Agency offices. In addition, local county courthouses, many state and probate courts, and some post offices accept passport applications. Necessary documents include: (1) a completed passport application (Form DSP-11); (2) proof of citizenship (birth certificate with raised seal or naturalization papers); (3) proof of identity (driver's license, employee ID card, or any other document with your photograph and signature); (4) two recent, identical, two-inch-square photographs (black-and-white or color); (5) $42 application fee for a 10-year passport (those under 18 pay $27 for a five-year passport). Passports are mailed to you in about 10 working days.

To renew your passport by mail, you'll need to complete Form DSP-82 and submit two recent, identical passport photographs and a check or money order for $35.

Canadians All Canadians need a passport and visa to enter Brazil. Visas are issued for stays of up to 90 days. To obtain a passport, send a completed application (available at any post office or passport office) to the Bureau of Passports, Complexe Guy Favreau, 200 Rene Levesque Blvd., Montreal, Quebec H2Z 1X4. Include $25, two photographs, a guarantor, and proof of Canadian citizenship. Applications can be made in person at the regional passport offices in 12 locations, including Edmonton, Halifax, Montreal, Toronto, Vancouver, and Winnipeg. Passports are valid for five years and are nonrenewable.

Britons All British citizens require a passport to enter Brazil. Visas are not required for stays of up to 90 days. Passport applications are available through travel agencies or a main post office. Send the completed form to a regional passport office. The application must be countersigned by your bank manager, or by a solicitor, barrister, doctor, clergyman, or justice of the peace who knows you personally. In addition, you'll need two photographs and the £15 fee.

Customs and Duties

On Arrival Visitors are allowed to bring into Brazil duty-free: (1) up to two liters of spirits; (2) two cartons of cigarettes; and (3) 25 cigars or 250 grams of tobacco. Household pets must be issued a visa before arrival and proof of vaccination against rabies must be provided.

On Departure If you are bringing any foreign-made equipment from home, such as cameras, it's wise to carry the original receipt with you or register it with U.S. Customs (Form 4457). Otherwise, you may end up paying duty on your return. There are no restrictions to the amount of local currency visitors may take out of Brazil.

U.S. Residents You may bring home up to $400 of foreign goods duty-free, as long as you have been out of the country for at least 48 hours. Each member of the family is entitled to the same exemption, regardless of age, and exemptions may be pooled. For the next $1,000 worth of goods, a flat 10% rate is assessed; above $1,400, duties vary with the merchandise. Included for travelers 21 or older are one liter of alcohol, 100 cigars (non-Cuban), and 200 cigarettes. Only one bottle of perfume trademarked in the United States may be brought in. However, there is no duty on antiques or works of art over 100 years old. Anything exceeding these limits will be taxed at the port of entry, and may be taxed additionally in the traveler's home state. Gifts valued at under $50 may be mailed to friends or relatives at home duty-free, but you may not send more than one package per day to any one addressee, and packages may not include perfumes costing more than $5, tobacco, or liquor.

Under the GSP (Generalized System of Preferences), certain goods that are 35% Brazilian-made can be imported by U.S. citizens duty-free outside the $400 allowance. This allowance does not pertain to many items, including most footwear, most textile articles (including clothing), watches, and some electronic, glass, and steel products. When making large purchases (such as gemstones) make sure you get a certificate from the store verifying that the item was crafted mostly in Brazil. On smaller purchases the store may just write "made in Brazil" on your receipt. On returning to the U.S. you should declare your purchases, writing "GSP" next to those items that qualify. For more information on how the GSP works you can write for the free booklet "GSP and the Traveler," U.S. Customs Service, Washington, DC 20229.

Canadian Residents Exemptions range from $20 to $300, depending on length of stay out of the country. For the $300 exemption, you must have stayed out of the country for one week. In any given year, you are only allowed one $300 exemption. You may bring in duty-free up to 50 cigars, 200 cigarettes, two pounds of tobacco, and 40 ounces of liquor, provided these are declared in writing to customs on arrival and accompany you in hand or checked-through baggage. Personal gifts should be mailed as "Unsolicited Gift—Value under $40." Get a copy of the Canadian Customs brochure, *I Declare*, for further details.

British Residents

Britons have two different allowances: one for goods bought in a duty-free shop, and the other for goods bought anywhere else in Rio. In the first category, you may import, duty-free: (1) 200 cigarettes or 100 cigarillos or 50 cigars or 250 grams of tobacco (these allowances are doubled if you live outside Europe); (2) two liters of table wine and, in addition, (a) one liter of alcohol over 22% by volume (most spirits), (b) two liters of alcohol under 22% by volume (fortified or sparkling wine), or (c) two more liters of table wine; (3) 50 grams of perfume and a quarter liter of toilet water; and (4) other goods up to a value of £32.

In the second category, you may import duty-free: (1) 300 cigarettes or 150 cigarillos or 75 cigars or 400 grams of tobacco; (2) five liters of table wine and one and a half liters of alcohol over 22% by volume, or five liters of table wine and three liters of alcohol under 22% by volume; (3) 75 grams of perfume and 375 milligrams of toilet water; and (4) other goods to the value of £250. Household pets brought into the United Kingdom must spend six months in quarantine; penalties are severe and strictly enforced.

Traveling with Film

If your camera is new, shoot and develop a few rolls before leaving home. Pack some lens tissue and an extra battery for your built-in light meter. Invest about $10 in a skylight filter and screw it onto the front of your lens. It will protect the lens and also reduce haze.

Film doesn't like hot weather. If you're driving in summer, don't store film in the glove compartment or on the shelf under the rear window. Put it behind the front seat on the floor, on the side opposite the exhaust pipe.

On a plane trip, never pack unprocessed film in check-in luggage; if your bags get X-rayed, say good-bye to your pictures. Always carry undeveloped film with you through security, and ask to have it inspected by hand. (It helps to isolate your film in a plastic bag, ready for quick inspection.) Inspectors at American airports are required by law to honor requests for hand inspection; abroad, you'll have to depend on the kindness of strangers.

The old airport scanning machines—still in use in some countries—use heavy doses of radiation that can turn a family portrait into an early morning fog. The newer models—used in all U.S. airports—are safe for anything from five to 500 scans, depending on the speed of your film. The effects are cumulative; you can put the same roll of film through several scans without worry. After five scans, though, you're asking for trouble.

If your film gets fogged and you want an explanation, send it to the **National Association of Photographic Manufacturers** (600 Mamaroneck Ave., Harrison, NY 10528). They will try to determine what went wrong. The service is free.

Language

The language of Brazil is Portuguese, not Spanish, and nothing makes Brazilians angrier than to be called Spanish-speaking.

However, the two languages are similar enough that if you speak Spanish you will be understood.

All hotels have at least some English-speaking staff and many restaurants have English translations of their Portuguese menus. But don't expect taxi drivers, street vendors, or shop clerks to speak English. Cabbies in particular can be a nuisance for tourists: The fare may increase if you don't speak Portuguese.

Staying Healthy

No serious health risks are associated with travel to Rio. If you have a health problem that might require purchasing prescription drugs while in Rio, have your doctor write a prescription using the drug's generic name; brand names vary widely from country to country.

The **International Association for Medical Assistance to Travelers** (IAMAT) is a worldwide organization offering a list of approved English-speaking doctors whose training meets British and American standards. For a list of physicians in Rio who are part of this network, contact IAMAT (736 Center St., Lewiston, NY 14092, tel. 716/754–4883; in Canada: 40 Regal Rd., Guelph, Ontario N1K 1B7, tel. 519/836–0102; in Europe: Gotthardstrasse 17, 6300 Zug, Switzerland). Membership is free.

Insurance

Travelers may seek insurance coverage in the following areas: health and accident, lost luggage, and trip cancellation. Your first step is to review your existing health and homeowner policies; some health-insurance plans cover health expenses incurred while traveling, some homeowner policies cover luggage theft, and some major medical plans cover emergency transportation.

Health and Accident Several companies offer coverage designed to supplement existing health insurance for travelers:

Carefree Travel Insurance (Box 310, 120 Mineola Blvd., Mineola, NY 11501, tel. 516/294–0220 or 800/645–2424) provides coverage for medical evacuation. It also offers 24-hour medical advice by phone, will help find English-speaking medical and legal assistance anywhere in the world, and offers direct payment to hospitals for emergency medical care.

Wallach and Company, Inc. (243 Church St. NW, Vienna, VA 22180, tel. 800/237–6615 or 703/281–9500) offers comprehensive medical coverage, including emergency evacuation for international trips of 10–90 days.

International SOS Insurance (Box 11568, Philadelphia, PA 19116, tel. 215/244–1500 or 800/523–8930) does not offer medical insurance but provides medical evacuation services and repatriation to its clients.

Travel Guard International (1100 Centerpoint Dr., Stevens Point, WI 54481, tel. 800/782–5151 or 715/345–0505), underwritten by Cygna, offers medical insurance with coverage for emergency evacuation when Travel Guard's representatives in the United States say it is necessary.

Lost Luggage Luggage loss is usually covered as part of a comprehensive travel-insurance package that includes personal-accident, trip-cancellation, and sometimes default and bankruptcy insurance. Several companies offer comprehensive policies:

Access America, Inc. (Box 807, New York, NY 10163, tel. 800/284–8300 or 212/490–5345), a subsidiary of Blue Cross–Blue Shield.

Near Services (1900 N. MacArthur Blvd., Suite 210, Oklahoma City, OK 73127, tel. 800/654–6700 or 405/949–2500).

Carefree Travel Insurance (*see* Health and Accident, above).

Travel Guard International (*see* Health and Accident, above).

Luggage Insurance On international flights, airlines are responsible for lost or damaged property only up to $9.07 per pound ($20 per kilo) for checked baggage, and up to $400 per passenger for unchecked baggage. If you're carrying valuables, either take them with you on the airplane or purchase additional insurance for lost luggage. Some airlines will issue additional insurance when you check in, but many do not. Rates are $1 for every $100 valuation, with a maximum of $400 valuation per passenger. Hand luggage is not included. Insurance for lost, damaged, or stolen luggage is available through travel agents or directly through various insurance companies.

Two companies that issue luggage insurance are **Tele-Trip** (tel. 800/228–9792), a subsidiary of Mutual of Omaha, and **The Travelers Insurance Co.** (Ticket and Travel Dept., 1 Tower Sq., Hartford, CT 06183, tel. 800/243–3174 or 203/277–2318). Tele-Trip operates sales booths at airports and also issues insurance through travel agents. It will insure checked luggage for up to 180 days and for $500–$3,000 valuation. For 1–3 days, the rate for a $500 valuation is $8.25; for 180 days, $100. Travelers Insurance will insure checked or hand luggage for $500–$2,000 valuation per person, also for a maximum of 180 days. Rates for up to five days for $500 valuation are $10; for 180 days, $85.

Before you travel, itemize the contents of each bag in case you need to file an insurance claim. Be certain to put your home address on each piece of luggage, including carry-on bags. If your luggage is stolen and later recovered, the airline must deliver the luggage to your home free of charge.

Trip Cancellation Flight insurance is often included in the price of a ticket when paid for by American Express, Visa, and other major credit and charge cards. It is usually included in combination travel insurance packages available from most tour operators, travel agents, and insurance agents.

Car Rentals

Avis (tel. 021/542–4249 or 021/398–3083 at the international airport), **Budget** (tel. 021/275–3244 or 021/398–3831 at the international airport), and **Hertz** (tel. 021/275–4996 or 021/398–3162 at the international airport) all operate in Rio. In addition, there are a number of reliable Brazilian car-rental companies, such as **Localiza** (tel. 021/275–3340 or 021/398–4455 at the international airport) and **Nobre** (tel. 021/541–4646 or 021/398–3862 at the international airport). Both Localiza and Nobre also have offices at the national Santos Dumont airport. If you plan to drive to other parts of the country, choose one of these larger firms, all of which operate nationwide.

Some companies charge a set daily rate with unlimited mileage, while others have a minimum charge plus mileage. The cost of renting a car for the day varies from $20 to $55, including insurance and taxes, depending on the size and model. You will pay more for automatic transmission. For an extra $12, you can hire a driver for an eight-hour shift.

Cars can be rented at the airport, your hotel can make arrangements, or you can go directly to the agencies—they all have offices on Avenida Princesa Isabel at the Leme end of Copacabana.

While an international driver's license is not required, it is best to have one: Rio's policemen sometimes "forget" the law.

Rio traffic is chaotic and can be dangerous unless you are alert. Besides the problem of the other drivers, there is the additional headache of potholed streets. Bus and taxi drivers are notorious; also watch out for motorcycles.

Air Pass

By far the best option for anyone planning extensive travel within Brazil is the **Brazil Air Pass,** offered by Varig (630 5th Ave., Room 1670, New York, NY, tel. 212/682–3100). This $330 pass gives you unlimited air travel for 21 days. All major cities are served, including São Paulo, Manaus, Brasília, Belém, Recife, and Búzios. The pass must be purchased outside of Brazil. Consult a travel agent or contact Varig directly.

Student and Youth Travel

The **International Student Identity Card (ISIC)** entitles students to youth rail passes, special fares on local transportation, and discounts at museums, theaters, sports events, and many other attractions. If purchased in the United States, the $10 cost of the ISIC also includes $2,000 in emergency medical insurance, plus $100 a day for up to 60 days of hospital coverage. Apply to the Council on International Educational Exchange (CIEE) (205 E. 42nd St., New York, NY 10017, tel. 212/661–1414). In Canada, the ISIC is available from the Federation of Students-Services (171 College St., Toronto, Ontario M5T 1P7) for CN$7.50.

Council Travel, a CIEE subsidiary, is the foremost U.S. student travel agency, specializing in low-cost charters and serving as the exclusive U.S. agent for many student airfare bargains and student tours. (CIEE's 80-page *Student Travel Catalog* and "Council Charter" brochure are available free from any Council Travel office in the U.S.; enclose $1 postage if ordering by mail.) In addition to the CIEE headquarters at 205 East 42nd Street, New York City, and a branch office in New York as well at 35 West 8th Street, there are Council Travel offices in Amherst, Austin, Berkeley, Boston, Cambridge, Chicago, Dallas, La Jolla, Long Beach, Los Angeles, Portland, Providence, San Diego, San Francisco, and Seattle.

The **Educational Travel Center** (438 N. Frances St., Madison, WI 55703, tel. 608/256–5551) is another student-travel specialist worth contacting for information on student tours, bargain fares, and bookings.

Students who would like to work abroad should contact **CIEE's Work Abroad Department** (205 E. 42nd St., New York, NY 10017, tel. 212/661–1414). The council arranges various types of paid and voluntary work experiences overseas for up to six months. CIEE also sponsors study programs in Latin America and Asia and publishes many books of interest to the student traveler. These include *Work, Study, Travel Abroad: The Whole World Handbook* ($8.95 plus $1 postage) and *Volunteer! The Comprehensive Guide to Voluntary Service in the U.S. and Abroad* ($4.95 plus $1 postage).

The Information Center at the **Institute of International Education** (IIE) (809 UN Plaza, New York, NY 10017, tel. 212/984–5413) has reference books, foreign-university catalogs, study-abroad brochures, and other materials that may be consulted by students and nonstudents alike, free of charge. The Information Center is open weekdays 10–4. IIE administers a variety of grant and study programs offered by U.S. and foreign organizations and publishes a well-known annual series of study-abroad guides, including *Academic Year Abroad, Vacation Study Abroad, Study in the United Kingdom and Ireland,* and *Management Study Abroad.* The institute also publishes *Teaching Abroad,* a book of employment and study opportunities overseas for U.S. teachers. For a current list of IIE publications, prices, and ordering information, write to the Institute of International Education Books (809 UN Plaza, New York, NY 10017). Books must be purchased by mail or in person; telephone orders are not accepted. General information on IIE programs and services is available from its regional offices in Atlanta, Chicago, Denver, Houston, San Francisco, and Washington, DC.

Traveling with Children

Publications

Family Travel Times is an 8- to 12-page newsletter published 10 times a year by TWYCH (Travel with Your Children, 80 8th Ave., New York, NY 10011, tel. 212/206–0688). Subscription includes access to back issues and twice-weekly opportunities to call in for specific information. Send $1 for a sample issue.

Great Vacations with Your Kids, by Dorothy Jordan (founder of TWYCH) and Marjorie Cohen, offers complete advice on planning a trip with children (toddlers to teens) and reports on special travel accommodations available to families ($9.95 paperback, E. P. Dutton, 2 Park Ave., New York, NY 10016, tel. 212/725–1818).

Kids and Teens in Flight is a brochure developed by the Department of Transportation. To order a free copy, call 202/366–2220.

Fly Rights, also published by the Department of Transportation, includes information on special services for children and the elderly. Call 202/366–2220 for a free copy.

Villa Rentals

At Home Abroad, Inc. (405 E. 56th St., Suite 6H, New York, NY 10022, tel. 212/421–9165). **Villas International** (71 W. 23rd St., New York, NY 10010, tel. 800/221–2260 or 212/929–7585). **Hideaway International** (Box 1270, Littleton, MA 01460, tel.

508/486–8955). **Villas and Apartments Abroad** (420 Madison Ave., Room 305, New York, NY 10017, tel. 212/759–1025).

Home Exchange See ***Home Exchanging*** by James Dearing ($9.95 paperback, Globe Pequot Press, Box Q, Chester, CT 06412, tel. 800/243–0495 or in CT, 800/962–0973).

Getting There All children, including infants, must have a passport for foreign travel; family passports are no longer issued. (For more information, *see* Passports and Visas, above.)

On international flights, children under two not occupying a seat pay 10% of adult fare. Various discounts apply to children 2–12. Reserve a seat behind the bulkhead of the plane, which offers more legroom and can usually fit a bassinet (supplied by the airline). At the same time, inquire about special children's meals or snacks, offered by most airlines. (See "TWYCH's Airline Guide" in the February 1988 issue of *Family Travel Times* for a rundown on children's services furnished by 46 airlines.) Ask your airline in advance if you can bring aboard your child's car seat. (For the pamphlet "Child/Infant Safety Seats Acceptable for Use in Aircraft," write the Community and Consumer Liaison Division, APA-200, Federal Aviation Administration, Washington, DC 20591, tel. 202/267–3479.)

Baby-sitting Baby-sitters can be arranged through most of the better hotels, though they may not speak English. Inquire at your hotel desk for further information.

Hints for Disabled Travelers

The **Information Center for Individuals with Disabilities** (Fort Point Place, 1st floor, 27–43 Wormwood St., Boston, MA 02217, tel. 617/727–5540) offers useful problem-solving assistance, including lists of travel agents who specialize in tours for the disabled.

Moss Rehabilitation Hospital Travel Information Service (12th St. and Tabor Rd., Philadelphia, PA 19141, tel. 215/329–5715) provides information on tourist sights, transportation, and accommodations in destinations around the world. The fee is $5 for up to three destinations. Allow one month for delivery.

Mobility International (Box 3551, Eugene, OR 97403, tel. 503/343–1284) has information on accommodations, organized study, etc., around the world.

The Society for the Advancement of Travel for the Handicapped (26 Court St., Penthouse Suite, Brooklyn, NY 11242, tel. 718/858–5483) offers access information. Annual membership costs $40, $25 for senior travelers and students. Send $1 and a stamped, self-addressed envelope.

Travel Industry and Disabled Exchange (TIDE, 5435 Donna Ave., Tarzana, CA 91356, tel. 818/343–6339) is an industry-based organization with a $15 per person annual membership fee. Members receive a quarterly newsletter and information on travel agencies and tours.

The Itinerary (Box 1084, Bayonne, NJ 07002, tel. 201/858–3400) is a bimonthly travel magazine for the disabled. Call for a subscription; it's not available in stores.

Access to the World: A Travel Guide for the Handicapped, by Louise Weiss, is useful but out of date. Available from Henry

Holt & Co., for $12.45 (tel. 800/247–3912, the order number is 0805 001417).

Access Travel, published by the U.S. Office of Consumer Affairs, is a free brochure that lists design features, facilities, and services for the handicapped at 519 airport terminals in 62 countries. To order, contact Consumer Information Center, Pueblo, CO 81009, tel. 800/948–3334.

"Fly Rights," a free brochure published by the Department of Transportation, offers airline access information for the handicapped as well as details on the services available for the elderly and children. To order, call 202/366–2220.

Hints for Older Travelers

The **American Association of Retired Persons** (AARP, 1990 K St. NW, Washington, DC 20049, tel. 202/872–4700) has two programs for independent travelers: (1) The Purchase Privilege Program, which offers discounts on hotels, airfare, car rentals, and sightseeing; and (2) the AARP Motoring Plan, which furnishes emergency aid (road service) and trip routing information for an annual fee of $33.95 per couple. The AARP also arranges group tours through two companies: **Olson-Travelworld** (5855 Green Valley Circle, Culver City, CA 90230, reservation tel. 800/227–7737) and **RFD, Inc.** (4401 W. 110th St., Overland Park, KS 66211, tel. 800/448–7010). AARP members must be over 50 years of age. Annual dues are $5 per person or per couple.

National Council of Senior Citizens (925 15th St. NW, Washington, DC 20005, tel. 202/347–8800) is a nonprofit advocacy group with some 4,000 local clubs across the country. Annual membership is $10 per person or $14 per couple. Members receive a monthly newspaper with travel information and an ID for reduced-rate hotels and car rentals.

Mature Outlook (6001 N. Clarke St., Chicago, IL 60660, tel. 800/336–6330), a subsidiary of Sears, Roebuck & Company, is a travel club for people over 50 years of age with hotel and motel discounts and a bimonthly newsletter. Annual membership is $7.50 per couple. Instant membership is available at participating Holiday Inns.

Club da 3ª Edade (The Third Age Club) (Rua da Assembléia 10, Sala 806, tel. 021/252–4512) is a Rio de Janeiro–based club for older people which provides entertainment, activities, and information.

"Travel Tips for Senior Citizens" (U.S. Dept. of State Publication 8970, revised Sept. 1987) is available for $1 from the Superintendent of Documents, U.S. Government Printing Office, Washington, DC 20402-9325, tel. 202/783–3238.

The International Health Guide for Senior Citizen Travelers, by W. Robert Lang, M.D., is available for $4.95 plus $1 for shipping from Pilot Books (103 Cooper St., Babylon, NY 11702, tel. 516/422–2225).

The Discount Guide for Travelers over 55, by Caroline and Walter Weintz, lists helpful addresses, package tours, reduced-rate car rentals, etc., in the United States and abroad. To order, send $7.95 to NAL/Cash Sales (Bergenfield Order Dept., 120 Woodbine St., Bergenfield, NJ 07021, tel. 800/526–0275).

"Fly Rights," a free brochure published by the Department of Transportation, offers details on the services available for the elderly and children as well as airline access information for the handicapped. To order, call 202/366–2220.

Further Reading

The Brazilians is a monthly English-language newspaper with articles on Brazilian arts, cultural events, economics, politics, and the Brazilian community in New York. For a single copy or subscription information write Box 985, New York, NY 10185 or call 212/382–1630.

For background and history on Rio and Brazil, try Bradford E. Burns's *A History of Brazil;* for an in-depth look at pre-Lenten celebrations there's *Carnival in Rio* by Albert Goldman. Errol-Lincoln Uyes's *Brazil,* a huge historical novel, follows two Brazilian families over five centuries. Other novels set in Brazil include Rona Jaffe's 1960 *Away from Home,* which is about a colony of expatriates living in Brazil and contains some excellent descriptions of Rio; and Peter Fleming's *Brazilian Adventure,* which chronicles a newspaperman's search through the jungles of central Brazil for a missing explorer. Fans of Gregory McDonald and the Fletch series can pick up *Carioca Fletch,* an entertaining mystery set in Rio.

A number of prominent Brazilian novelists have had their works translated into English, and these are now widely available in bookstores. Try Jorge Amado's colorful, bawdy works set in the author's native northeastern section of Brazil. Two of the most popular are *Dona Flor and Her Two Husbands* and *Gabriela, Clove and Cinnamon* (both have been made into films). Márcio Souza's semihistorical novels are also great fun; *The Emperor of the Amazon* deals with a madcap revolutionary at the turn of the century, while *Mad Maria* describes the attempt to build a railroad across the jungle and the political and business intrigue surrounding this.

Bruce Weber's *O Rio de Janeiro: A Photographic Journal* captures the beauty, diversity, and sensuality of Rio's residents in a collection of mostly black-and-white photos.

Arriving and Departing

From the U.S. by Plane

Airports All international flights, and most domestic flights, arrive and depart from the **Galeão international airport.** The airport is approximately 45 minutes from the beach area where most of Rio's hotels are located.

The **Santos Dumont airport,** located just outside downtown Rio, serves the Rio–São Paulo air shuttle and a few air-taxi firms. Santos Dumont is 20 minutes from the beaches and walking distance from downtown.

Airlines **Pan Am** and Brazil's **Varig** have daily service to Rio from New York and Miami. Pan Am's connecting flights serve most areas in the United States. **Japan Air Lines** flies twice a week between Los Angeles and Rio, and the Argentine airline **Aerolineas Argentinas** has regular service from the United States with a stop in Rio. Varig, Aerolineas Argentinas, and **Canadian Airlines International** offer direct service between both Toronto and Montreal and Rio.

Flying Time Flying time between Miami and Rio is 8½ hours, the New York–Rio flight is slightly over 9 hours, and flying time on the Los Angeles–Rio route is 13 hours. Travelers from the U.S. East Coast have a one- to three-hour time difference (this varies because Brazil goes on daylight saving time as the U.S. is going off).

Enjoying the Flight Most flights from North America leave at night and arrive in Rio the next morning, a bonus for travelers who have no difficulty sleeping aboard planes. For sleepers, the window seats are usually best, while those who like to move about the cabin should ask for aisle seats. Bulkhead seats (adjacent to the exit signs) have more legroom, but seat trays are attached to the arms of your seat rather than to the back of the seat in front.

Discount Flights The most common discount fare is the APEX (advance purchase) ticket, which must be bought in advance, usually 21 days before your trip, and normally requires a minimum stay of seven days and a maximum of 30. Cancellation or a last-minute change in your travel plans, however, will subject you to penalties.

There are also attractively priced discount packages to Rio, which include the plane, hotel, and sometimes other extras like meals and ground transportation. These are generally the least expensive, often giving you the entire package for less than you would pay for a regularly priced plane ticket alone. Ask a travel agent what is available. *The New York Times* Travel section also lists a wide selection of package tours (and charter flights) on its advertising pages; this is especially helpful in case you can't find what you're looking for in your local newspaper.

There are also charter flights to Rio that do not include accommodations and offer more flexibility in terms of length of stay. The **Brazilian American Cultural Center** (BACC), for example, offers discounted rates on regularly scheduled flights. For a nominal membership fee, you can enjoy considerable savings—and be in touch with folks who know and love Brazil. For more information, contact the BACC (20 W. 46th St., New York, NY 10036, tel. 800/222–2746 or 212/242–7837).

Smoking If smoking bothers you, ask for a seat far away from the smoking section. If you are on a U.S. airline and the attendant tells you there are no nonsmoking seats, insist on one: Federal Aviation Administration regulations require domestic airlines to find seats for all nonsmokers.

Between the Airport and Hotels Your initial steps upon emerging from customs at Rio's international airport can be confusing. Taxi drivers with a smattering of English will assault you, offering to take you wherever you want to go; many, however, will take you for the proverbial "ride" and charge you a horrendous fee. To be safe, stick to either the special airport taxis or to buses. Remember that traffic is worst into town from the airport from 7 to 10 AM, and worst out to the airport from 5 to 8 PM.

By Bus Air-conditioned buses park curbside outside customs; for about $1 they will take you to the beaches—Copacabana, Ipanema, Leblon, São Conrado, and Barra da Tijuca—where the majority of Rio's hotels are located. The trip takes about an hour, and drivers follow the beachfront drives, stopping at all hotels. If you are going to a hotel inland from the beach the driver will stop at the nearest corner (but remember, you'll have to handle your own luggage). Buses leave from the airport every half hour from 5:20 AM to 11 PM. Buses to the airport leave from the Hotel Nacional in São Conrado every half hour from 6:30 AM to 11 PM.

By Taxi Special airport taxis are operated by two firms, **Transcoopass** (tel. 021/270–4888) and **Cootramo** (tel. 021/270–1442), both of whom have booths in the arrival area of the airport. Fares to all parts of Rio are posted at the booths, and you pay in advance in the range of $7–$10.

Also trustworthy are the white radio taxis parked in the same area, which charge on the average 20% less than the special airport cabs. Avoid all yellow taxis.

If you are coming to Rio from São Paulo via the air shuttle, you will be landing at Rio's downtown Santos Dumont airport. Here the same transportation options exist as at the international airport. Again, stick to the special buses, the airport taxis, or the radio cabs, and avoid the yellow city cabs.

From the U.S. by Ship

For cruise lines that regularly serve Rio, *see* Cruises in Before You Go. Several round-the-world cruises also stop in Rio, and it is often possible to book just one segment of the trip. Consult a travel agent for schedules.

There are also some mixed cargo/passenger ships that call at Rio. **Ivaran Lines** (1 Exchange Plaza, New York, NY 10006, tel. 212/809–1220) offers a 17-day trip departing from New York, stopping in Savannah and Miami. Fares start at $3,850 for a double cabin.

From the U.K. by Plane and Ship

By Plane Depending on the time of year, the time difference between Great Britain and Rio is three or four hours, and flights take around 11 hours. Most flights leave Europe in the early evening and arrive in Rio early in the morning. Returning, most flights depart Rio in the late afternoon or early evening and arrive in Europe in the early afternoon.

By Ship Although cruises are not usually scheduled between Britain or Europe and Brazil, European ships offer shorter cruises up and down the Brazilian coast during the Northern Hemisphere winter, and it is possible to book on when the ships come over for the season, usually in November, and when they return in April. Consult a travel agent for details and schedules. Rio is also a port of call for the *Queen Elizabeth II* on her round-the-world cruises.

Getting Around Brazil

By Bus Regular, generally good bus service is available between the city and other tourist destinations in the state and the rest of the country. Long-distance buses leave from the Rodoviária Novo Rio station, Avenida Francisco Bicalho 1, São Cristóvão, near the port area. Any local bus marked Rodoviária will take you to the bus station. Tickets can be purchased at the depot or, for some destinations, from a travel agent. Buses to Petrópolis and Teresópolis also leave from the more conveniently located Menezes Cortes terminal near Praça XV downtown; tickets can be purchased at the station.

By Car Before taking the wheel into your own hands be aware that driving in Brazil is only for the brave. Brazil's economic problems have left little money for highway maintenance, and as a result roadways are in dire need of repair. Although the highway to São Paulo is generally good, there is always some section undergoing (or in need of) repair. On top of potholed highways, you will have to deal with the Brazilian driver, statistically the deadliest in the world. Also, keep in mind that Brazil is a huge country, and driving to cities outside of the state of Rio de Janeiro can be very time-consuming. Some distances: Rio–São Paulo, 429 km; Rio–Brasília, 1,150 km; Rio–Belém, 3,250 km.

Whether you are taking a bus or driving, try to avoid trips outside of Rio on the weekends from December to March. This is holiday season, and Rio's residents flock to beach and mountain resorts on the weekends, clogging the roads and turning the bus depot into a tropical bedlam.

By Plane For any extensive travel in Brazil the Brazilian Air Pass, available only outside Brazil, is highly recommended (*see* Air Pass in Before You Go, above).

By Train Train travel in Brazil is not generally recommended. Rail links in Brazil are limited, and trains are not known for either their comfort or punctuality. Other than a number of packed commuter trains to the suburbs, the only long-distance service from Rio is to São Paulo (nightly) and to Belo Horizonte (Friday and Sunday evenings). Tickets must be purchased about 10 days in advance at the Estação Pedro II station, commonly referred to as Central, located at Praça Christian Otoni alongside Avenida Presidente Vargas downtown. You can get information over the phone by calling 021/233–1494 or 021/233–3390, but you're unlikely to reach anyone who speaks English.

Staying in Rio

Important Addresses and Numbers

Tourist Information The Rio de Janeiro city tourism department, **Riotur,** is located at Rua da Assembléia 10, 8th and 9th floors, downtown, near the Praça XV Square. You can also obtain information by phoning 021/242–8000 weekdays 9–6. In addition, Riotur has information booths at the Sugarloaf cable car station (Av. Pasteur 520, Urca, open 8–8), Marinha da Glória (Atêrro do Flamengo, Glória, tel. 021/205–6447, open 8–5), and the Rodoviária Novo Rio (the main bus depot at Av. Francisco Bicalho 1, São Cristovão, tel. 021/291–5151, open 6 AM–midnight).

The Rio de Janeiro state tourism board, **Turisrio,** is also located downtown at Rua da Assembléia 10, 7th and 8th floors. For information call 021/252–4512 weekdays 9–6. Turisrio also runs the information counters in the arrivals section of the international airport, which operate from 5 AM to 11 PM, tel. 021/398-4073 or 398-4077.

Brazil's national tourism board, **Embratur,** is headquartered in Rio near the Túnel Rebouças (inconveniently far from beach neighborhoods and hotels) at Rua Mariz e Barros 13, Praça da Bandeira, tel. 021/273-2212. From the beach neighborhoods take a taxi; a mass of viaducts and thoroughfares make it inaccessible on foot.

Consulates

The **U.S. Consulate** (Av. President Wilson 147, downtown, tel. 021/292-7117). The **Canadian Consulate** (Rua Dom Gerardo 35, 3rd floor, downtown, tel. 021/233-9286). The **British Consulate** (Praia do Flamengo 284, 2nd floor, Flamengo, tel. 021/552-1422).

Emergencies

The **police** emergency number is 190. The line should be answered by multilingual staff, but unless you can communicate in Portuguese (or get by well in Spanish) you are best off seeking the help of your hotel in an emergency.

If you need a doctor, your hotel will be able to recommend one who speaks English, and the better hotels will have a doctor on duty. The English-speaking **Rio Health Collective** (tel. 021/225-9300, ext. 44) has a 24-hour medical referral service that can direct you to reliable specialists, including dentists, who speak English.

There are three large emergency hospitals in Rio: **Miguel Couto** (Rua Mario Ribeiro 117, Gávea, tel. 021/274-2121), **Rocha Maia** (Rua General Severiano 91, Botafogo, tel. 021/295-2095), and **Souza Aguiar** (Praça da República 111, downtown, tel. 021/296-4114 or 242-4539). Health care at all of these hospitals, however, is unreliable, and they should be avoided unless there is absolutely no other choice.

English-Language Bookstores and Publications

Most large bookstores have a section of English-language books, and the **Siciliano** bookstores have a large selection. They have branches at the Barra Shopping mall (tel. 021/325-1787) and São Conrado Fashion Mall (tel. 021/322-0637); in Ipanema at Rua Visconde de Pirajá 511 (tel. 021/239-3497), and in Copacabana at Av. Nossa Senhora de Copacabana 830 (tel. 021/255-3054).

Both of Rio's airports also have English-language books and periodicals on sale. Some of the hotels also have a small selection. Also available at the larger newsstands and in top hotels are the *Miami Herald*, the *International Herald-Tribune*, the *Wall Street Journal*, the *Financial Times*, *Time* magazine, and *Newsweek*. Best bets for foreign publications are the newsstands found along Avenida Rio Branco, downtown; on the Praça General Osório and Praça da Paz, Ipanema; and on Praça Serzedelo Correia and Avenida Nossa Senhora de Copacabana near the corner of Avenida Prado Junior, Copacabana.

Late-Night Pharmacies

Many pharmacies stay open until 10 or 10:30 PM. Four are open 24 hours a day: **Farmácia Piaui** (Av. Ataulfo de Paiva 1283, Leblon, tel. 021/274-8448); **Farmácia Piaui** (Rua Barata Ribeiro 646, Copacabana, tel. 021/255-7445); **Drogaria Cruzeiro** (Av. Nossa Senhora de Copacabana 1212, Copacabana, tel. 021/287-3636); **Farmácia do Leme** (Av. Prado Junior 237, Copacabana, tel. 021/275-3847).

Travel Agencies **American Express** (Av. Atlântica 2316A, tel. 021/235–1396; and at Praia do Botafogo 228, Bldg. A, Room 51, tel. 021/552–2243). **Wagons Lits** (Av. Rio Branco 156, Room 310, tel. 021/262–3721).

Telephones

Local Calls Bright orange pay phones are liberally scattered along Rio's streets. To use them you must buy tokens, called *fichas*, on sale at newsstands or shops located near the phones. Insert the token in the clearly marked slot and wait for a dial tone. Each ficha permits a three-minute connection, after which you will be cut off. It's best, therefore, to insert more tokens than you think you will need; any not used will be returned when you hang up. Dial 100 for a local operator and 102 for directory assistance.

To place a wake-up call from a phone booth, dial 134; for the correct local time, dial 130.

Calls within Brazil To place a long-distance call to another part of Brazil, dial 0 before the area code followed by the telephone number. To dial from a pay phone, you must use the blue-colored DDD phones, which require special tokens. For directory assistance in another part of Brazil, dial the area code plus 102. You can send a telegram within Brazil by calling 135.

International Calls To place an international call direct, dial 00, followed by the country code, city code, and telephone number. Country codes are listed at the front of the phone book, or you can dial 000333 for information regarding international calls. For assistance from an English-speaking international operator, or to place a collect international call, dial 000111. Your hotel can also dial for you; many hotels will allow you to make an international call even if you are not a guest, adding on a surcharge.

You can also make long-distance calls from a telephone-company public station located at: the international airport (open 24 hours); the domestic Santos Dumont airport (open 6 AM–11 PM); the main Rodoviária Novo Rio bus terminal (open 24 hours); Avenida Nossa Senhora de Copacabana No. 462 (open 24 hours); in Ipanema at Rua Visconde de Pirajá 111 (open 6:30 AM–11 PM); downtown at Praça Tiradentes No. 41 (open 24 hours); and at the Menezes Cortes bus station on Rua São José (open weekdays 6:30 AM–10 PM).

Direct-dial calls to the U.S. and Canada cost around $2.75 per minute, and to Great Britain about $3.27 per minute.

Mail

Postal Services and Rates Post offices are open weekdays 8–6 and Saturday 8–noon. Some branches stay open later, and the post office at the international airport never closes. Telegrams can be sent from any post office. Letters to the United States take about a week to arrive; to Europe, about 10 days. Express post, registered mail, and parcel services exist for both domestic and international mail. Postcards to any foreign country cost about 70¢ to mail; letters up to 20 grams cost about 88¢.

Receiving Mail Normally, you should have mail sent to you at your hotel. However, if you don't know ahead of time where you will be staying,

American Express (Av. Atlântica 2316A, 22041 Rio de Janeiro, RJ, Brazil, tel. 021/235–1396) will hold mail for its clients.

Tipping

In your hotel, tip the maid 50¢–$1 per day; the concierge, a few dollars; porters, 50¢–$1. In restaurants a 10% service charge is routinely added to your bill; it's customary, however, to leave an additional 5% (or more), particularly in better restaurants. Taxi drivers are not usually tipped, but the fare is often rounded up a reasonable amount. If the driver has been helpful or has handled your luggage, tip a few dollars (some drivers will demand a certain amount per bag, but this is not a regulation). Shoe shiners, gas station attendants, and car tenders should be given about 20¢. Tour guides generally receive about $1.

Opening and Closing Times

Banks are open weekdays 10–4:30. Money exchanges are open weekdays 9–5 or 5:30.

Government offices are usually open weekdays 9–5 or 6, although some close for an hour or two in the middle of the day.

Business offices are open weekdays 9–6.

Museum hours vary, but as a rule most are open Tuesday–Saturday in the morning and afternoon with a break for lunch.

Shopping centers are open Monday–Saturday 10–10. Department stores are open weekdays 9 AM–10 PM, Saturday 9–6:30.

Getting Around Rio de Janeiro

In theory, moving from one place to another in Rio should be easy. In practice, however, getting around in Rio can be a colossal headache, especially during the hot summer months. Squeezed in between mountains and the ocean, Rio has always been a nightmare for city planners. The neighborhood of Copacabana has only 109 streets along which an estimated 600,000 vehicles plod each day. If traffic stops on one of these streets it invariably clogs up dozens of others. The result is the infamous carioca traffic jam, which can occur at any time of day, leaving exasperated motorists pounding their car horns in the midst of 90° heat. Parking is another major problem. For a city of 5.6 million, Rio has amazingly few parking garages, which results in drivers leaving their vehicles anywhere they will fit, including sidewalks.

This situation plays havoc with even the most well-intentioned plans and is the main reason why cariocas seldom, if ever, show up on time. The best way to deal with this is to smile.

By Bus Local buses in Rio are inexpensive and will take you anywhere you want to go, but for tourists there are definite liabilities. The principal one is the threat of being robbed. During high season the city buses are infested with pickpockets and purse snatchers in search of tourists. When riding buses keep cameras and other valuables out of sight, place shoulder bags over your chest in front of you, put wallets in a front pocket, and hold onto purses tightly. You enter a Brazilian bus at the rear and exit at the front, paying in the middle when you pass through a turnstile. This is a favorite moment for petty thieves, who strike as tourists reach for their wallets and then race to the back of the bus, jumping out the rear door. Have your fare in your hand when you go to the turnstile, and use small bills (most fares are in the range of 10¢). Also, should you be victimized, never react. Many of these thieves are armed.

Obviously, riding buses under these conditions is not ideal, and most hotels now recommend that their guests avoid city buses, with two exceptions: the safer and more comfortable *frescão* and *jardineira* bus lines. The air-conditioned frescãos serve the beach neighborhoods where tourists stay, providing transportation between the beaches, downtown, and Rio's two airports. Fares range from 50¢ to $1. These buses, which look like highway buses, stop at regular bus stops but also may be flagged down wherever you see them. Also recommended are the jardineira buses, open-sided vehicles that follow the beach drive from Copacabana to São Conrado, and also take passengers to the Barra da Tijuca neighborhood. Fares are about 17¢, and white posts along the street mark jardineira bus stops. These buses, which look like old-fashioned streetcars, were introduced specifically for tourists and have become a major hit. They offer excellent views of the scenery and drive slowly along the beach avenue, a welcome relief to anyone who has ridden the regular city buses, whose drivers are considered the city's most reckless. Also, the jardineiras have so far escaped the plague of petty thieves.

By Subway Rio's subway system, called the Mêtro, operates Monday through Saturday 6 AM to 11 PM, closed on Sunday. Unfortunately, it is not yet finished. The part that is completed, though, offers the fastest and most comfortable transportation in the city. The air-conditioned cars whisk passengers between the Botafogo neighborhood (a 10-minute taxi ride from Copacabana) and downtown. A second line connects downtown with the city's northern neighborhoods, but this area is far from the beaches and of little interest to tourists.

Construction is under way on an extension of the Botafogo line to Copacabana and Ipanema, which should be completed in 1991. Until then the problem for tourists will be getting from the beach neighborhoods to the Botafogo station. The best bet is to take a taxi there. Buses marked *integração* also go directly to the Botafogo station. There are subway stations close to the Sambadrome, where the annual Carnival parade takes place, and Maracanã Stadium, where soccer matches are held. In the stations and in each car are maps showing the subway stops.

A single Mêtro ticket costs 19¢, a double costs 34¢. Combination Mêtro–bus tickets allow you to ride special buses to and from the Botafogo station: The M-21 runs to Leblon via Jardim Botânico and Jóquei, while the M-22 goes to Leblon by way of Túnel Velho, Copacabana, and Ipanema. To ride the subway, insert the ticket with the magnetized strip into the slot at the turnstile.

By Taxi Taxis are plentiful and cheap in Rio and are the most convenient mode of transportation available to tourists. Dealing with cabdrivers, however, is not always a pleasant experience. Few of them speak English, and most will attempt to increase the fare for tourists. Because of Brazil's high inflation, fares change constantly and it is impossible to keep meters adjusted. Taxis are required to post a chart noting the latest fare adjustments on the inside of the left rear window. The driver may try to tell you that the chart is out of date. Don't believe it. Also, beware of the meter itself. When the driver resets the meter he raises a flag, which will have either the number one or two on it (for digital meters the numbers one and two appear in red). Number two means 20% more but can only be used in certain circumstances: between 10 PM and 6 AM, on Sundays and holidays, during the month of December, in the neighborhoods of São Conrado and Barra da Tijuca, or when climbing steep hills. In most cases, it should be on number one. Cabbies also like to tell tourists that the number two means double the fare. Not true.

If you want to take a cab and avoid a hassle over the fare, ask your hotel to call a radio cab or use one of the taxis that routinely serve hotel guests. Radio cabs charge 30% more but are honest, reliable, and usually air-conditioned. Other cabs working with the hotels will also charge more, normally a fixed fee explained before you leave. In both cases you are trading price for peace of mind, a bargain in Rio.

By Car Driving in Rio for first-time visitors is not recommended. The carioca flair for driving is usually enough to leave most tourists shaking in their shoes. In addition, there are the traffic jams and the endless confusion of the city's streets, all of which have strange-sounding Portuguese names, although not all of them have street signs, making finding addresses a great adventure. If you wish to have the convenience of an automobile without the headache of having to drive it, hire a car and driver. Auto-rental firms will supply a driver for an additional $12–$15 for eight hours a day (beyond eight hours, the rate is $4 an hour). Two special taxi firms, **Transcoopass** (tel. 021/270–4888) and **Cootramo** (tel. 021/270–1442), charge $9 an hour for car and driver.

Guided Tours

Orientation Tours All guests of Rio's hotels receive pamphlets on the various sightseeing tours available in the city. While there are many companies that offer these tours, the acknowledged leader is **Gray Line,** whose office is located in the Rio Sheraton Hotel, Avenida Niemeyer 121, Vidigal, tel. 021/274–7146. Gray Line excels in transportation (three types of air-conditioned buses ranging from large to small) and in guides. Many of the other operators cater to Brazilian tourists and have little expertise in conducting tours in foreign languages. Gray Line's guides, however, are superb and definitely speak your language. The tours available include the following: Sugarloaf and the Botanical Gardens (4 hours, $18); Corcovado and the Tijuca Forest (4 hours, $17); City Tour (4 hours, $13); Rio by Night (6 hours, $40); Soccer Game (4 hours, $17); Samba (4 hours, $40); Macumba (Brazil's version of voodoo) (5 hours, $38); Santa Cruz Fort and Niterói (4 hours, $15); Helicopter Ride (20 minutes, $55); Museums of Rio (4 hours, $15); Petrópolis (6 hours, $20). In addition to Gray Line, other good operators are **BTR** (tel. 021/235–1320) and **Combratur** (tel. 021/541–6599).

Special-Interest Tours Peter O'Neill, a respected travel agent and longtime member of Rio's foreign community, organizes tailor-made tours for groups. He specializes in trips for nature lovers, and in the past has arranged visits to Rio's Tijuca Forest with guides from the

Brazilian Foundation for the Conservation of Nature. Longer expeditions have included trips to the Amazon, the mineral spas in Minas Gerais, and the historical towns of Paratí and Salvador. Call **Marlin Tours,** tel. 021/255–4433.

Upon request, Carlos Roquette, a Brazilian history professor, conducts, in English and French, historical tours of Rio's neighborhoods for $20 (tel. 021/322–4872).

Boat Trips Boat tours are available to nearby islands. The tropical-islands tours depart from the fishing village of Itacuruçá, about 90 minutes by car from Rio. Brazilian schooners, *saveiros*, are used, and the day-long trips include lunch and time for swimming at some of the beautiful deserted beaches on the 36 islands of Sepetiba Bay. The trips are offered by Rio-based operators; the two best are run by **Sepetiba Turismo** (tel. 021/235–2893) and **Gray Line** (tel. 021/274–7146). The cost is about $40 and includes ground transportation to Itacuruçá. Tourists may also arrange their own transportation to the village, where trips on schooners are available at about half the price of the guided tours, although without English-speaking guides or other frills. (*See* Costa Verde in Chapter 9 for more information on Sepetiba Bay.)

Personal Guides Personal English-speaking guides are not common in Rio. **Marlin Tours** (tel. 021/255–4433), which caters to English-speaking tourists, and **Rio Custom Tours** (tel. 021/274–3217), linked to an American-owned travel agency, are the best options.

Security

Better safe than sorry should be your motto while in Rio. Although not every tourist in Rio is a crime victim, petty theft is an always-present threat, so take precautions. If you are victimized, the police emergency number is 190. Multilingual operators should be on duty, but if possible, ask someone at your hotel to help you.

Whenever you can, leave valuables in your hotel room or safe. Don't be ostentatious in your dress, and don't wear expensive jewelry or watches. Keep cameras out of sight in bags.

Don't walk alone at night on the beach. Be aware of Rio's hillside shantytowns, which in some cases are close to hotels and tourist attractions; don't walk in front of them. If at all possible don't take city buses except for the air-conditioned frescão buses or the open-sided jardineiras. In particular avoid the Santa Teresa streetcar, and the 553 bus around the Inter-Continental and Nacional hotels. Also, don't get involved with drugs. Penalties in Brazil for possession of drugs are severe, and dealers are the worst of the worst.

2 Portrait of Rio

Carnival

by Edwin Taylor

Since 1979, Edwin Taylor has written extensively on Rio de Janeiro and Brazil. In addition to travel and business articles for American and European magazines and newspapers, he has co-authored two books, one on Rio and one on Brazil, and is editor and publisher of two highly regarded newsletters on Brazil, Brasilinform *and* Brazil Travel Update.

Like any great event, Carnival has its buildup. It starts in November when the weather warms, the beaches fill, and a certain air of expectation settles over Rio. The shoe-shine boys of Copacabana pick up the mood and add an extra snap and shuffle to the steady rhythm they beat out with their rags and fingers. In December the tourists arrive, and makeshift samba bands begin to appear along the beachfront. By January it is more than expectation. Seamstresses are working into the morning hours to prepare costumes for the grand parade of the samba schools, sidewalk vendors are hawking confetti, streamers, noisemakers, and masks, and throughout Rio the sounds of Carnival are growing louder.

When it finally arrives on the Friday before Ash Wednesday, usually in February but sometimes in March, it comes with the rush of thousands of dancing feet and the rhythmic eruption of a multitude of drums, triangles, and whistles. Carnival is more than Rio's premier event, it is the greatest party on Earth—uninhibited, vibrant, and unabashedly sexy.

Although spontaneity is the soul of Carnival, the party does have a structure. It begins on Friday night and continues until the dawn of Ash Wednesday, four days and five nights of nonstop partying. On the first two nights, the focus is on the Carnival balls, where thousands of revelers crowd into ballrooms across the city and samba madly until the dawn. On the nights of Sunday and Monday, however, the balls take second stage to the main attraction of Carnival, the parade of the samba schools.

Samba Schools

While they are called schools, education is the furthest thing from the minds of samba-school members. In reality the schools are neighborhood clubs known as schools because when they were first formed in the 1920s they practiced in schoolyards. In the beginning the schools were a disorganized crowd of samba dancers who paraded along downtown streets. Quickly, however, costumes and dance routines were added, then a marching percussion band, called the *bateria,* to provide accompaniment for the dancers, all of this gradually evolving over the decades into the modern samba-school parade.

Today there is little that could be called amateurish about either the schools or the parade. The elaborate costumes and the gaudy floats topped by scantily clad women have given an air of Las Vegas to the event. But behind the surface glitter is a complex and sophisticated operation. The parade is above all a competition between the participating samba schools, the culmination of an entire year's planning and preparation. To win, however, requires more than simply dancing well and singing in tune. Each school adopts a theme to represent during the parade, and each must use all of the elements at its disposal to interpret this theme. In general, themes revolve around historical events or personalities, famous books or popular celebrities. They must, though, deal with some aspect of Brazilian culture.

Once a theme is chosen, the samba school begins to meld the elements of the parade to fit it. The music, and principally its lyrics, are matched to the theme, as are the costumes to be worn by dancers and band members, and the floats. The school's directors plan and chart the composition of the various wings, called *alas*, of dancers that will comprise the school. Each wing must interpret a part of the theme, and each must be a visual complement to the entire moving mass of up to 5,000 dancers and musicians. In recent years the visual aspect has acquired as much importance as the music and dance. Composers and choreographers are taking a backseat to the aesthetic demands of the samba schools. Gaining in importance has been the *carnavalesco*, a combination designer/art director/football coach who has the final responsibility for putting a coherent, organized, and visually attractive school on Avenida Marques do Sapucai.

All of this takes more than just time and labor. It also requires a great deal of money, up to $500,000 for a leading samba school. Originally the schools were financed entirely by the members, who each chipped in to pay for individual costumes. Today, however, the total cost has outstripped the limited means of school members, the majority of whom are poor. Although participants still contribute large sums, the schools now receive an annual subsidy from the city tourism board. Many are also financed by Rio's mobsters, the men who run the city's illegal numbers game, who use their samba-school association to curry favor with the masses.

The Parade

Unfortunately for tourists, the rising costs of staging the parade have also pushed up the price of viewing. Seats in the 85,000-capacity Sambadrome, the impressive samba parade stadium, now go for $138 for grandstand seats and $210 for numbered chairs in the section reserved for tourists, a place of honor that most foreign visitors would be happy to forsake. Seats in other sections are far cheaper, as low as $10, but by the time tourists arrive these are all sold out. For this reason, visitors are usually better off if they are traveling with a group tour and have purchased their tickets abroad as part of the package. Otherwise you will be forced to buy from a scalper upon arrival in Rio, and you may be sure you will get no bargains. The most reliable sources of tickets are those recommended by your hotel. Be wary of anyone approaching you with tickets for sale.

And finally it is ready. After a year of preparation, the samba schools take to Avenida Marques do Sapucai on the Sunday and Monday nights of Carnival. There are 18 of them in Group IA, the major leagues of the samba schools. (There is also a Group IB which parades on other nights at the Sambadrome, and Groups IIA and IIB, which parade along one of downtown's main streets, Avenida Rio Branco. All of these, however, are considered inferior to the Group IA schools and tend to attract small crowds.) On each of the two nights, nine of the top schools parade, starting at 8 PM and continuing until noon the next day, 16 hours of dance, music, and spectacle.

On these nights, Rio is transformed into a wonderland of fantasy and dreams. In the shantytowns, sequined princesses, gilded kings, and tassel-topped clowns emerge from the shacks to make their way down the darkened hillside paths. On the city's south side, home to the middle and upper-middle class, glittering figures climb into family cars, vans, and station wagons. (Once the province of the poor, the samba schools today have become chic among affluent cariocas with the result that they have evolved from being nearly all black to a racial and social mixture that is a microcosm of Rio itself.)

As the participants make for the parade route, so do the spectators. For tourists, the best transportation choices are the subway or the buses that leave from the major hotels. While the buses are more convenient, they are also more expensive ($15 round-trip). In addition, you will have to return when your bus departs for the hotels, which may be too early or too late depending on your reaction to the parade. The subway operates 24 hours a day during Carnival, and there are two stations close to the Sambadrome. If you have a parade ticket for an even-numbered gate, get off at the Praça Onze station; for odd-numbered gates, get off at Estação Central do Brasil. An added attraction of the subway is that it is used by samba-school members, giving you an opportunity to rub shoulders with the dancers themselves. Taxis will also take you to the Sambadrome, but for an exorbitant fee. If you have rented a car, don't even think about driving. There is no parking nearby and most streets in the neighborhood of the stadium are blocked off on parade nights.

Comfort should be the primary concern of any first-time viewer of the parade. The parades are long and there are sometimes tiring gaps between the schools as well as unexpected problems, such as the breakdown of a float, which cause delays. Even if you decide to see only two schools, you will spend at least three hours sitting on the bare concrete of the grandstand, squeezed in by other spectators on either side. Take something comfortable to sit on, plus an umbrella in case it rains (the grandstand is uncovered and brief downpours frequently occur during the parade). If you are going to be watching the parade during its daylight portion, bring sunscreen, sunglasses, and a hat or visor. There are concession stands, but the lines are usually long, so if possible bring a thermos with something to drink. If you are not in the tourist section, however, you should avoid drinking too much, since the bathrooms are deplorable. No matter what section you are in, bring your own toilet paper.

The parade itself will undoubtedly surprise you. Nothing like it exists anywhere in the world, and most tourists find themselves caught up in the infectious enthusiasm of the spectators. What makes this event special is the combination of the rhythmic samba, the intricate and sensuous dance routines, the blazing colors of the schools spread out along the half-mile avenue, and the rousing cheers and shouts that greet the dancers. It is a hypnotic spectacle of sound and color that will at first rivet you to your seat until gradually you slip into the spirit of the samba, tapping your feet, clapping your hands, and finally rising to your feet, swaying and chanting with the thousands around you.

But while you are being initiated into the rites of samba, the professionals below you are engaged in a head-to-head competition. This is serious business, and to the winning school and its fans go bragging rights for an entire year. Scattered along the parade route are judges who carefully note each school's performance, watching to see if the school is singing in tune, if the theme is adhered to throughout, if the various wings are well coordinated, and checking on dozens of other prickly details known to true samba fans. When it's over the points are added up and the winner declared at a ceremony that immediately becomes one more day of celebration. On the Saturday following Ash Wednesday the three top finishers in each of the samba-school groups parade once more, an event that offers tourists a chance to see the very best schools without having to sit through the also-rans. For this reason, even though the competition is over, many consider the Saturday parade to be the most viewable of the three days of parading.

Street Carnival

Not all of Rio's Carnival is located within the confines of the Sambadrome. Much of what goes on is immune to schedules or planning. It simply happens. Huge block parties erupt on streets in Copacabana and Ipanema, with entire blocks roped off to allow the participants to express their joy. On Avenida Rio Branco, loosely organized neighborhood groups called *blocos* dance in gyrating masses along the street each day and night of Carnival (one word of caution:

street Carnival is fun and contagious, but leave your valuables in the hotel).

In the beach neighborhoods, traditional Carnival bands known as *bandas* march out at all hours, attracting thousands of passersby who dance along after the band. The liveliest is the banda of Ipanema, whose fun-loving spirit usually overcomes the havoc it creates with traffic on the neighborhood's streets. To catch a ride with one of these bands, hang out at Posto 6, the beach area at the Ipanema end of Copacabana near the Rio Palace Hotel, or at A Garôta de Ipanema bar in Ipanema, on the corner of ruas Vinicius de Morais and Prudente de Morais.

The Balls

And of course there are the balls. They begin the week before Carnival with the somewhat sedate (for a Carnival ball) Night in Hawaii at the Yacht Club, one of Rio's most exclusive clubs. By the Friday night of Carnival, however, all inhibitions have been discarded.

Carnival balls are definitely not for the prudish. Dress as if you were going to an orgy and you will probably fit right in. Men wear shorts and T-shirts, while women wear garments that would warm the heart of Hugh Hefner—corsets, garter belts, and stockings are popular, as are skimpy bikinis. In general, the less the better, and nudity among women is not uncommon, especially after 2 AM, when things really heat up.

Occasionally you will see someone in an elaborate costume at the balls, but this is an increasing rarity. The fancy-dress costumes are usually saved for competitions held on all four days of Carnival at private clubs and hotels. Although the costumes are often spectacular, costing into the thousands of dollars, these competitions tend to be drawn out and boring. If you want to attend one, however, ask at your hotel for a schedule.

Getting into a Carnival ball usually requires buying tickets well in advance, an impossibility for most tourists. As a result, a thriving black market has sprung up to deal with foreign visitors. Your hotel will be able to tell you where and how to buy tickets, which, at the better balls, will cost between $15 and $55 per person. You may also go to the ball itself and attempt to buy a ticket at the entrance. If you are successful the price should be around $5, but be prepared for a long wait. Lengthy lines of ticket seekers form at the entrance to the better balls, and not everyone gets in.

There are literally scores of balls during the five nights of Carnival, as every private club, nightclub, or meeting hall becomes a venue. The smaller balls tend to be less elaborate in decorations and costumes but may also be friendlier and more comfortable. The large, popular balls are always oversold, and thousands of revelers end up back to back and belly to belly in an ambience that is closer to a sauna than a ballroom. There is no noticeable air-conditioning at the balls, and the room temperature soars to well over 100°. Nonstop pounding samba music makes it nearly impossible to talk or be heard. Eating and drinking is also a problem as huge lines form at concession stands (and also at bathrooms). Obviously there must be something else to compensate for all this discomfort. There is—sex. Few parties in the world are so openly aimed at promoting sexual contact—the main reason why many Brazilians stop attending Carnival balls after they are married. This is a singles world, and to guarantee attendance promoters pack the halls with beautiful young women who pay half price or less (there are always more women than men at the large balls).

The major balls are held at two sites. The Scala nightclub (Av. Afrânio de Melo Franco 296, tel. 021/239–4448) is home to the Champagne Ball (the Thursday before Carnival), the Red and Black Ball (held Friday and always the wildest), the City Ball (Saturday), and the Gala Gay Ball (Tuesday). Monte Libano (Av. Borges de Medeiros 701, tel. 021/239–0032), a private club, hosts Carnival's last major ball on Tuesday night, the Night in Baghdad Ball.

If you don't happen to enjoy being squeezed in between sweating seminude bodies for several hours (the balls start at 11 PM and end around 5 AM), you will probably be better off avoiding the bigger parties. Among the smaller ones, the best is the Pão de Açucar Ball (tel. 021/541–3737 or 021/295–3044) held atop Sugarloaf Mountain on Friday night. For around $75 a person, you will have all the fun of a Carnival ball without the liabilities. Crowds are smaller, many participants attend in costume, it is outdoors, the temperature on the mountaintop is pleasant, and the view of the city below is unbeatable. Additionally, the Pão de Açucar Ball is the most magnificent in terms of costumes.

3 Exploring Rio de Janeiro

Orientation

by Edwin Taylor

Rio de Janeiro is divided into three main zones: downtown (Centro), the north zone (Zona Norte), and the south zone (Zona Sul). The north is a highly populated area of mostly low-income neighborhoods with pockets of prosperity. It is located far from the beach and other areas of interest to tourists. Ringing the north zone is a huge poverty belt, the northern suburbs where more than 3 million people live, often in wretched conditions. Out of these suburbs come the majority of the samba schools that are the driving spirit for each year's Carnival.

For tourists, nearly all of Rio's attractions are found in the more affluent south zone, the neighborhoods located on or near the beach. It is here, from the bayside Botafogo neighborhood to the distant Barra da Tijuca, that hotels, restaurants, shopping, and nightlife all are concentrated.

Ocean and bayside streets run the entire length of the south zone, winding along the undulating contours of Rio's coastline. The names change from one neighborhood to another, but all these streets and roads fall under the general heading of "along the beach" or *pela praia,* a direction known to all taxi drivers. The main drags are Avenida Atlântica in Copacabana, avenidas Vieira Souto and Delfim Moreira in Ipanema/Leblon, and Avenida Sernambetiba in the Barra da Tijuca. Distances from one beach to another vary, but in most cases you will find that a taxi is the best means of transportation. Carioca engineers have built enough tunnels over the years to connect all parts of this mountainous city, but traffic often comes to a dead halt, and arriving anywhere on time can be a minor miracle.

During daylight hours the center of Rio life focuses on the beaches, the most active of which remains Copacabana. To sense the carioca spirit, spend a day on Copacabana Beach and the sidewalk cafés that populate its beachfront drive, Avenida Atlântica. Ipanema beach life is more restrained and cliquish, and thus harder for outsiders to penetrate; also, there are only three beachside bars in the entire length of Ipanema and its western extension, Leblon. The more distant southern beaches, beginning with São Conrado and extending past the Barra to Grumari, are rich in natural beauty and increasingly isolated and empty the farther south you go.

Although Rio is more than 400 years old, it is in every respect a modern city. The overwhelming majority of the city's historic structures have fallen victim to the wrecking ball, leaving only a handful of sites that can be visited by tourists. Space is the perennial problem of Rio, a city of 5.6 million inhabitants squeezed between mountains and the ocean. To compensate, on several occasions landfill has been taken from the mainland to fill in parts of the bay and thus extend the city proper. In this process many historical areas have simply disappeared, and others have fallen prey to development needs. In Rio, for one building to go up inevitably means another must come down first.

The little that is left of Rio's historical past is found in and around the downtown area in churches and other buildings scattered about the myriad streets that make up the city center. Organized tours, both walking and in sightseeing buses, are available and are highly recommended. The scattered na-

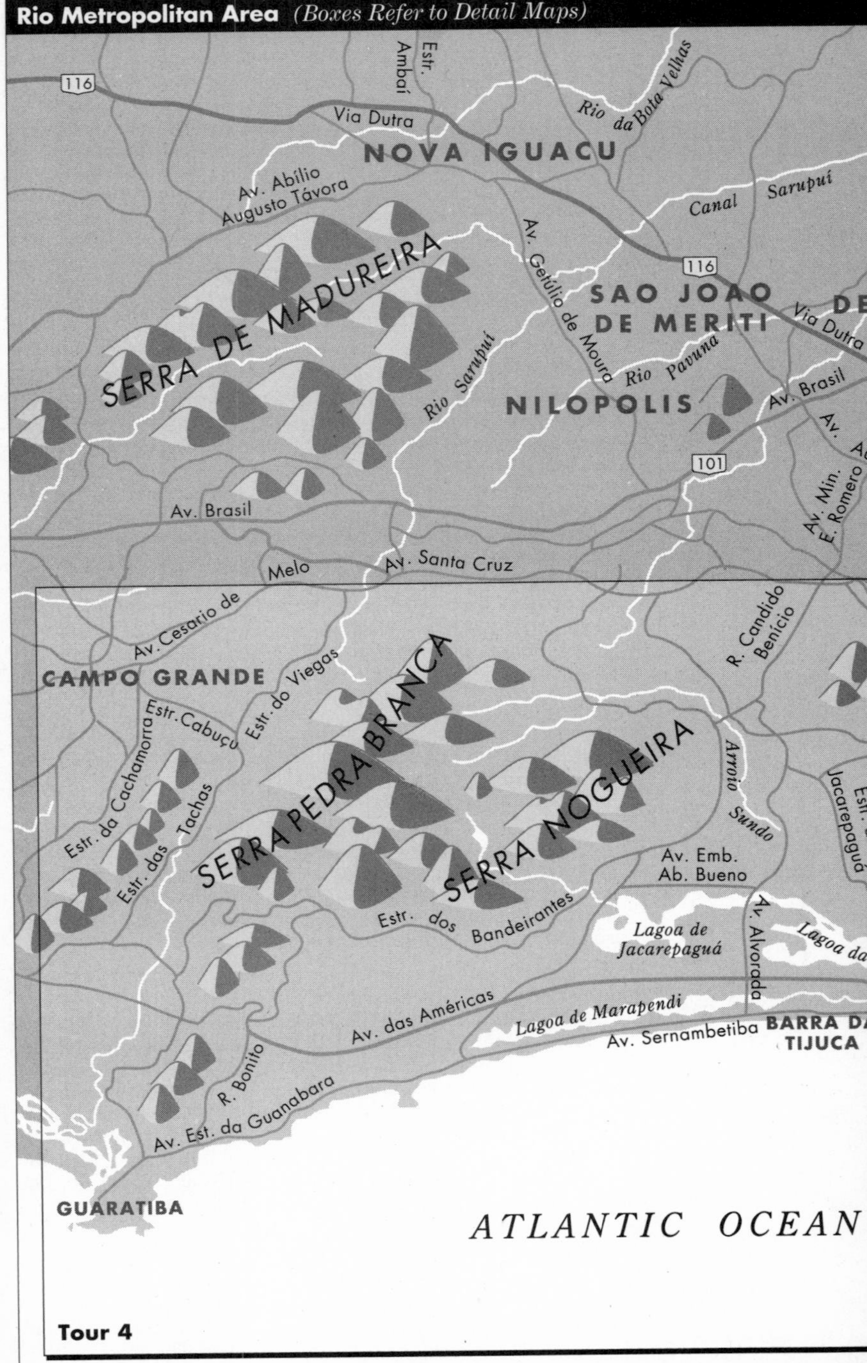

Rio Metropolitan Area (Boxes Refer to Detail Maps)
116
Estr. Ambaí
Via Dutra
Rio da Bota Velhas
NOVA IGUACU
Av. Abílio Augusto Távora
Canal Sarupuí
Av. Getúlio de Moura
116
SAO JOAO DE MERITI
Via Dutra
SERRA DE MADUREIRA
Rio Sarupuí
Rio Pavuna
NILOPOLIS
Av. Brasil
Av. Min. E. Romero
101
Av. Brasil
Av. Santa Cruz
Av. Cesario de Melo
R. Candido Benício
CAMPO GRANDE
Estr. do Viegas
Estr. Cabuçu
SERRA PEDRA BRANCA
SERRA NOGUEIRA
Estr. da Cachamorra
Estr. das Tachas
Arroio Sundo
Estr. de Jacarepaguá
Av. Emb. Ab. Bueno
Estr. dos Bandeirantes
Lagoa de Jacarepaguá
Av. Alvorada
Lagoa da
Av. das Américas
Lagoa de Marapendi
Av. Sernambetiba
BARRA DA TIJUCA
R. Bonito
Av. Est. da Guanabara
GUARATIBA
ATLANTIC OCEAN
Tour 4

Rio Iguaçu
Via Washington Luis
Av. Pres. Kennedy
N
0
4 miles
0
6 km
Ilha de Paquetá
UQUE
CAXIAS
Estr. do Galeão
Ilha do Governador
Av. Brasil
Guanabara
de
Baía
SAO GONCALO
Ilha do Fundão
101
Av. Itaoca
Clube
Rio-Niterói
Av. Brasil
Av. Suburbana
Am. Calvac
R. 24
de Maio
R. Bela
Av. Pres. Vargas
Tour 1
104
NITEROI
RIO DE JANEIRO
102
Sugarloaf
BOTAFOGO
COPACABANA
SAO CONRADO
LEBLON
IPANEMA
Tours 2 & 3

ture of these sites, plus the sometimes undesirable nature of their surroundings, makes individual sightseeing problematic at best. Also, walking along downtown streets can be less than pleasant during the hot summer months, when high pollution levels are joined by soaring temperatures and humidity. Air-conditioned sightseeing buses are a welcome relief on such days. For a listing of companies that offer city tours, *see* Guided Tours under Staying in Rio in Chapter 1.

Admission to most of Rio's museums, churches, and other sites is free. If there is an entrance fee, it is usually in the range of 5¢ or 10¢ or less.

Tour 1: Historical Rio

Numbers in the margin correspond with points of interest on the Tour 1: Historical Rio map.

Cariocas are fond of saying that Brazil is a country that has no memory, a glib phrase used to explain away the absence of historical neighborhoods in a city that dates back to the 16th century. Less kind commentators say that cariocas should be shot for letting their historical monuments vanish into dust and debris. Like it or not, many Brazilians seem to have little interest in their nation's history and have not bemoaned the destruction of their city's architectural heritage. Only recently have efforts begun to preserve what is left, a process that, while clearly late, is at least a step in the right direction.

Restoration work is being concentrated in the port area and on the nearby downtown streets, the area first settled by Rio's Portuguese colonizers. Funding is a major problem, however, and already some of the projects first completed are suffering from poor maintenance. For this reason it is impossible to say exactly what will be around in the future. Rio's handful of visitable museums are also cash short and undergoing seemingly endless reforms. These headaches, though, should not dissuade visitors from venturing downtown in search of the city's past.

If you are not on an organized tour, the best approach to visiting the historical sites is to take the subway (if you are staying in Copacabana, Ipanema, São Conrado, or the Barra, take a taxi to the Botafogo Mêtro station; if you are staying in Flamengo or Glória, there are subway stations in both of these neighborhoods), but remember that the subways do not operate on Sundays. Your first stop is the Catete station, where a
1 half block from the exit on Rua do Catete 179 is the **Catete Palace,** the former official residence of Brazil's presidents and today the **Museu da República** (Museum of the Republic). This elegant granite-and-marble 19th-century building became the presidential residence after the 1889 military coup that overthrew the monarchy and installed the Republic of Brazil. All of Brazil's presidents lived in the palace until 1954, when then-president Getúlio Vargas committed suicide in his palace bedroom. The palace was closed after Vargas's death until 1960, the year the capital was shifted from Rio to the newly constructed city of Brasília and the palace converted to a museum. Today its three floors house presidential memorabilia, including period furniture and paintings, from the proclamation of the Republic in 1889 to the end of Brazil's latest military regime in 1985. On the second floor a diplomatic reception room is pre-

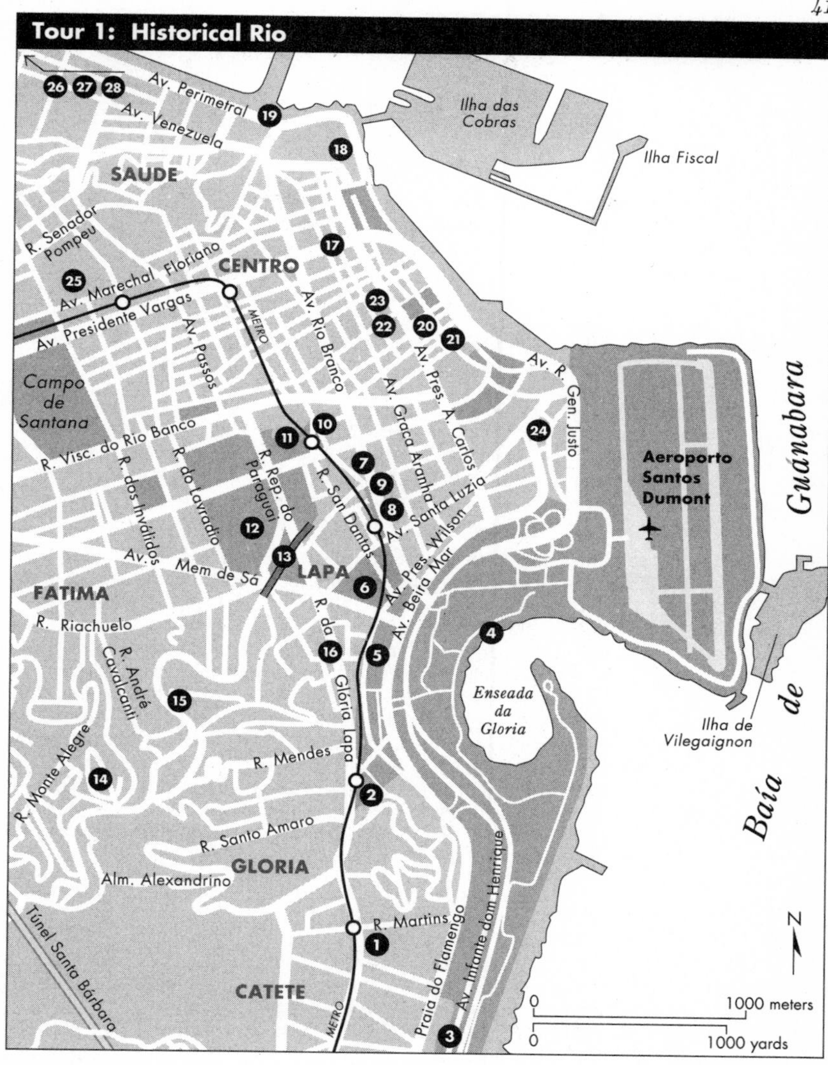

Beco do Comércio, **23**
Biblioteca Nacional, **8**
Carioca Aqueduct, **13**
Catedral Metropolitana, **12**
Catete Palace, **1**
Chácara do Ceu Museum, **15**
Cinelândia, **6**
Flamengo Parkway, **3**
Ingreja Candelária, **17**
Jardim Zoológico, **28**
Lapa neighborhood, **16**
Largo da Carioca, **10**
Maracanã Stadium, **26**
Monumento aos Pracinhas, **4**
Museu do Palácio do Itamarati, **25**
Museu Historico Nacional, **24**
Museu Nacional, **27**
Museu Nacional de Belas Artes, **9**
Nossa Senhora da Glória do Outeiro, **2**
Nossa Senhora do Carmo, **22**
Paço Imperial, **21**
Praça XV, **20**
Praça Mauá, **19**
Praça Paris Parkway, **5**
Santa Teresa, **14**
Santo Antonio Convent, **11**
São Bento Monastery, **18**
Teatro Municipal, **7**

served, while on the third the Vargas bedroom is maintained exactly as it was the day he died. The museum offers an intriguing glance at the world of refinement and formal manners that once characterized life at the top of Brazil's political ladder. It was closed in 1984 for an extensive renovation but is scheduled to reopen at the end of 1989. *Rua do Catete 179, tel. 021/225-4302. Call to see if it has reopened.*

One subway stop north of Catete is the Glória station and the
2 nearby **Nossa Senhora da Glória do Outeiro** church. This elegant 1720 church, with its bell tower and carved ceiling, is a prime example of colonial Brazilian baroque architecture. It stands sentinellike atop a small hill, with an unobstructed view of the downtown area. The eight-sided church was built on the site where, according to legend, a hermit with the assistance of two angels sculpted a statue of Our Lady of Glória that was later credited with miraculous powers. This in turn led to the construction of the church, which became the favorite of the royal family. Dom Pedro II, emperor of Brazil from 1831 to 1889, was married in this church. Each year on August 15, the church's saint's day, Glória comes into her full glory, shining in the night sky with a crown of white lights. *Outeiro de Glória is open weekdays 8–noon and 1–5.*

The view from Glória includes the bay and two large public
3 parks. The **Flamengo Parkway** in Flamengo Park, known popularly as the **Atêrro,** or "Landfill," flanks the bay beginning in the Flamengo Beach neighborhood and ending in Glória. It was built through landfill and lovingly designed by Brazil's master landscape architect Roberto Burle Marx. Long paths used for jogging, walking, and bicycling wind through the park, and there are also public tennis and basketball courts and playgrounds for children. On weekends the freeway that runs alongside the park is closed to traffic, and the entire area, from the rows of apartment blocks facing the bay to the beach along the bay, becomes one enormous public park where cariocas gather with their families to mingle, gossip, and stretch out on the grass.

Directly across from the Glória church is the **Glória Marina.**
4 Just beyond the marina is the imposing **Monumento aos Pracinhas** (Monument to the Brazilian Dead of World War II), two soaring columns flanking the tomb of an unknown soldier. Brazil was the only Latin American nation to take a combatant's role in the war, sending troops to fight alongside the U.S. Fifth Army in Italy. A small museum (open 10–6) relates the country's war effort. The second park visible from the Glória
5 church viewpoint is the **Praça Paris Parkway,** a formally landscaped park with fountains and a pool, designed to be a carioca version of a Parisian park. Lately, however, the park has been abandoned by the city and is now inhabited by Rio's homeless.

6 The next subway stop after Glória is **Cinelândia,** a downtown landmark marked by a conglomeration of movie theaters and a large open space that has become Rio's version of London's Hyde Park. Political debates and speeches are a continuous phenomenon at Cinelândia, with rival groups sometimes coming to blows.

7 On the outer edge of Cinelândia is the **Teatro Municipal** (Municipal Theater, Praça Floriano 210, tel. 021/210-2463), a scaled-down version of the Paris Opera House. The theater is located

at the beginning of **Avenida Rio Branco,** the main thoroughfare of downtown. Modeled after the Champs-Elysées, Rio Branco was constructed in 1905 with 115 classical three- and five-story buildings. Time and progress, however, have eliminated all but 10 of those original structures. The most impressive of the survivors is the theater, which in its fabled history has seen performances by many of this century's leading ballet stars and opera singers, including Nijinsky, Pavlova, and Callas. Today it still offers a complete yearly program of ballet, symphonic music, and opera, although for tourists its main attraction is the downstairs **Café do Teatro,** one of the city's most unusual restaurants (*see* Chapter 6). Across the street from the theater
8 are the Victorian **Biblioteca Nacional** (National Library, Av. Rio Branco 219, tel. 021/240–9229) and the French neoclassical
9 **Museu Nacional de Belas Artes** (Museum of Fine Arts). The museum houses works by Brazil's leading 19th- and 20th-century artists, including canvases by the country's best-known modernist, Cândido Portinari. *Av. Rio Branco 199, tel. 021/240–0160. Open Tues. and Thurs. 10–6:30, Wed. and Fri. noon–6:30, weekends and holidays 3–6.*

10 Five blocks down Avenida Rio Branco is the **Largo da Carioca,** a large public square that is also the site of the next subway station. Street vendors hawk their wares in the midst of a constant ebb and flow of pedestrians, all of this below two of Rio's important historical monuments. Atop a low hill overlooking the
11 Largo is the **Santo Antonio Convent.** The convent was completed in 1780, but parts of its construction date from 1608, making it the oldest surviving structure in Rio. Its baroque interior contains priceless colonial art, including wood carvings and wall paintings. The next-door **São Francisco da Penitência** church dates from 1739, and while small, it is famed for its wood sculptures and the rich gold leaf that covers its interior. The small hill on which the two sit is all that remains of a much larger hill that was removed for landfill. The resulting empty space has been filled in by a phalanx of modern government office buildings, the most notable of which is the airy headquarters of Brazil's state-owned oil company, **Petrobrás,** looking as if it were built of aluminum-coated Lego blocks. *Santo Antonio Convent, Largo da Carioca, tel. 021/262–0129. Open Mon.–Sat. 7 AM–6 PM, Sun. 9–11 AM and 4–6 PM. São Francisco da Penitência church, Largo da Carioca 5, tel. 021/262–0197. Open weekdays 1–5 PM.*

Continuing down Avenida República do Chile are two other Rio
12 landmarks, the **Catedral Metropolitana** (Metropolitan Cathedral) and the city's 18th-century aqueduct. The cathedral resembles an American space capsule from the early 1960s, the period when the building was designed and construction began on it. It was inaugurated unfinished in 1976 on the 300th anniversary of the diocese of Rio. Work still continues, albeit at a snail's pace.

A stone's throw from the cathedral, straddling Avenida Mem
13 de Sá, is the classic form of the **Carioca Aqueduct** (known to Brazilians as the **Arcos da Lapa**), an imposing structure of 36 colossal stone arches built in 1723 to carry water from the hillside neighborhood of Santa Teresa to the downtown area. In 1896 the city transportation company took over the then-abandoned aqueduct and converted it to a viaduct, laying trolley tracks across its length. Since then, Rio's distinctive trolley

cars (called *bondes* because they were financed by foreign bonds) have carried passengers back and forth between Santa Teresa and downtown. Until recently the trip was a favorite with tourists, but Rio's soaring crime rate has made this particular diversion virtually off-limits. The open-sided, slow-moving cars make the work of pickpockets and purse snatchers particularly easy. We recommend that you take a taxi to Santa Teresa, but if you want to take the trolley, leave anything of value that could attract a thief's attention in your hotel.

The trolleys depart from a station in front of the Petrobrás building and cross the aqueduct before meandering through
14 the cobblestone streets of **Santa Teresa,** Rio's most delightfully eccentric neighborhood. Gabled Victorian mansions are intermingled with alpine chalets and more prosaic dwellings, often hanging at unbelievable angles from the flower-encrusted hillside. Once an escape route for runaway slaves, Santa Teresa in the late 19th century became a home for Rio's wealthy, whose aging mansions you'll see throughout the neighborhood. To connect their homes with the city below the residents built elaborate public staircases, which survive today, offering spectacular views from the neighborhood's streets. All of this can be seen from the vantage of a trolley car but, again, a far safer approach would be to take a taxi.

15 One of Santa Teresa's most popular attractions is the **Chácara do Ceu Museum,** an outstanding modern-art collection left by one of Rio's greatest patrons of the arts, Raymundo de Castro Maya. The museum was once Castro Maya's home, and today both it and his remarkable collection are open to the public. Included are originals by such 20th-century masters as Picasso, Braque, Dalí, Degas, Matisse, Modigliani, and Monet. It also contains works by Brazil's leading modernists, such as Portinari, Volpi, and Di Cavalcanti. The grounds of the museum offer Santa Teresa's finest views of the bay and downtown with the aqueduct in the foreground. *Rua Murtinho Nobre 93, tel. 021/232–1386. Open Tues.–Sat. 2–5, Sun. 1–5.*

Time Out Santa Teresa's special flavor has attracted artists and intellectuals to its eclectic slopes. Their hangout is the **Bar do Arnaudo,** a nondescript bar and restaurant specializing in regional dishes from Brazil's northeast but whose main appeal is as a neighborhood listening post. *Rua Almirante Alexandrino 316-B, tel. 021/252–7246. Open 11:30 AM–11 PM. Closed Mon.*

To exit Santa Teresa, take a cab back down the hill and pass
16 through the **Lapa neighborhood,** located on the far side of the aqueduct's arches from downtown. In the first part of this century, Lapa was the center of Rio nightlife, a fabled bohemia of bars, clubs, and cabarets. Today striptease clubs line its main street, **Avenida Mem de Sá,** but on side streets you will see the neighborhood's distinctive architecture—four- and five-story apartment buildings with wrought-iron balconies, and sometimes ornate statuary on the facades, a carioca version of New Orleans's French Quarter.

Exit Avenida Mem de Sá and Lapa alongside the **Praça da República,** a large, near-downtown park facing **Avenida Presidente Vargas,** the broad avenue that connects downtown with the tunnels leading through Rio's mountainous spine to the beaches of the southern zone. Flanked by office buildings

on either side, Presidente Vargas is packed with cars day and night, funneling motorists into and out of the downtown area. At its beginning, closest to the bay, stands the solid form of the
17 **Igreja Candelária** (Candelária church). The classic symmetry of Candelária's white dome and bell towers casts an unexpected air of sanity over the chaos of downtown traffic. This unusually beautiful church, with its imposing architecture and equally imposing location, has long been a favorite wedding site among Rio's wealthy and famous. A Candelária wedding can be sure to attract at least one or two cabinet members and on occasion the president himself. Construction on the church began in 1775, and while it was formally dedicated by the emperor in 1811, work on the dome was not completed until 1877. *Praça Pio X, tel. 021/233-2324. Open weekdays 7:30–noon and 1–4:30* PM, *Sat. 7:30–noon, and Sun. 9* AM *until the end of noon mass.*

Candelária once faced the bay, whose waters virtually lapped at the church's front doors. Landfills have since pushed back the water, but this area in the blocks north and south of Candelária is still the historical center of Rio and contains the city's best-preserved colonial structures. Five blocks toward
18 the bay is the **São Bento Monastery,** whose ornate interior with gold-leaf-covered wood carvings is extraordinarily rich and beautiful. Getting there is half the fun. The monastery is located on a slight elevation that can only be reached by elevator. Go to **Rua Dom Gerardo No. 40,** a store where the elevator is located. One flight up is the monastery and grounds. The view of Guanabara Bay from here is one of the most peaceful in Rio. *Open daily 5–11:30* AM *and 1–6* PM.

Peace and quiet, however, is the antithesis of the street scene
19 just west of São Bento in the **Praça Mauá** port area. Ships, sailors, and longshoremen make for a rowdy combination, day and night. Sex shows and prostitutes are the square's main attractions, although an ambitious urban-renewal project aimed at turning the Mauá area into a tourist attraction is under way.

20 On the south side of Candelária is **Praça XV,** site of a number of historical buildings, including the former imperial palace. This square, known during colonial days as Largo do Paço, was the center of the imperial government that ruled Brazil for most of the 19th century. The square gets its modern name from the date of the declaration of the Republic of Brazil, November 15, 1889. To reach Praça XV from the São Bento Monastery, walk along Avenida Primeiro de Março.

21 The dominating structure in the square is the **Paço Imperial,** one of Rio's few restored colonial buildings. This two-story structure is notable for its thick stone walls and entranceway, and courtyard paved with huge stone slabs. The paço was built in 1743, and for the next 60 years it was the headquarters for Brazil's viceroys, appointed by the Portuguese court in Lisbon. When King João VI arrived, he converted it into his royal palace. With Brazil's declaration of independence and the founding of the Empire of Brazil, the paço became the imperial palace and was home to emperors Pedro I and II. After the monarchy was overthrown the palace became Rio's central post office, eventually losing that function as well until it was finally saved from oblivion by the restoration work of the 1980s. Today it is a cultural center, concert hall, and the city's principal venue for visiting art exhibitions. The paço also contains a large

three-dimensional model of downtown Rio, and every Tuesday at noon it hosts lunchtime concerts. *Praça XV, tel. 021/232-8333. Open daily 11–5.*

Facing Praça XV across Avenida Primeiro de Março are two
22 18th-century churches. The larger of the two, **Nossa Senhora
do Carmo,** was built in 1761 to serve as Rio's first Metropolitan Cathedral. Both of Brazil's emperors were crowned here. Next door is the smaller **Nossa Senhora do Monte do Carmo,** circa 1770, noted for its baroque facade.

Behind Avenida Primeiro de Março is a network of narrow
23 streets and alleys highlighted by the **Beco do Comércio,** a pe-
destrian street flanked by restored 18th-century buildings and homes, now converted to offices. The best known is the **Telles de Menezes** building (Praça XV 34) whose famous arch, the **Arco dos Telles,** links this fascinating street with Praça XV.

Time Out Cozy restaurants and sidewalk cafés are scattered throughout the streets behind Avenida Primeiro de Março. On Beco do Comércio a popular stop for lunch or drinks is the **English Bar,** where you may partake of Old World cuisine in a New World historical setting. *Beco do Comércio 11, tel. 021/224-2539. Open weekdays noon–4* PM *for lunch, until 8* PM *for drinks. Closed weekends.*

---

24 A few blocks south of Praça XV is the **Museu Historico Nacional**
(National History Museum), an intriguing collection of colonial buildings that has the potential to become Rio's most interesting historical site. Unfortunately it has yet to live up to this promise. What is now a museum began as a half-finished fortress in 1603. Other buildings, new wings, and unending improvements have created the present sprawling complex combining architectural styles from the 17th, 18th, and 19th centuries. The museum's archive, the most impressive in Brazil, includes rare documents and colonial artifacts. Much of this, however, is shut away in sections undergoing constant "renovations," a euphemism for the standard problem of Rio's museums: lack of funding to prepare and maintain exhibits. In 1988, after much delay, the museum unveiled the first of what is planned to be a series of modular showcases dividing Brazil's history into distinct periods. The first section, called "Brazil as a Colony," is now on permanent display. *Praça Marechal Ancora, tel. 021/240-7978. Open Tues.–Fri. 10–5:30, weekends and holidays 2:30–5:30.*

To complete the historical tour, return to the Largo da Carioca
subway station and take the Mêtro north to the Presidente Var-
25 gas stop. Three blocks west from the station is the **Museu do
Palácio do Itamarati** (Itamarati Museum) (Av. Marechal Floriano 196, tel. 021/291-4411), built in 1854 and for 80 years the home of Brazil's foreign ministry. This neoclassic structure is now a museum devoted to Brazil's diplomatic history, although it is seldom open. Call in advance.

Next take the subway to the Maracanã stop, site of Rio's huge,
26 180,000-seat **Maracanã Stadium.** Within walking distance of
the soccer stadium is **Quinta da Boa Vista,** an open area where
27 Rio's zoo and the city's most fascinating museum, the **Museu
Nacional** (National Museum), Brazil's largest natural history museum, are located. The museum, a former imperial palace dating from 1803, features exhibits on Brazil's past and its

flora, fauna, and minerals. What will entrance most tourists, however, are the landscaped parks, pools, and marble statues on the grounds of this palace-turned-museum. *Quinta da Boa Vista, tel. 021/264–8262. Open Tues.–Sun. 10–4:45.*

28 Next door the **Jardim Zoológico** presents animals from Brazil's wilds in their natural habitats. There are beautiful Amazon birds, jaguars, monkeys, boa constrictors, and alligators. *Quinta da Boa Vista, tel. 021/254–2024. Open Tues.–Sun. 9–4:30.*

Tour 2: The Bay and Sugarloaf

Numbers in the margin correspond with points of interest on the Tours 2 and 3: The Bay, Sugarloaf, Corcovado, and the Tijuca Forest map.

If you arrive in Rio by plane, the first body of water you will see on the way to your hotel is the vast 147-square-mile **Guanabara Bay,** where the first Portuguese explorers anchored their ships in 1500. Guanabara is an Indian name meaning "arm of the sea," and it was along the banks of this bay that the city of Rio de Janeiro took shape and grew. Virtually the only evidence of the bay's historical importance that still remains are two small forts that guard its narrow entrance, Santa Cruz (17th century) and the São João (19th century).

Today Guanabara Bay is the transit point for oceangoing ships entering and leaving Rio's port, the second largest in South America. Although it is still beautiful to look at, its waters have been polluted by an estimated 1.5 million tons of industrial waste and raw sewage that is dumped into the bay daily. Once the playground of Rio's wealthy, the bay-side beaches are no longer fit for bathing, and tourists should avoid any contact with them. The principal attraction of the bay is the views it offers of Rio, best seen on day cruises.

In addition to views of Rio from the water, bay cruises also provide a cool-off from the oppressive summer heat of the city. Boat trips are available at both ends of the fare scale. Inexpensive ferries and only slightly more expensive hydrofoils toil and scoot across the bay at regular intervals. If you are traveling in a group, you may be interested in renting a *saveiro* (schooner) with crew for a day's outing on the bay. For information on boat rentals call the Glória Marina (tel. 021/265–0797 or 285–2247).

1 There are 84 islands in the bay, the largest of which is **Paqueta,** once the site of holiday homes for Rio's upper class. Today Paqueta's main attraction is its slow pace of life, a welcome contrast to the urban swirl of Rio. Cars are banned from the island and transport is by bicycle or horse-drawn buggy (a buggy trip around the island costs $3). You can make the trip in 90 minutes by ferry or in 15 minutes by hydrofoil. Both depart from the
2 **Estação dos Barcos** at Praça XV, downtown. *Ferries (tel. 021/231–0396) run Mon.–Sat. 5:30 AM–11 PM, Sun. 7:10 AM–11 PM. Tickets: 10¢ each way. Hydrofoils (tel. 021/231–0339) operate weekdays 10–4, weekends 8–5. Tickets: 50¢ each way.*

3 For cariocas the only reason to visit **Niterói** across the bay is to admire the view of Rio. The best views are from Niterói's bay-side beaches beginning with **Icarai** and continuing on to
4 **Jurujuba.** Beyond Jurujuba on the coastal highway is the **Santa**

Tours 2 and 3: The Bay, Sugarloaf, Corcovado, and the Tijuca Forest

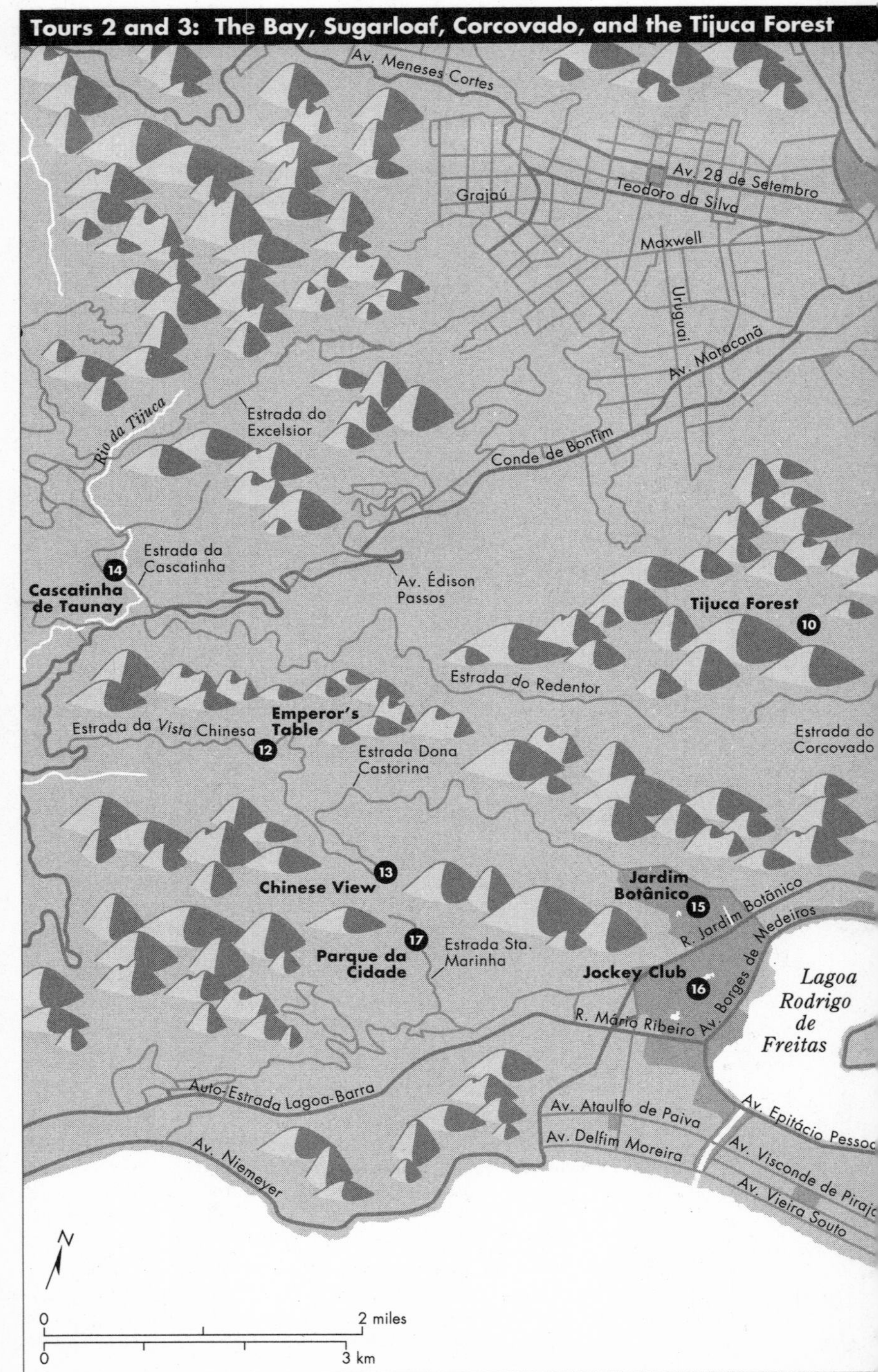

Baía de Guanabara
Paquetá 1
Niterói 3
Santa Cruz Fort 4
São Luis Gonzaga
Quinta da Boa Vista
Av. Osvaldo Aranha
Figueira de Melo
Av. Francisco Bicalho
Av. Perimetral
Vidal de Negreiros
Alm. Cochrane
Av. Presidente Vargas
Av. Rio Branco
R. Haddock Lobo
R. Visc. do Rio Banco
Av. Henrique Valadares Relacão
Av. Mem de Sá
2 Estação dos Barcos
Av. Eng. Freyssinet
Túnel Santa Bárbara
Alm. Alexandrina
Largo do Boticário 9
R. das Laranjeiras
Praia do Flamengo
Marquês de Abrantes
Velho Cam. do Chico
11 Dona Marta Viewpoint
Estrada Mirante Dona Marta
8
orcovado
Túnel Reboucas
Casa Rui Barbosa 7
São Clemente
Museu do Indio 6
R. Voluntários da Pátria
R. Visconde de Silva
R. Mena Barreto
Av. Pasteur
Sugarloaf 5
Av. Princesa Isabel
Av. Henrique Dodsworth
R. Baratas Ribeiro
Av. Atlântica
ATLANTIC OCEAN

Cruz Fort, time-honored guardian of the entrance to Guanabara Bay. In its three centuries, the well-preserved fort has also served as a military prison. Its most famous prisoner was 19th-century Italian revolutionary Giuseppe Garibaldi, who learned the art of guerrilla warfare while fighting with a separatist movement in the south of Brazil. The galleries, dungeons, and courtyards of this sprawling fort are fascinating to explore, but access is difficult since the fort is still controlled by the military. (Call tel. 021/711–0166 or 711–0462 for information.) Sightseeing tours usually have better luck in gaining admittance. For this reason, and because of the distances involved in visiting Niterói from Rio (a car or taxi is essential), organized tours are the best option (*see* Staying in Rio in Chapter 1).

From the cable car ride to the top to the unsurpassed views on
5 all sides, a trip to **Sugarloaf** is not to be missed. Give it as much time as possible. This soaring 1,300-foot granite block standing at the mouth of Guanabara Bay was originally called *pau-nd-acugua* by the Indians, meaning "high, pointed peak." To the Portuguese the Indian phrase was similar to their *pão de açucar,* or "sugarloaf," and the rock's shape reminded them of the mold used to refine sugar into the conical form known as a sugarloaf.

The first recorded climb of Sugarloaf was accomplished by an Englishwoman, Henrietta Carstairs, in 1817. The ascent remained difficult until 1913, when a two-stage cable car line was inaugurated. In 1972, the original cars were replaced by larger, Italian-made bubble cars holding 75 passengers each and offering 360-degree views. Today these cars move smartly up and down the mountain in two stages, the first stopping at the **Morro da Urca,** a smaller mountain (705 feet high) in front of Sugarloaf, and the second continuing on to the summit. Each stage takes three minutes, and over 1,300 passengers can be transported each hour. There has never been an accident with the cable car system.

The various viewpoints on Urca Mountain and Sugarloaf offer unobstructed vistas of most of the city below, and each view changes with the passage of the day. Sunsets are awe inspiring, and at night the lights below are an unforgettable sight. On its western side, Sugarloaf offers views of Copacabana, Ipanema, Leblon, and surrounding mountains. At the foot of the mountain sentinel are Botafogo and Flamengo with Corcovado and the Christ statue in the background. To the north lies the bay, the bay bridge, and the beaches of Niterói.

While the summit is reserved for viewpoints, the first-stage stopping point on Morro da Urca has developed into an entertainment center. Here you will find a 45-minute, 2,500-slide audiovisual show on the sights and sounds of Brazil. Called the "Brazil Experience," it is shown hourly from 9 AM to 8 PM, with a sound track available in English. Each Monday night, Beija Flor, one of Rio's top samba schools, gives a lively samba show at the Urca amphitheater starting at 10:30 PM (*see* Chapter 8). Shows with Brazilian singers or rock groups also are held periodically atop Urca, and each year the mountain is the site of one of Carnival's most elegant and beautiful balls (*see* Chapter 2).

Time Out Urca Mountain is also home to an international restaurant called, appropriately enough, **Sugarloaf.** Large picture windows overlook the bay; go up in the afternoon for a late lunch at the restaurant, then wait for the sunset. Reservations are usually not necessary, but to be on the safe side call in advance. *Tel. 021/541–3737. Open noon–7 PM, until 11 PM on nights when there are shows on the mountain.*

During high season, from January to March, long lines often form for the trip on the cable cars. For the remainder of the year, the wait is seldom more than 30 minutes. *Cable cars: Praia Vermelho. Tickets: about $1. 8 AM–10 PM daily.*

Close to Sugarloaf in the Botafogo neighborhood are two small
6 but intriguing museums. The **Museu do Indio** (Indian Museum) displays Brazilian Indian costumes, headdresses, and handicrafts. *Rua das Palmeiras 55, tel. 021/286–8799. Open Tues.–Fri. 10–5, weekends 1–5.*

7 A short distance away is the **Casa Rui Barbosa,** the former home, now turned museum, of one of Brazil's most important 19th-century statesmen and politicians. A leading liberal of his time, Barbosa was the guiding genius behind Brazil's first constitution following the overthrow of the monarchy. This pink mansion houses memorabilia of Barbosa's life, including an extensive library, which is often consulted by scholars from Brazil and abroad. *Rua São Clemente 134, tel. 021/286–1297. Open Tues.–Fri. 10–4:30, weekends and holidays 2–5.*

Tour 3: Corcovado and the Tijuca Forest

An eternal argument among Brazilians and tourists is which view is better, that from Sugarloaf or from its "rival,"
8 **Corcovado.** Corcovado Mountain has two advantages: at 2,300 feet it is nearly twice as high as Sugarloaf and offers an excellent view of Sugarloaf itself. Corcovado, however, is all view and has none of the added attractions of Sugarloaf. Whichever you favor, don't leave Rio without making the trip up to the top of Corcovado, where the powerful image of Christ with arms outstretched crowns the summit.

Although it seems unthinkable today, there was once a Corcovado without a Christ statue. Prior to this century, getting to the top was also a major challenge. The sheer 1,000-foot granite face of Corcovado (the name means "hunchback" in Portuguese and refers to the mountain's shape) has always been a difficult undertaking for climbers, far more troublesome to scale than Sugarloaf. To make the summit accessible, a railroad was constructed in 1885, later joined by a road. It was not until 1921, the centennial of Brazil's independence from Portugal, that someone had the idea of placing a statue on top (an earlier scheme to put a statue of Christopher Columbus here on the 400th anniversary of the discovery of America never got under way).

The project was handed over to a team of French artisans headed by sculptor Paul Landowski. The idea was to build a statue of Christ with his arms apart as if he were embracing the city. It took 10 years, but finally on October 12, 1931, the **Crito Redentor** (Christ the Redeemer) statue was inaugurated. The figure stands 100 feet tall atop a 20-foot pedestal and weighs 700 tons. A 1981 cleanup of the statue and the installation of a powerful lighting system have enhanced the forceful presence of this unique image, visible night and day from most of the city's neighborhoods.

There are two ways of reaching the top of Corcovado, either by the recently renovated cogwheel train or by the winding road that climbs the mountain. The train is the more interesting of the two, providing a close look at the thick mountain vegetation during the steep, 2.3-mile ascent, lasting around 20 minutes. The train is comfortable and the view spectacular but, as at all tourist attractions, keep your eyes on your valuables when entering and leaving the cars. If you wish to go up by the road, you will need to either rent a car, hire a taxi, or go with a sightseeing tour (some tours use the train or a combination of train and bus). Of these, a tour is the safest choice, giving you the best price (around $20), an English-speaking guide, plus the assurance that you won't be ripped off.

Should you go by train, it is likely that there will be at least a 30-minute wait at the **Cosme Velho train station,** reached quickly by taxi from any point in the south zone of Rio. If the wait is
9 longer, take advantage of it to visit the **Largo do Boticário,**
your first right up the hill from the train station off Rua Cosme Velho. The homes along this shady, tree-lined cul-de-sac look as if they are relics from some past century. In fact, only one of the homes dates from earlier than the 1920s. Knowing this, however, doesn't spoil the magic spell of this pleasant and relaxing stroll.

Whether you arrive by train, bus, or car, there will still be a formidable climb up long and steep staircases before you reach the summit where the statue and viewpoints are located (there are no elevators or ramps for wheelchairs). Once you have reached the summit, all of Rio stretches out before you. The view, from left to right, includes Rio's north zone, the international airport, downtown, Copacabana, Ipanema, the Rodrigo de Freitas Lagoon, and the Jockey Club. Most striking is the view of the bay, the bay islands, Sugarloaf, and the mountains on the far side. The best time to visit, lines permitting, is the late afternoon shortly before sunset. The effect of the reddening sun against the buildings, bay, and ocean is stunning. One by one, the lights of the city come on, in contrast to the darkened bulk of Sugarloaf and the surrounding water. *Train station: Rua Cosme Velho 513, tel. 021/285–2533. Trains leave every 30 min daily 8* AM*–8* PM*. Late-afternoon trains are the most popular; on weekends be prepared for a long wait. Nominal fee.*

Surrounding Corcovado is a dense, beautiful tropical forest
10 called the **Tijuca Forest.** Many of Rio's most breathtaking viewpoints are located along the 60 miles of narrow, winding roads that pass through this national park. The most famous are the
11 **Dona Marta Viewpoint,** located on the way up the mountain and providing a full view of Sugarloaf, Botafogo, and the bay; the
12 **Emperor's Table,** supposedly the site where Brazil's last emperor, Pedro II, brought his court for picnic lunches, and from where you have a view of the Rodrigo de Freitas Lagoon; and
13 the **Chinese View,** farther down the road with a view similar to, but less dramatic than, that of the Emperor's Table.

The forest was once part of a private estate belonging to a Brazilian nobleman and is studded with exotic trees, thick jungle
14 vines, and a delightful waterfall, the **Cascatinha de Taunay.** Beyond the waterfall is the small but distinctive **Mayrink Chapel,** with an altar painting by Brazil's most famous 20th-century artist, Cândido Portinari.

Time Out Extraordinary views, an unspoiled natural setting, and the cool air at the higher elevations make the forest a prime site for picnicking. Cariocas routinely gather around the waterfall and at other spots along the road for weekend picnic lunches. The park is also home to an attractive rustic restaurant, **Os Esquilos (The Squirrels).** The international cuisine here is at least acceptable, and the setting on parklike grounds surrounded by the tranquillity of the forest is perfect. An excellent tea is served in the afternoon. *Estrada Escragnolle, Km 2, Floresta da Tijuca, no phone. Open Tues.–Sun. 11 AM–7 PM.*

The forest and its viewpoints require private transportation, either by sightseeing tour bus (again the best option), rental car, or taxi.

15 The road through the forest exits in the south zone, next to another of Rio's striking natural attractions, the **Jardim Botânico** (Botanical Garden). The 340-acre garden contains over 5,000 species of tropical and subtropical plants and trees, including 900 varieties of palm tree. The garden was created by Portuguese King João VI in 1808, during his exile in Brazil. While waiting for the British to rid Portugal of Napoleon's armies, the king decided to "civilize" what he considered the backwoods town of Rio. The Royal Botanical Garden was one of his favorite projects, and to make it grow he awarded medals to those who brought him exotic plants and exempted farmers from paying duties on imported species. In 1842 the garden gained its most impressive adornment, the **Avenue of the Royal Palms,** an 800-yard-long double row of 134 soaring royal palms that graces the edge of the garden next to **Rua Jardim Botânico.** Other attractions are the statues scattered throughout the grounds, an 1820 bronze fountain, and mammoth Victoria Regia water lilies from the Amazon, which measure 21 feet around. There are also ponds, sprawling ficus trees, and a small greenhouse filled with insectivorous plants, including Venus's-flytraps. The garden makes for a marvelous afternoon stroll—especially on a hot day, when its temperature is usually a good 10° cooler than on the street. *Rua Jardim Botânico 1008. Open daily 8:30–6.*

16 Across Rua Jardim Botânico from the garden is Rio's **Jockey Club** (Praça Santos Dumont 31, tel. 021/274–0055), a racetrack that doubles as a private club, although being a member today is not the privilege that it once was. While the club has slipped somewhat in status, it has retained what must be the most beautiful view from the stands of any racetrack in the world. You don't have to bet, or even like horses, to enjoy looking out at the lush green of the Botanical Garden and the granite majesty of Corcovado. For $1 tourists can gain entry to the members' stands, where lunches and dinners are served at track-side tables or in the air-conditioned restaurant with its crystal chandeliers. Races start at noon on weekends and at 7:30 PM on Monday and Thursday. The first Sunday of August is reserved for the Brazilian Derby, the country's Kentucky Derby and Ascot.

Continuing up Rua Jardim Botânico you enter the neighborhood of Gávea, a newly popular enclave of Rio's upper middle class that climbs the mountainsides at its edges. At the end of Estrada de Santa Marinha, one of the neighborhood's winding streets

17 reached via Estrada da Gávea, is the **Parque da Cidade,** or City Park. The large hilly park is popular for weekend picnics, and also is home to the **Museu da Cidade** (City Museum), a 19th-century two-story house that was once the residence of a nobleman. The museum contains a century-by-century account of Rio's development since its founding in the 1500s. Objects, furniture, and clothing from different periods are on display. *Estrada de Santa Marinha, tel. 021/322–1328. Open Tues.–Sun. noon–4:30.*

Tour 4: The Beach Neighborhoods

Numbers in the margin correspond with points of interest on the Tour 4: The Beach Neighborhoods map.

From the bay to its farthest ocean boundaries, Rio is home to 23 beaches, an almost continuous 45-mile stretch of white sand. While you probably won't be able to fit all of this tour into one day, you should leave time to explore the city's different beaches and their neighborhoods during your visit to Rio. The tour starts at the bay beaches of Flamengo and Botafogo and then continues roughly south and then west along the coast.

1 **Flamengo** and **Botafogo.** For most of Rio's history, these two bay-side beaches were the city's prime location for bathing. Pollution and population shifts have changed that, and today the two are minor attractions next to the huge Flamengo Parkway (*see* Tour 1, above).

Flamengo is a neighborhood of aging apartments of little interest to visitors. During the years Rio served as Brazil's capital, Botafogo was the site of Rio's glittering embassy row. The embassies are gone now, transferred to Brasília, but the mansions that housed them remain scattered along Botafogo's tree-lined streets. The neighborhood also contains many of Rio's better small restaurants. Among the neighborhood's more interesting streets, lined with the mansions built in Botafogo's heyday, are **Mariana, Sorocaba, Matriz,** and **Visconde de Silva.**

Time Out One of Botafogo's many fine restaurants is the boisterous **Café Pacifico,** Rio's only Mexican restaurant, home to tacos, enchiladas, and tostadas. *Rua Visconde de Silva 14, tel. 021/246–5637. Open weekdays noon–3 PM and 6:30 PM to 2 AM.*

2 **Copacabana.** Maddening traffic, unbearable noise, packed apartment blocks, and one of the world's most famous beaches —this is Copacabana, a Manhattan with bikinis. More than 300,000 people are squeezed into the buildings that line Copacabana's 109 streets. The privileged live on beachfront **Avenida Atlântica,** famed for its wide mosaic sidewalks, hotels, bars, and cafés. A walk along the classic two-mile crescent curve of the beach is a must. On Copacabana you see the essence of Rio beach life, a cradle-to-grave lifestyle that begins with toddlers accompanying their parents to the water and ends with graying seniors walking hand in hand along the beach sidewalk. In between, cariocas meet, gossip, flirt, date, play, dance, read, and, according to rumor, even conduct business deals on the beach. Copacabana's main hotels are located on Avenida Atlântica. Here you'll find the modern, soaring high rise of the **Meridien** (No. 1020) at the start of the beach; the

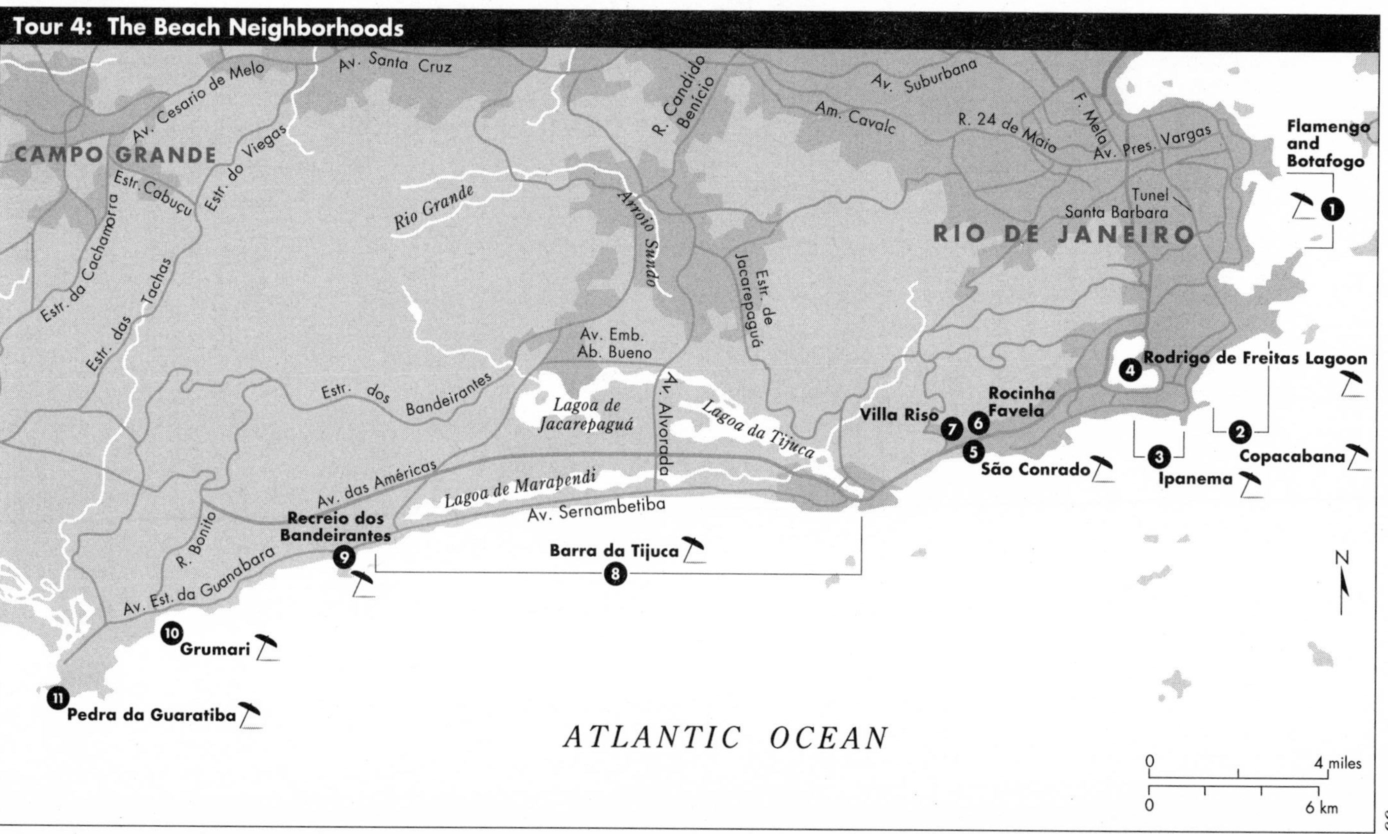
Tour 4: The Beach Neighborhoods
CAMPO GRANDE
Av. Cesario de Melo
Av. Santa Cruz
R. Candido Benício
Av. Suburbana
Am. Cavalc
R. 24 de Maio
F. Mela
Av. Pres. Vargas
Flamengo and Botafogo
1
Tunel Santa Barbara
RIO DE JANEIRO
Estr. Cabuçu
Estr. do Viegas
Estr. da Cachamorra
Estr. das Tachas
Rio Grande
Arroio Sundo
Estr. de Jacarepaguá
Av. Emb. Ab. Bueno
Estr. dos Bandeirantes
Lagoa de Jacarepaguá
Av. Alvorada
Lagoa da Tijuca
4 Rodrigo de Freitas Lagoon
Rocinha Favela
Villa Riso
7
6
5
São Conrado
3
Ipanema
2
Copacabana
Av. das Américas
Lagoa de Marapendi
Av. Sernambetiba
R. Bonito
Recreio dos Bandeirantes
9
Barra da Tijuca
8
Av. Est. da Guanabara
10 Grumari
11 Pedra da Guaratiba
N
ATLANTIC OCEAN
0
4 miles
0
6 km

Rio Othon Palace (No. 3264) in the middle; and the ornate **Rio Palace** (No. 4240) at the far end. Between the Meridien and the Rio Othon Palace are two of Copacabana's older, more traditional hotels: the sedate **Ouro Verde** (No. 1456); and the landmark **Copacabana Palace** (No. 1702), the city's first (and still most famous) luxury hotel, where princes and tycoons gambled away fortunes in the wild 1930s and '40s, when casino gambling was legal in Rio.

Two blocks from the beach and running parallel to it is **Avenida Nossa Senhora de Copacabana,** the neighborhood's main commercial street, whose sidewalks are always crowded with the colorful characters that give Copacabana its special flavor. Shopping in string bikinis is considered normal here.

Time Out Stop in for a drink at one of Avenida Atlântica's outdoor cafés. The draft beer is cold and cheap, the view of Copacabana beach life is unmatched, and if you are looking for company you will find it here. Avoid ordering meals at these sidewalk bar/restaurants, however. Food is overpriced and of poor quality. Stick to beer and snacks. The cafés are open all day and into the morning hours. Try **Lucas** (Av. Atlântica 3744, tel. 021/247–1606); **Rio-Jerez** (Av. Atlântica 3806, tel. 021/267–5644); or **Terraço Atlântico** (Av. Atlântica 3431, tel. 021/521–1296).

---

3 **Ipanema.** At one time Copacabana was the most exclusive address in Rio, but when the neighborhood filled up, Rio's upper crust moved on to the next beach south, Ipanema. Today, Ipanema, nearby **Leblon,** and the blocks surrounding the near-
4 by **Rodrigo de Freitas Lagoon** comprise Rio's money belt. For a close-up look at Rio's most posh apartment buildings, stroll down beachfront **Avenida Vieira Souto** and its extension **Delfim Moreira,** or take a drive around the lagoon on **Avenida Epitácio Pessoa,** a street that many consider Rio's most beautiful. On Vieira Souto, don't be surprised if you see a long line of limousines pulling up to the **Caesar Park** hotel (No. 460), the neighborhood's leading hotel and a frequent stopping point for visiting dignitaries and international celebrities. The tree-lined streets between Ipanema Beach and the lagoon are among the most peaceful and attractive of the city. Nothing, though, quite matches the lagoon for raw natural beauty. The calm water, the surrounding mountains covered with green vegetation, and Corcovado and the Christ statue take your breath away. If possible plan your day so that you pass by the lagoon at sunset. If you are an early riser or a jogger, the view at sunrise is also exceptional. For sophistication, stroll down the **Rua Garcia D'Avila,** where most of Ipanema's trend-setting boutiques are clustered. Other "in" addresses of Rio's trendiest neighborhoods are **Praça da Paz, Rua Vinicius de Morais, Farme de Amoedo,** and **Anibal Mendonça.** Here you'll find chic boutiques, jewelry stores, and top restaurants.

Time Out The streets of Ipanema and Leblon are literally filled with small bars, fast-food outlets, and a neighborhood specialty—stand-up fruit-juice bars, where you can experiment from a wide variety of fresh tropical fruits blended together into delicious concoctions. On the beachfront, however, the lone watering hole in Leblon is the **Caneco 70,** a good stop for a beer or cooling orange juice. The upstairs tables have the best view of the beach action, while the downstairs tables have the closest view of Rio's promenading beautiful people. *Av. Delfim Moreira 1026, tel. 021/294–1180. Open 10* ***AM–4:30 AM.***

Have you ever wondered if there really *was* a Girl from Ipanema? There was and still is, and although she no longer lives in Rio, her memory is well preserved. The song was inspired by then-carioca schoolgirl Heloisa Pinheiro, who caught the fancy of songwriter Tom Jobim and his pal lyricist Vinicius de Morais as she walked home from school past the two bohemians sitting in their favorite bar. The two then turned out one of the century's top pop classics. That was in 1962, and today the bar has been renamed A **Garôta de Ipanema** (Girl from Ipanema) and is one of Ipanema's most "in" addresses for drinks and conversation. The street is named after Morais, now dead. Jobim is still writing songs, while Heloisa is a still-beautiful businesswoman and mother of four living in São Paulo. Drop in for a beer and a taste of Rio's modern history. *Rua Vinicius de Morais 49-A, tel. 021/267–8787. Open daily 11* ***AM–3 AM.***

São Conrado and the Southern Beaches. For a wonderful outing, take a cab from Ipanema to the fishing village of **Pedra da Guaratiba,** 45 minutes away. The drive starts out by climbing **Avenida Niemeyer** at the end of Ipanema where the imposing **Dois Irmaos Mountain** stands. The road hugs the rugged cliffs with spectacular sea views on the left before snaking down to sea level again in São Conrado, a natural amphitheater surrounded by forested mountains on three sides and the beach and ocean on the fourth.

5 **São Conrado** is a mostly residential neighborhood divided, starkly, between high- and low-income families. Wealthy cariocas live on the valley floor in plush condominiums, while the high ground has been taken over by Rio's largest shantytown,
6 **Rocinha.** Called *favelas,* these hillside slums are present throughout the south zone of Rio and are the result of the city's chronic housing problem coupled with the unwillingness of many of the city's poor to live in distant working-class neighborhoods. As a result an estimated 1 million people live in Rio's 480 favelas. Living conditions vary from one slum to another but are always precarious. The shacks are made of either wood and cardboard hammered together, or of bricks and makeshift mortar. Most of these dwellings have electricity, and in some cases there is running water, but there is no sewage and the slums are always subject to flooding and landslides when the summer rains come. The favelas are crime centers and of late have become heavily involved in Rio's drug trade.

Tourists should consider favelas off-limits, though you can safely drive by and look to get an idea of just how deplorable life in a shantytown is. Rocinha in particular is impressive, a teeming anthill of over 80,000 people living in a compact space spilling down the mountainside.

São Conrado is also home to more pleasant sights. Hang gliders float overhead preparing to land on the beach, while in the middle of the small valley is the exclusive Gávea Golf and Country Club. The far end of São Conrado is marked by the towering presence of **Gávea Mountain,** a huge flat-topped granite block. Next to it is **Pedra Bonita,** the mountain from which the gliders depart. In the 18th century the valley was a sugar plantation
7 and the original plantation house, **Villa Riso,** is still intact and

open to visitors. It offers a complete program including a tour of the beautiful grounds and the well-preserved house, a show of Brazilian folk music and dances, and a buffet lunch of Brazilian fish and meat dishes. The staff all dress in clothing from Brazil's colonial period. *Estrada da Gávea 728, tel. 021/322–0899 or 322–1444. Cost: $20, including lunch and transfer. Tour: Tues. 12:30–4. Call in advance for reservations.*

Continuing along the coast from São Conrado, the road becomes an elevated viaduct hanging half over the water, with views of the ocean on the left and sheer mountain cliffs on the right, where sumptuous homes hang at precarious angles.
8 Emerging from a tunnel you enter **Barra da Tijuca,** Rio's suburbia. This flat, open area is free of the space limitations that plague the rest of the southern zone and is undergoing development. Condominium complexes are springing up along the beach, while inland the city's largest shopping centers and supermarkets have already made the Barra their home. Drive along the beachfront avenue, **Sernambetiba,** which extends for 11 miles (the Barra beach is the longest of Rio's beaches). On the left is the pounding surf while in the distance to the right are mountains with numerous fresh-water lagoons in between.
9 At the end is a massive rock that marks the **Recreio dos Bandeirantes,** a small cove popular for bathing.

From here the road again climbs, following the undulating
coastline to the small surfers' beach **Prainha,** and beyond that
10 to the crown jewel of Rio's beaches, **Grumari.** From Grumari, a
potholed road climbs almost straight up through the thick forest, finally emerging at the top of a hill overlooking the vast
11 **Guaratiba flatlands.** Down the hill is the fishing village of **Pedra**
da Guaratiba, site of some of Rio's finest, albeit rustic, seafood
restaurants, including **Quatro Sete Meia** (*see* Chapter 6).

Time Out In addition to the view of the flatlands and ocean below, the final viewpoint also offers a delightful rest stop, the **Vista Alegre Bar.** While you are enjoying the view, you can also enjoy an excellent *caipirinha* (the potent but tasty Brazilian drink made out of ground lime, crushed ice, and sugarcane alcohol) at this richly ambient, hole-in-the-wall bar. Open daily 8 AM–10 PM.

What to See and Do with Children

Hotels with pools are usually the best choice if you are traveling with children. The more activities the better, and Rio's two resort hotels, the **Rio Sheraton** and the **Inter-Continental Rio** (*see* Chapter 7), are the city's most popular with families because of their multiple pools, sports facilities and programs, and varied dining and entertainment options. In addition, the Sheraton is the only hotel in Rio with a playground. The city, meanwhile, offers other attractions of interest to children.

A visit to the **Barra Shopping** center (*see* Malls in Chapter 4) is a guaranteed hit with youngsters. The mall has a mini-amusement park with rides and all the extras, including cotton candy (*algodão doce* in Portuguese). The mall also has Rio's only bowling alley and, believe it or not, an indoor ice-skating rink.

Boat trips in the bay (*see* Tour 2, above) offer an exciting and time-consuming distraction. The horse-and-buggy trip around the island of **Paqueta** is definitely recommended.

During **Carnival,** many private clubs hold children's balls in the afternoon. These are delightfully tame and innocent, virtually the only balls where the primary emphasis is on wearing costumes, often elaborate ones. Ask at your hotel for help in gaining admittance to one of these balls.

Many of Rio's **parks** have been taken over by the homeless and beggars, making them unattractive for foreign tourists. Exceptions are the **Flamengo Parkway,** or **Atêrro** (*see* Tour 1, above), and the **Tijuca Forest** (*see* Tour 3, above).

Rio also has a large and complete amusement park, the **Tivoli Park,** located on the banks of the lagoon. It also offers every stomach-churning ride imaginable. *Lagoa Rodrigo de Freitas. Open Thurs. and Fri. 2–8 PM, Sat. 3–11 PM, and Sun. 10–10.*

Rio's prime viewpoints, **Sugarloaf** and **Corcovado,** are fascinating for all ages (*see* Tours 2 and 3, above). On occasion, the amphitheater atop Sugarloaf has special plays or musical shows for children, although in Portuguese.

The colonial show at **Villa Riso** (*see* Tour 4, above) and Rio's **zoo** (*see* Tour 1, above) are fine spots to bring your children.

Off the Beaten Track

Getting close to the samba cult is a wish of many first-time and even repeat visitors to Rio caught up in the fascinating rhythms and dance of Brazil's national music. It is actually not that difficult to achieve. To get your feet wet, go on Friday or Saturday night to **Avenida Sernambetiba** in the Barra da Tijuca where a multitude of trailers sell food and drink along the beachfront. Two or three of these trailers each weekend night host what are called *pagodes* by samba aficionados. A pagode is a samba jam session, where musicians, many of them top professionals, drop in and perform for an appreciative hand-clapping, toe-tapping audience. It is good clean fun beneath the stars, fueled by cold beer and fried fish and lasting, if the mood's right, until nearly dawn.

For the ultimate samba experience join a samba school for Carnival and dance down the avenue in a glittering costume during the samba-school parade. Each year several members of Rio's foreign community do exactly that. If you are in Rio at least a week before Carnival, call **"RioLife,"** the newsletter of Rio's English-speaking community, at 021/580–8498. They will be able to get you in touch with a member of the community who is dancing with a samba school. If you make it, expect to pay at least $100 for your costume, but the experience will be unforgettable.

If you enjoy adventure, go to **São Conrado** on a Sunday and wait on the far end of the beach, where the hang gliders land. If you ask them they will take you by car up to the jumping-off point, a wooden platform atop the Pedra Bonita Mountain, overlooking São Conrado. From the platform you have one of Rio's most incredible views, looking straight down at the lush green valley of São Conrado, the ocean, and surrounding mountains. More impressive, though, is the jump itself. For $60 you can take a tandem ride.

The spiritual side of Rio is shown graphically by the interior of the **Igreja Penha** (Church of Penha). Perched high atop a mountain in Rio's north zone, the church is the focus of pilgrims who climb its 365 steps on their knees as an expression of gratitude for divine cures. The inside is hung with crutches and silver charms representing parts of the body that were cured, supposedly thanks to the intervention of Our Lady of Penha. The view from the top is superb. *Largo da Penha 19. Open 7 AM–5 PM.*

Another side of Rio's spiritual life can be seen in **macumba,** an African-inspired religious cult somewhat reminiscent of Caribbean voodoo. Macumba ceremonies are a fascinating mix of throbbing drums, dancing, and chanting that drives participants into trances. Unfortunately, spectators are not generally permitted at these ceremonies, but a few tour companies have organized macumba tours. The best is the Gray Line (tel. 021/274–7146 or 021/294–1444) tour, which leaves every Friday night for a four-hour visit to a *terreiro,* a site of macumba ceremonies. The cost is $40 per person. If you are in Rio on **New Year's Eve,** don't miss the macumba ceremony on Copacabana Beach. As midnight approaches, the beach becomes a swaying, chanting mass of devotees dressed in the cult's traditional white. Gathered around candle-lit altars set up in the sand, they wait for the stroke of midnight to race to the water and throw offerings of flowers, perfume, and jewelry to sea goddess Iemanjá.

Sightseeing Checklists

This list includes both attractions that were covered in the preceding tours and additional attractions that are described here for the first time.

Historical Buildings and Sites

Beco do Comércio (*see* Tour 1: Historical Rio). Subway stop: Largo da Carioca.

Carioca Aqueduct (*see* Tour 1: Historical Rio). Subway stop: Largo da Carioca.

Lapa Neighborhood (*see* Tour 1: Historical Rio). Subway stop: Largo da Carioca.

Largo do Boticário (*see* Tour 3: Corcovado and the Tijuca Forest).

Teatro Municipal (*see* Tour 1: Historical Rio). Subway stop: Cinelândia.

Biblioteca Nacional (*see* Tour 1: Historical Rio). Subway stop: Cinelândia.

Paço Imperial (*see* Tour 1: Historical Rio). Subway stop: Largo da Carioca.

Praça XV (*see* Tour 1: Historical Rio). Subway stop: Largo da Carioca.

Santa Cruz Fort (*see* Tour 2: The Bay and Sugarloaf).

Santa Teresa Neighborhood (*see* Tour 1: Historical Rio).

Villa Riso (*see* Tour 4: The Beach Neighborhoods).

Churches

Candelária Church (*see* Tour 1: Historical Rio). Subway stop: Largo da Carioca.

Glória Church (*see* Tour 1: Historical Rio). Subway stop: Glória.

Metropolitan Cathedral (*see* Tour 1: Historical Rio). Subway stop: Largo da Carioca.

Nossa Senhora da Lampadosa Chapel. Located downtown near Praça Tiradentes, five blocks north of Largo da Carioca, is this small, 18th-century chapel built by slaves. It was here that Tiradentes, the leader of Brazil's first revolt against Portuguese rule, heard mass before he was executed in 1793. Today Tiradentes is a national hero, and the nearby square where he was executed bears his name.

Nossa Senhora do Carmo Church (*see* Tour 1: Historical Rio). Subway stop: Largo da Carioca.

Santo Antonio Convent (*see* Tour 1: Historical Rio). Subway stop: Largo da Carioca.

São Bento Monastery (*see* Tour 1: Historical Rio). Subway stop: Largo da Carioca.

São Francisco da Penitência (*see* Tour 1: Historical Rio). Subway stop: Largo da Carioca.

São Francisco de Paula Church. The paintings within this 1756 church are its main attraction. Some are religious works by Brazil's most famed 18th-century painter, Mestre Valentim da Fonseca e Silva. Others are a who's who of 19th-century Brazilian politicians and noblemen. The church faces the south side of the Largo de São Francisco, downtown.

Museums

Casa Rui Barbosa (*see* Tour 2: The Bay and Sugarloaf).

Catete Palace (*see* Tour 1: Historical Rio). Subway stop: Catete.

Chácara do Ceu Museum (*see* Tour 1: Historical Rio).

City Museum (*see* Tour 3: Corcovado and the Tijuca Forest).

Indian Museum (*see* Tour 2: The Bay and Sugarloaf).

Museum of Fine Arts (*see* Tour 1: Historical Rio). Subway stop: Cinelândia.

Museum of Modern Art (Av. Infante Dom Henrique 85, Flamengo Parkway, tel. 021/210–2188). The museum's entire collection was destroyed in a 1978 fire. The beautiful building is now open only to host occasional film screenings and traveling art exhibits. Check to see if there is an event being held while you are in town.

National History Museum (*see* Tour 1: Historical Rio). Subway stop: Largo da Carioca.

National Museum (*see* Tour 1: Historical Rio). Subway stop: Maracanã.

Parks and Gardens

Jardim Botânico (*see* Tour 3: Corcovado and the Tijuca Forest).

Flamengo Parkway (*see* Tour 1: Historical Rio). Subway stop: Flamengo or Glória.

Parque da Catacumba. Located off the western edge of Avenida Epitácio Pessoa, the road that circles the Rodrigo de Freitas Lagoon, is this pleasant, statue-filled park. The lagoon is also surrounded by a jogging path and has several tennis courts.

Parque da Cidade (*see* Tour 3: Corcovado and the Tijuca Forest).

Praça Paris Parkway (*see* Tour 1: Historical Rio). Subway stop: Glória.

Quinta da Boa Vista (*see* Tour 1: Historical Rio). Subway stop: Maracanã.

Tijuca Forest (*see* Tour 3: Corcovado and the Tijuca Forest).

Other Places of Interest

Jockey Club (*see* Tour 3: Corcovado and the Tijuca Forest).

Maracanã Stadium (*see* Tour 1: Historical Rio). Subway stop: Maracanã.

Jardim Zoológico (*see* Tour 1: Historical Rio). Subway stop: Maracanã.

4 Shopping

by Edwin Taylor

Rio de Janeiro is one of South America's premier shopping cities, with excellent opportunities to buy everything from simple souvenirs to luxury items such as fine jewelry and elegant clothing. Besides the variety of products available in Rio's stores, there is also a wide choice of shopping ambiences. Shoppers can stroll down city streets lined with fashionable boutiques, wander through modern, air-conditioned malls, or barter with the vendors at street markets and fairs.

Brazil's four-digit inflation and weak currency have added to the allure of Rio's shops by driving down the dollar value of prices. Due to tight restrictions on imports, however, you will find no bargains on non-Brazilian products (in most cases they will be more expensive than at home). In addition, U.S. citizens are not required to pay duty on many items of which 35% or more was made in Brazil (*see* Customs and Duties in Before You Go, Chapter 1). This is a country where it is best to buy native. There is no sales tax in Brazil; the price you see is what you will pay.

Remember to always pay for your purchases in Brazilian currency. If you pay in dollars you will be given an exchange rate that is good for the shop but terrible for you. The same is true for credit card purchases which, while convenient at the time of purchase, will turn out to cost you a bundle due to the unfavorable exchange rate used to convert *cruzado* prices to dollars. Bargaining is reserved for street fairs and street vendors.

Stores outside of shopping centers are generally open weekdays from 9 or 10 AM to 6 or 7 PM, and on Saturdays from 9 or 10 until noon. In the malls, shopping continues from 9 or 10 AM until 10 PM Monday through Saturday. There is no midday break for naps in Brazil, although a few shops (such as galleries) may close for an hour or two around lunchtime.

Gift Ideas

Stones, both precious and semiprecious, leather goods, cotton fashions, and handicrafts are all good buys in Brazil. The variety and quality of Brazilian gemstones is stunning, but if you want to spend less on a gift, souvenir shops have ashtrays, bookends, ornamental eggs, carved animals, and jewelry made of agate and other varieties of colored quartz. Soapstone containers and carvings are also inexpensive.

Leather shoes are a true bargain in Rio. You can find chic, finely finished leather handbags and clothing in trendy boutiques, or sturdy top-stitched rawhide totes at the street markets. Cotton, linen, and silk are all produced in Brazil. You will find fashions in these fibers ranging from sophisticated classics to colorful casual wear. Summer fashions are a Rio specialty, and shops are filled with inexpensive and creative bikinis, shorts, and dresses with an emphasis on the daring. Tiny string bikinis are a carioca trademark and can be found for sale everywhere, including from vendors on the beach itself.

Another favorite among tourists is the lace and embroidery from the northeast of Brazil, available in the form of dresses and blouses, tablecloths, and hand towels. Handicrafts from the neighboring state of Minas Gerais and other regions of Brazil also make unique souvenirs. All can be found at **Pé de Boi** (Rua Aníbel de Mendonça 108, Shop C). Indian handicrafts are also sold in many souvenir stores, although their authenticity is sometimes dubious. The **Artindia** shop downtown (Av. Presidente Wilson 164), run by Brazil's Indian Bureau, Funai, has a small selection, but you can be sure the items are for real. A variety of local painters and artisans also sell their creations at regularly scheduled street markets.

Music is a key component of the Brazilian character, and the first introduction of foreigners to the country often comes through popular Brazilian tunes. Shops selling records and tapes are scattered around the city and can be found in all the malls.

One typical but often overlooked gift idea is the delicious, dark-roasted coffee. For last-minute shoppers, it is sold in convenient carry-on cartons at the airport.

Shopping Districts

Ipanema is the most fashionable shopping district in Rio, with a seemingly endless array of exclusive boutiques. Cool summer clothing in natural fibers, appropriate for the climate, is the top item here.

Many of Ipanema's shops are concentrated in arcades, the majority of which are located along Rua Visconde de Pirajà. Try **Forum de Ipanema** at number 351 near the Praça da Paz square; **Quartier de Ipanema** at number 414; the upscale **Galeria 444** at number 444; and **Vitrine de Ipanema** at number 580.

Ipanema is also home to three big names in gems: **H. Stern, Amsterdam-Sauer,** and **Roditi** are all located conveniently next door to each other along Rua Visconde de Pirajà.

Although **Copacabana** has lost some of its former glamour, attractive shops still line Avenida Nossa Senhora de Copacabana and the side streets. Here you'll find a number of souvenir shops, bookstores, and branches of some of Rio's better stores, although for top of the market jewelers head for beachfront Avenida Atlântica.

Shopping **downtown** provides a mixture of quality outlets for men's and women's wear and stores aimed at the bargain hunter. The best choices for both are concentrated on several pedestrian streets on either side of Avenida Rio Branco from Avenida Presidente Vargas to Cinelândia, where a branch of the **Mesbla** department store is located.

Street Markets

Flea Markets Known in Rio as the **Hippie Fair,** the colorful handicraft fair held every Sunday from 9 AM to 6 PM on Ipanema's Praça General Osório is the most popular among foreign visitors. Here you are usually buying directly from the artisan. Paintings and wood carvings, leather bags, sandals and clothing, batik fashions, jewelry, hand-printed T-shirts, rag dolls, knickknacks, and even furniture are on sale. Finely crafted items are mixed in with basic junk. One noisy, popular booth sells samba percussion instruments.

A smaller **fair** is set up every Thursday and Friday downtown at Praça XV from 8 AM to 6 PM, with leather goods, handmade cotton clothes, embroidery, decorations, knickknacks, jewelry, and straw bags. Similar articles are on sale on weekdays downtown at the **Largo da Carioca.**

The latest addition to Rio's street fairs is also the most convenient for the majority of tourists. In the evenings along the median of Copacabana's beachfront drive, **Avenida Atlântica,** artisans spread out their wares across from Copacabana's hotel strip, with the action concentrated in front of the Rio Othon Palace hotel. Here, from nightfall until the customers go home, you will find paintings, carvings, handicrafts, sequined dresses, hammocks from the northeast, and souvenir T-shirts. The fair is popular not only because of its convenience but also because it serves as a meeting point for tourists from around the world.

On Saturdays there is an **open-air antiques fair** during daylight hours on **Praça Marechal Ancora,** downtown near **Praça XV.** Here you can purchase china and silver sets, old watches, Oriental rugs, chandeliers, rare books, all types of paintings and art objects, and even old records. The fair moves out to the **Casa Shopping Center** in Barra da Tijuca on Sundays.

The **Feira Nordestino (Northeastern Fair),** held every Sunday morning at the Campo de São Cristóvão from 6 AM to 1 PM, is a different type of experience. Although there are embroidery and lace articles, hammocks, wood-block prints, and leather footwear from Brazil's northeast on sale, the fair is not aimed at tourists, or even at cariocas. It is a social event for northeasterners living in Rio, who gather to hear their own distinctive music, eat and purchase regional foods, and buy tools and cheap clothing. The crowded, noisy market offers a glimpse of another side of Brazil not often seen by tourists.

Food Markets If you have the time you should also stop by one of Rio's ubiquitous outdoor food markets, where everything from fruits and vegetables to fresh fish and pots and pans is sold. These street markets are a traditional aspect of Rio that has not changed in decades. Fairs are held every day of the week on predetermined streets, from early in the morning until noon (prices fall as closing approaches). The most convenient for tourists are the Friday **Ipanema Fair** at Praça Nossa Senhora da Paz, and the Thursday **Copacabana Fair** at Rua Ronald de Carvalho, between Avenida Nossa Senhora de Copacabana and Rua Barata Ribeiro.

Specialty Stores

Art For collectors as well as tourists looking for distinctive gifts, Brazilian art has great appeal. Rio's galleries provide a good cross section of contemporary Brazilian art, from the brightly colored canvases of primitivists to the more cerebral work of Brazil's modernists. Not widely known outside of Brazil, the country's artwork is currently undervalued with excellent investment potential. The following galleries can be counted on to contain a worthwhile, representative sampling.

Bonino is the most traditional, best-known, and most visited of Rio's art galleries. It has been around for some 30 years and is very active, with a high turnover of shows. *Rua Barata Ribeiro 578, Copacabana, tel. 021/235–7831. Open weekdays 10–noon and 3–9, Sat. 10–7.*

Contorno is a more eclectic gallery, but the art it displays is certainly Brazilian. *Shopping Center da Gávea, Rua Marquês*

Rio Shopping

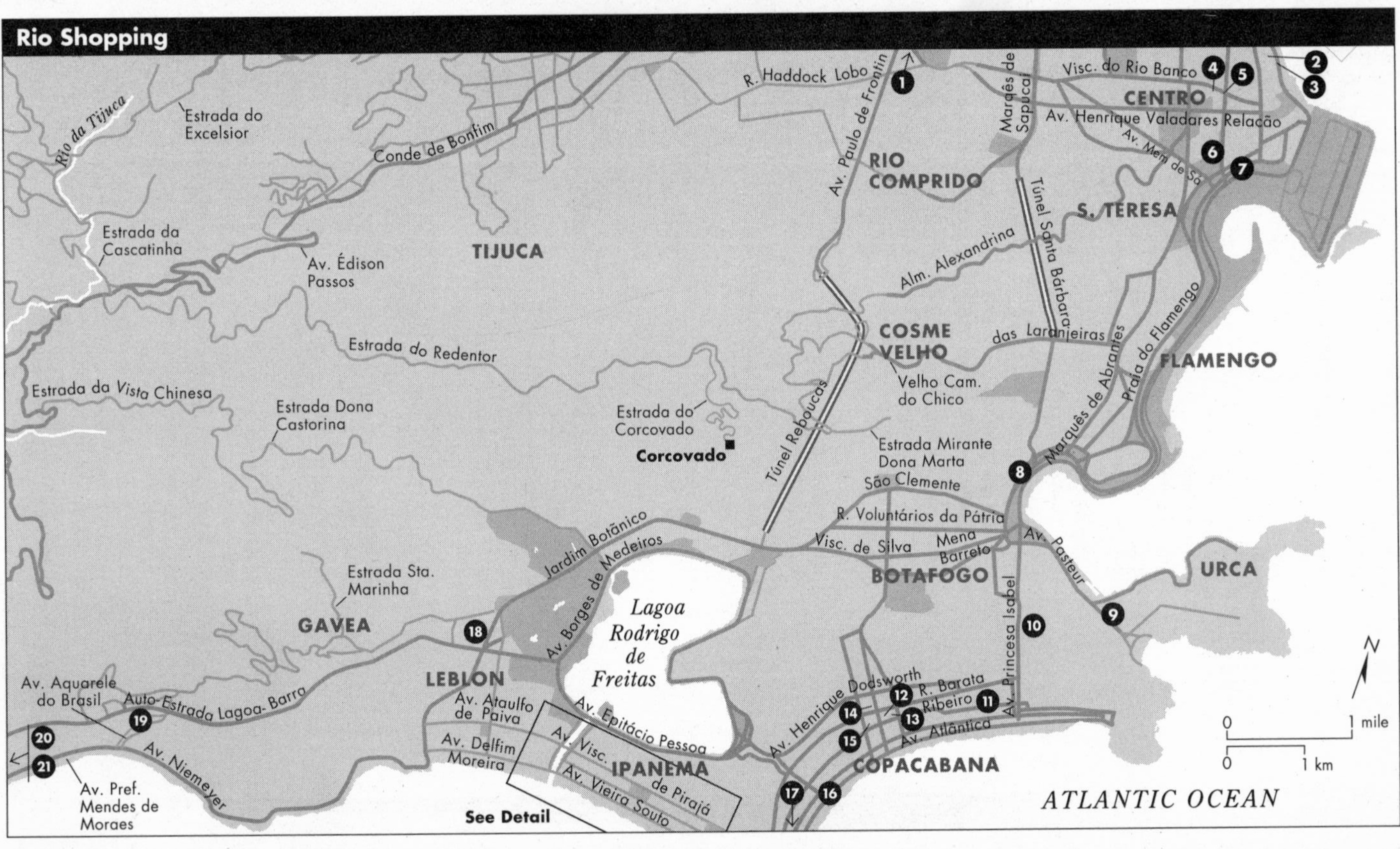

Ipanema Shopping

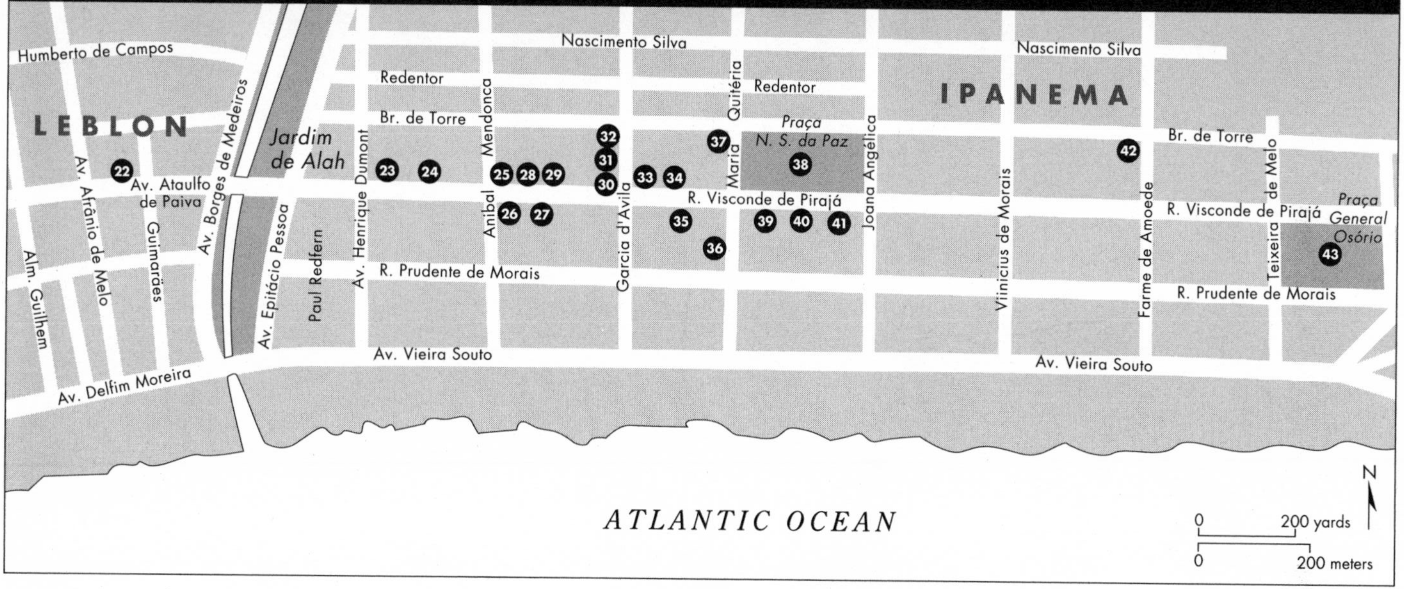

Amsterdam-Sauer, **29**
Artindia, **7**
Asparagus, **36**
Avenida Atlântica, **16**
Barra Shopping, **21**
Bee, **18**
Bonino, **14**
Bum Bum, **35**
C&A, **15**
Casa Shopping Center, **20**
Copacabana Food Fair, **11**
Dá no Pé, **13**
Dijon, **33**
Evelyn's, **24**
Formosinho, **12**
Forum de Ipanema, **40**
Galeria 444, **34**
Galeria de Arte Jean-Jacques, **9**
Hippie Fair, **43**
H. Stern, **28**
Ipanema Food Fair, **38**
Krishna, **31**
Largo da Carioca, **4**
Leonardo da Vinci, **5**
Mesbla, **6**
Mr. Wonderful, **26**
Northeastern Fair, **1**
Pé de Boi, **25**
Praça XV de Novembro, **2**
Praça Marechal Ancora, **3**
Quartier de Ipanema, **39**
Richard's, **37**
Rio Design Center, **22**
Rio Sul, **10**
Roditi, **30**
Rotstein and Pucci, **41**
São Conrado Fashion Mall, **19**
Sears, **8**
Shopping Center Cassino Atlântico, **17**
Shopping Center da Gávea, **18**
Spy & Great, **32**
Thomas Cohn, **42**
Vitrine de Ipanema, **23**

de São Vicente 52, Gávea, tel. 021/274–3832. Open daily 10–12:30 and 2–7.

The Gávea mall is also home to several other excellent galleries, of which the best are **Ana Maria Niemeyer, Beco da Arte, Borghese, Bronze, Paulo Klabin, Saramenha,** and **Toulouse.**

Galeria de Arte Jean-Jacques specializes in paintings by Brazilian primitive artists. *Rua Ramon Franco 49, Urca, within walking distance of the Sugarloaf cable car station, tel. 021/542–1443. Open Tues.–Sat. 11–8.*

Gravura Brasileira shows work by the most important names in Brazilian contemporary art. *Shopping Center Cassino Atlântico, Av. Atlântica 4240, Copacabana, next to the Rio Palace hotel, tel. 021/267–3747. Open weekdays 10–9 and Sat. 2–6.*

Also in the Cassino Atlântico are the **Gauguin, Investiarte, Maria Augusta, Mini Gallery, Ralph Camargo, Versailles** galleries; **Aktuel** features sculpture.

The **Rio Design Center** (*see* Malls, below) in Leblon contains several galleries, including **Borghese, Beco da Arte, Montesanti, Museum,** and **Way.**

Thomas Cohn shows contemporary, avant-garde Brazilian art. *Rua Barão da Torre 185-A, Ipanema, tel. 021/287–9993. Open weekdays 2–8 and Sat. 4–8.*

Books **Leonardo da Vinci** (Av. Rio Banco 185, down the ramp at subsolo No. 2, tel. 021/533–2237), a fabulous bookstore with books in several languages, has a broad selection of art books. It is located downtown, near Largo da Carioca.

Clothing
Women's **Krishna** (Rua Garcia D'Avila 101, near the H. Stern headquarters) specializes in classic, feminine dresses and separates, many in linen and silk. Silk dresses costing as much as $200 are still a good buy by international standards. Also featuring classics, **Asparagus** (Rua Carlos Goes 234, Leblon; and Rua Maria Quitéria 59B, Ipanema) is known for its knit fashions. Stylish, comfortable cotton jersey dresses go for $40–$60. **Spy & Great** (Rua Garcia D'Avila 58 and Rua Garcia D'Avila 121, Ipanema) is known for its casual fashions, many in denim. **Evelyn's** (Rua Visconde de Pirajá 550, Shop J, Ipanema; Av. Nossa Senhora de Copacabana 471, Shop A, Copacabana; and a half a dozen other locations around Rio) has bright cotton jersey separates for around $20.

Other top shops for women's casual wear with branches in the leading malls include **Smuggler, Yes Brasil, Smash,** and **Toot.**

Many boutiques carry bikinis—**Cantão** has a good selection of colors and styles—but the market leader in beachwear is **Bum Bum,** with two Ipanema stores at Rua Vinicius de Morais 130 and Rua Visconde de Pirajá 437. Another favorite is **Agua na Boca** (Rua Visconde de Pirajá 444, Ipanema). Bikinis and cutaway one-piece suits sell for $10–$15.

Men's For men, classic, elegant casual fashions are the specialty at **Richard's** (Rua Maria Quitéria 95, Ipanema). Sophisticated linen trousers and jackets cost a little over $100 apiece. Other stores carrying handsome, quality men's clothing include **Dijon** (Rua Garcia D'Avila 110, Ipanema; and Rua Barata Ribeiro numbers 496-A, 560-F, and 752-E in Copacabana); **Philippe**

Martin (Rua Visconde de Pirajá 338, Ipanema); and **Van Gogh** (Rua Visconde de Pirajá 444, Ipanema). Trendy, but quality, men's fashions can be found at **Mr. Wonderful** (Rua Visconde de Pirajá between Rua Anibal de Mendonça and Rua Garcia D'Avila, Ipanema).

Men's, Women's, and Children's **Bee,** at Rua Visconde de Pirajá 483, offers original, casual designs for men, women, and children; T-shirts start at $15. **Benetton, Cantão, Dimpus,** and **Fiorucci** carry both men's and women's fashions at numerous stores throughout Rio and at the major malls. Rio's department stores (*see* Department Stores, below) all carry large selections of men's, women's, and children's clothing.

Jewelry Brazil is one of the world's largest producers of gold and the largest supplier of colored gemstones, with important deposits of aquamarines, amethysts, diamonds, emeralds, rubellites, topazes, and tourmalines.

You will have no problem finding either jewelry stores or salespeople in Rio. Stores are found at the airports, on all major shopping streets, in the malls, and at leading hotels. But unless you are an expert it's wise to do your gem shopping at one of Rio's reputable jewelers. Although you may find lower prices in souvenir stores, your purchases could turn out to be nothing more than colored glass. By international standards the prices are already extremely attractive, so don't take any chances.

The top names in jewelry in Rio are **H. Stern** and **Amsterdam-Sauer.** At the H. Stern world headquarters at Rua Visconde de Pirajá 490 in Ipanema, you can see exhibits of rare gemstones and take a free tour demonstrating how raw stones are transformed into sparkling jewels. Transportation is provided from the major hotels.

Amsterdam-Sauer and **Roditi** have large outlets next door to H. Stern. Other reliable jewelers are **Masson, M. Rosenmann, Maximino, Natan, Sidi, Moreno, Gregory and Sheehan,** and **Ernani G. Walter.**

For costume jewelry, try the Sunday Hippie Fair in Ipanema (*see* Street Markets, above). Here you will find creations not only in silver and precious stones but also original items made of acrylic, feathers, seashells, and bone.

Leather Leather goods, especially shoes, are an excellent buy in Rio. The shopping malls all have a good selection. At the Rio Sul shopping center, **Germon's** and **Sagaró** carry high-quality, dressy women's shoes, and **Altemia Spinelli** and **Birello** carry both men's and women's dress shoes. Also at the Rio Sul, **Victor Hugo** and **Santa Marinella** specialize in handbags for women. **Beltrami,** with stores at the Rio Sul and the São Conrado Fashion Mall, carries fine women's shoes and bags, as do **Bottega Veneta** and **Nazaré,** both at the Shopping Center da Gávea.

In Ipanema you will find fashionable footwear at **Roland Rivel, Mariazinha,** and **Soft Shoes,** all at the Forum de Ipanema arcade on Praça Nossa Senhora da Paz. Nearby at Rua Visconde de Pirajá 371, **Rotstein** and **Pucci** have a large variety of exclusive and casual women's shoes and bags.

With stores all over town, **Sapasso** and **Polar** are the two largest shoe-store chains, with footwear for men, women, and children. For low prices you can't beat **Formosinho** and **Dá no Pé,** which sell stock ends of export models. Formosinho, with men's and women's shoes, has three stores along Rua Visconde de Pirajá and one at Avenida Nossa Senhora de Copacabana 582. A Dá no Pé shop (women's shoes only) is on the same block (Av. Nossa Senhora de Copacabana 614).

The first name in leather clothing in Rio is **Frankie Amaury,** located in the Shopping Center da Gávea.

Other places to find leather bags, sandals, and belts are the handicraft fairs held on Sunday at the Praça General Osório in Ipanema and on Thursdays and Fridays at Praça XV downtown (*see* Street Markets, above). Although some are finely crafted, most are rustic and rough-hewn.

Malls

Rio's shopping malls are modern and attractive, based on the American model, with a growing number of dining and entertainment options. Most of Rio's fashionable stores, including the large department stores and the leading boutiques, have a branch at one or more of the malls. Hours are generally from 9 or 10 AM to 10 PM, Monday through Saturday.

Of the malls near the Copacabana–Ipanema–Leblon neighborhoods, **Rio Sul** (Av. Lauro Müller 116) in Botafogo has the most to offer. The city's best boutiques and traditional clothing stores are represented in its more than 400 shops. You will also find plenty of shops selling home decorations, records, tapes, books, and gifts, in addition to branches of the C&A and Mesbla department stores and a large supermarket. Besides snack bars and a café, there is a *churrascaria* barbecue restaurant. Free bus service is available to and from the larger hotels.

Right on the beach at the Ipanema end of Copacabana, adjoining the Rio Palace hotel, is the **Shopping Center Cassino Atlântico** (Av. Atlântica 4240). Here you will find a concentration of antiques stores, art galleries, and souvenir shops, as well as a pleasant atrium café and a small tea room.

The **Rio Design Center** (Av. Ataulfo de Paiva 270) in Leblon specializes in interior decorating, with several attractive furniture and home furnishings showrooms. Of more interest to tourists, however, are the several art galleries and antiques stores. The center also frequently exhibits Brazilian arts and crafts, such as ceramics and tapestries.

The **Shopping Center da Gávea** (Rua Marquês de São Vicente 52) in Gávea has a mixture of fashionable clothing stores—both small boutiques and branches of larger chains—as well as many leather goods stores, home furnishings and furniture showrooms, and top art galleries. The mall has three movie theaters and several fast-food outlets.

The **São Conrado Fashion Mall** (Autoestrada Lagoa Barra) is located near the Inter-Continental and Nacional hotels in São Conrado. Most of its shops sell fashionable clothes, mainly for women, but clothing for men and children is also available. There are a few gift, stationery, and interior-decorating stores, and a fitness center and ballet studio, too. Since the mall is within walking distance of the nearby hotels, it has unfortunately attracted the attention of petty thieves. Take special care when leaving the mall. Hold onto your purchases and keep an eye out for the innocent-looking children who ask for money on the sidewalk.

Barra Shopping (Av. das Américas 4666) is the largest and most complete of Rio's malls. Although it is located in Barra da Tijuca (10–15 minutes by car or bus from Ipanema), shoppers from all over town head for this large complex. Here you will find hundreds of boutiques (all of Rio's finest fashion stores are represented here) and larger stores, including branches of Mesbla, Sears, and C&A department stores. There are also three movie theaters, an extensive play area for children with rides and games, Rio's only bowling alley and only ice-skating rink, banking and postal services, and a variety of restaurants and fast-food outlets, including a McDonald's. The mall provides air-conditioned buses to and from most hotels. English-speaking staff are also available at the mall to help tourists. Virtually anything you would find in the shops of Ipanema you will also find at Barra Shopping, with the advantages of convenience and air-conditioning, although lacking a bit in character and ambience.

Casa Shopping (Av. Alvorada 2150), located next door to Barra Shopping, specializes in decorations and home furnishings. Several excellent restaurants have opened branches here, including the Rodeio churrascaria, one of Rio's best barbecue houses (*see* Chapter 6). Three movie theaters operate here, and on Sundays there is an antiques fair (*see* Street Markets, above).

Department Stores

Mesbla, Rio's largest department-store chain, has concentrated its efforts in recent years on fashionable, mostly casual clothing and accessories for men, women, and children. But it also has a large and attractive home-furnishings department and a wide selection of toys, records, cosmetics, musical instruments, and sporting goods. *Main store: Rua do Passeio 42/56, downtown. Open weekdays 9 AM–10 PM and Sat. 9–7. Branches: Rio Sul and Barra Shopping malls. Open Mon.–Sat. 9 AM– 10 PM.*

Sears department stores carry the chain's own line of fashions and have a large cosmetics section. Other good departments include sporting goods, hardware, appliances, furniture, home furnishings, and records. *Main store: Praia de Botafogo 400, the bay drive in Botafogo. Open Mon.–Sat. 10–6:30. Branch: Barra Shopping. Open Mon.–Sat. 10–10.*

Due to its size, **C&A** is classified as a department store, but it sells only clothing—for men, women, and children, including accessories, shoes, and a sporting line. *Av. Nossa Senhora de Copacabana 749 and in the Rio Sul and Barra Shopping malls. All are open 9 AM–10 PM.*

5 Sports, Fitness, Beaches

Participant Sports and Fitness

by Edwin Taylor

As befits the home of revealing swimwear, Rio is also a world-class fitness center. On any day of the year you will find thousands of cariocas jogging along the beaches, exercising on the sand, or indoors pumping iron or performing aerobics at one of the city's 3,000 fitness centers. This all-encompassing concern with exercise is a natural extension of the cariocas' passion for the body beautiful. But while Rio's residents will strain for hours to sculpt the perfect body, they have little interest in participant sports; as a result there is a dearth of tennis courts, golf courses, and other public sports venues.

Biking

Although bicycle riding is popular along the beachfront, you will have to supply your own bike. One shop tried to rent bikes but soon gave up on the idea as several customers forgot to return them. No one else has tried.

Fishing

Fishermen consider the waters off Brazil among the best in the world for blue-water, or deep-sea, fishing. Blue and white marlin, sailfish, yellow tuna, and *dourado* (a Brazilian game fish) are all caught here. Smaller fish include red snapper, grouper, flounder, sea bass, and snook. Licenses are not required, and there is no official season, although the best fishing occurs between November and mid-February.

While the fishing is good, it is not cheap. All the equipment is imported, and there are only a handful of boats that will take you out. A day's fishing (10–12 hours) including boat rental, crew, bait, and equipment comes to around $1,000 for a group of four to six. The following charter companies dominate the market: **Captain's Yacht Charters** (Rua Conde de Lages 44, Room 602, tel. 021/252–1155), about $1,150 per day; **International Marine Service** (Marina da Glória, tel. 021/205–8646), about $1,210 per day; **S. P. Nautica** (Marina da Glória, tel. 021/285–2540), about $960 per day; and **Assessória Náutica** (Marina da Glória, Box 1, tel. 021/265–0797), about $1,000 per day.

Golf

Rio is not a golfer's paradise. There are only two private country clubs in the city and no public courses. Another three private courses exist in the state of Rio, one at the Frade Hotel near the city of Angra dos Reis and the other two in the mountain resort cities of Petrópolis and Teresópolis.

Rio's two courses welcome tourists but only during the week; to play on the weekend you must be the invited guest of a member. The courses charge $30 for green fees ($50 on the weekend), plus $8 for a set of rented clubs. They are the **Gávea Golf and Country Club,** Estrada da Gávea 800 (next to the Inter-Continental Hotel), tel. 021/322–4141; and the **Itanhanga Golf and Country Club,** Estrada da Barra da Tijuca 2005 (in the Barra da Tijuca neighborhood), tel. 021/399–0507. The memberships of both clubs are dominated by Rio's foreign community, especially Americans, Europeans, and Japanese.

Hang Gliding

Hang gliding has a strong following in Rio. The city's bird-men and -women jump off the Pedra Bonita Mountain in São Conrado near the Inter-Continental Hotel. If you are interested in jumping in tandem with an experienced hang glider, get in touch with the **Rio Hang Gliding Association** (Associação de Vôo Livre, Av. Rio Branco 156, Room 1119, tel. 021/220–4704). For $60 you can experience the sensation of jumping off a wooden platform 1,700 feet in the air and gliding down to the valley below.

Health and Fitness Clubs

There is no shortage of fitness centers in Rio; at last count there were 22 along the 10 blocks of Ipanema's main commercial street, Visconde de Pirajá. Three of the city's better hotels also offer top-quality exercise rooms and gyms: the Rio Sheraton, Inter-Continental, and Rio Palace. The **Top Bell Club,** with branches in the Sheraton and the Inter-Continental, accepts guests of other hotels for aerobics classes or weight lifting. The cost is $11 per hour.

Serious swimmers will find the best hotel pools at the Inter-Continental, Rio Sheraton, Nacional, Rio Palace, and Copacabana Palace. Few of the older hotels on Copacabana have pools, and those that do tend to have no more than wading pools with the same true for the hotels of Ipanema. The city's better private health clubs all have Olympic-size pools, but none of them receives tourists on a regular basis. If you ask your hotel to call one of them, though, something could probably be arranged.

Hiking

Hiking trails run throughout the **Tijuca Forest,** although most of them are unmarked. For information contact the **Camping Club of Brazil** (Rua Senador Dantas 75, 29th Floor, tel. 021/262–7172), which also organizes trekking tours. Rio is also home to two excursion clubs that organize mountain climbing, spelunking, and white-water rafting in the area. Contact **Clube Excursionista Carioca** (Rua Hilario da Gouveia 71/206, tel. 021/541–3531) or **Centro Excursionista do Rio de Janeiro** (Av. Rio Branco 277/805, tel. 021/220–3548).

Jogging

At all hours of the day and night, cariocas can be seen running along the city's streets and sidewalks. The best time for jogging is in the morning or the early evening when the temperature is lower. The favorite spots are the beachfront sidewalks in Copacabana and Ipanema, the pathways of the downtown Flamengo Park, and the path that encircles Ipanema's Rodrigo de Freitas Lagoon. A more difficult location to reach, but one of the best, is the Tijuca Forest on the road to Corcovado. Here, in addition to beautiful views, the forest's higher elevation ensures cool, refreshing temperatures.

Squash

Squash has grown quickly in recent years and there are now several squash clubs in the city. The favorites are the **Rio Squash Club** (Rua Cândido Mendes 581, Glória, tel. 021/242-0642), **Speed Squash** (Rua Senador Pompeu 78, Barra da Tijuca, tel. 021/233-1578), and the **K. S. Academy** (Av. Armando Lombardi 663, Barra da Tijuca, tel. 021/399-8540).

Tennis

Rio has few public tennis courts, and all of them have waiting lists that extend for weeks. If you want to play you will have to use one of the city's private tennis centers or the lighted courts at the Rio Sheraton, Inter-Continental, or Nacional hotels, the only hotels with tennis courts (you don't have to be a guest at the hotels to book their courts).

The best tennis centers are **Lob Tênis** (Rua Stefan Zweig 290, Laranjeiras, tel. 021/205-9997), the closest to Copacabana and Ipanema; **Clube Canavera** (Av. das Américas 487, tel. 021/399-2192), in Barra da Tijuca; and **Centro Carioca de Tênis** (Rua Timboacu 765, tel. 021/392-7009), in the distant neighborhood of Jacarepagua.

Court fees rarely exceed $2 an hour; an additional 50¢ tip is appropriate for the ball boy.

Water Sports

As a seaside resort city, Rio should be a center for water sports. Sadly, what is available is limited, and sometimes difficult to arrange. Recently, however, a few entrepreneurs have begun setting up tents on the beach in Barra da Tijuca and Ipanema where they rent surfboards and Windsurfers. Otherwise, if you are interested in sailing, surfing, windsurfing, or scuba diving, your best bet is to go to the **Glória Marina** (tel. 021/265-0797), near downtown, where equipment for these sports can usually be found for rent.

For Windsurfers or sailboats for hire, contact **Escola de Vela** at the marina (tel. 021/285-3097). For scuba diving, contact one of the following firms, which rent equipment and boats: **Centro de Atividades Subaquáticas** (Glória Marina, tel. 021/265-0797); **Ponto Mar** (Rua Prof. Alfredo Gomes 3, tel. 021/266-6066); and **Subshop** (Rua Barata Ribeiro 774, tel. 021/235-5446).

Spectator Sports

Horse Racing

Races are held year-round at Rio's **Jockey Club** (Praça Santos Dumont 31, Gávea, tel. 021/274-0055) beginning Monday and Thursday at 7:30 PM and weekends at noon. The big event of the year, the **Brazilian Derby,** is held the first Sunday of August.

Soccer

Volleyball and basketball have taken on added importance due to the success of Brazilian teams in international competitions, but the first love of any carioca sports fan remains his soccer team. Rio, like the rest of Brazil, is soccer mad. Team loyalties are fierce and passed on from one generation to another. The top three teams are **Flamengo** (currently the best and most popular), **Fluminense,** and **Vasco da Gama.** Play between these three is soccer at its finest, with the greatest rivalry between Fluminense and Flamengo.

Even if the game doesn't turn you on, the 180,000-seat **Maracanã Stadium** is impressive, and the crowd itself is half the spectacle. Well before the game drums begin beating in various parts of the stadium and maintain their tom-tom rhythm right through to the end. When goals are scored, firecrackers and smoke bombs explode and rooters wave huge homemade flags featuring their team's colors. The Maracanã crowd is good-natured and the stadium is safely constructed, so don't worry about stories you may have read of soccer disasters.

State and city championships usually occur between March and September, but don't ask for an advance schedule—they don't exist. The national championships, involving all of Brazil's better teams, start in October and continue to the final game, the Super Bowl of soccer, in December or January. Should you be in town the day a Rio team takes the national championship, hold on to your seat: The celebration will make Carnival seem tame.

During the season the top game each week is played on Sunday starting around 5 PM. The easiest way to see a game is through one of the guided tours offered by all of the leading tour operators whose brochures are available at hotel desks. If you want to go on your own, take a cab or the subway to Maracanã, located just north of downtown. Check first at your hotel to find out who is playing and the availability of tickets. Admission to the grandstand is only about 50¢, but you may not enjoy rubbing shoulders with the masses and sitting on a hard concrete slab; reserved seats are around $2 and far more comfortable.

Beaches

The following is a listing of Rio's primary beaches, traveling roughly south and then west along the coast from downtown. All are public and all, except Prainha and Grumari (the most westward), are served by buses and taxis. There are no public rest rooms or changing rooms, although you may use the rest rooms at nearby restaurants and cafés.

Despite increased security (especially near the major hotels), theft is still a big problem on Rio's beaches. Don't bring any valuables with you, and try not to leave your towel or beach chair unattended.

The Bay Beaches

Beaches fronting Rio's Guanabara Bay (principally **Botafogo** and **Flamengo**) are nice to look at, but don't go near the water. Years of uncontrolled industrial and sewage dumping have made the bay's waters unfit for bathing. Even sunbathing or strolling here is not recommended. Most of the bathers come from Rio's poorer neighborhoods, and a foreign tourist would be an obvious target for crime.

Copacabana

The aging queen of Rio beach life, Copacabana is the recognized tourist beach, fronted by the bulk of Rio's better hotels. You can swim here, although pollution levels are not always perfect and there is a strong undertow—stay close to shore. Lifeguard stations are found once every kilometer along the beaches.

On any summer weekend Copacabana is packed with thousands of bathers. The beach for most of its extension is wide enough to handle not only sunbathers but entire soccer fields marked out in the sand (watch out for flying balls!). Sidewalk trailers sell beverages and snacks, but don't eat anything that's cooked on the premises: Hygiene is nonexistent. On the sand itself vendors weave through the crowds selling beverages, ice cream, and souvenirs. Beach chairs and umbrellas, if not supplied by your hotel, may be rented. By the end of the afternoon the litter on the sand is enormous, a problem that exists on all the city's beaches.

At the Sugarloaf end of Copacabana is **Leme,** really no more than a natural extension of Copacabana. Here a rock formation extends into the water, forming a quiet cove less crowded than the rest of the beach and good for bathing. Avoid the opposite end of Copacabana, near the Copacabana Fort, where an ever-present stench will extinguish forever your romantic notions of Copacabana.

Ipanema

The most chic of Rio's beaches, Ipanema and its extension, **Leblon** (the two are divided by a canal), are favored by affluent cariocas, especially those who live in the million-dollar apartments across the street. The water, however, can be a serious problem. Pollution levels on Leblon Beach in recent years have reached the point where bathing has occasionally been prohibited. Repairs on the beach's ocean outfall system at the end of 1988 corrected this problem for the time being.

Swimmers should also be aware that there is an undertow here, although it is not as strong as at Copacabana. Trailers and vendors are well represented in Ipanema, but you'll find only a handful of cafés and restaurants along the beachfront avenue.

Arpoador, the Copacabana end of Ipanema, is good for surfing, as is the end of Leblon, next to Dois Irmaos Mountain.

São Conrado

Continuing west, the next beach over from Ipanema, São Conrado, lies in a natural amphitheater surrounded on three sides by forested mountains including the imposing flat-topped Gávea Mountain. Its natural beauty and safe swimming have made São Conrado popular among the golden youth of Rio, who are also attracted by the hang gliders who jump off Pedra Bonita Mountain and float down to a landing site on the beach.

The Gávea Golf and Country Club runs through the middle of São Conrado, the Inter-Continental and Nacional hotels are both located here, and the Rio Sheraton is nearby. Unfortunately, São Conrado is also home to Rio's largest *favela* (shantytown), and sewage from the slum runs freely into the ocean at the end closest to Ipanema. Bathers should stay on the far end, near the hang-glider landing point. At this end you will also find trailers selling fresh-fruit drinks.

Barra da Tijuca

Rio's longest beach is the 11-mile Barra da Tijuca, known to cariocas as simply the Barra. Water pollution is not a problem here, and for most of its length, the Barra beach escapes the crowds (it is almost deserted on weekdays) that flock to Copacabana, Ipanema, and São Conrado. The exception is the first four miles of the beach, where the construction of apartment buildings has been concentrated. While there are fewer vendors here than on the other beaches, there are innumerable trailers along the beachfront Avenida Sernambetiba.

The waves here tend to be strong, so swim with caution. Lately several entrepreneurs have begun setting up large tents on the beach where they rent surfboards and Windsurfers.

Recreio dos Bandeirantes

Located at the far end of the Barra beach is the Recreio, a half-mile stretch of sand anchored by a huge rock, which creates a small protected cove. Its quiet, secluded nature makes it popular with carioca families, who fill it on weekends. The calm, pollution-free water, with no waves or currents, is good for bathing, but don't try to swim around the rock—it's bigger than it looks.

Prainha

The length of two football fields, this vest-pocket beach is a favorite for surfers who take charge of it on the weekends. The swimming here is good, but keep alert for flying surfboards!

Grumari

If you enjoy the beach, you should find a way to spend an afternoon at Grumari, but keep it a secret. What preserves this spectacular beach, the most beautiful and unspoiled of Rio, is precisely the fact that it has not yet been "discovered" (it was, however, featured in Michael Caine's movie *Blame It on Rio*). Located 30 minutes from Ipanema on a road that hugs the coastline, Grumari, like Prainha, can be reached only by car (there is no regular bus service here, and taxis pass infrequently). Grumari doesn't have the amenities of the other beaches—no trailers or vendors, only two unimpressive snack bars—but it does have a glorious beach and quiet cove backed by low hills covered with tropical vegetation.

6 Dining

Introduction

by Edwin Taylor

Sophisticated cariocas have always considered themselves more European than South American, or even Brazilian. The result can be seen in the city's restaurants, which are heavily European in their cuisine, so much so that there are more French restaurants than Brazilian ones. This European bias has more to do with carioca notions of status than with the quality of native cooking. Traditional Brazilian food may be hard to come by, but when it is found it can make for a delicious dining experience.

Among visitors the most popular Brazilian restaurants are the *churrascarias*, or steak houses, especially those serving meat *rodízio*-style. Rodízio in effect means "going around," and that is precisely what waiters do at these unique establishments. For a set price you get all the meat and side dishes you can eat as waiters circulate nonstop, carrying skewers laden with charbroiled hunks of beef, pork, and chicken. The meat is sliced at your table; as soon as one waiter departs, another arrives with a fresh cut. On and on it goes until you say stop.

Another favorite is the traditional weekend lunch, where Brazilians gorge themselves at one sitting for the entire day. *Feijoada*, a huge meal that combines black beans, rice, cuts of pork and pork sausage, fresh oranges, and hot peppers, is offered by most hotel restaurants every Saturday. Sunday is customarily the day for *cozido*, a dish of broiled vegetables and potatoes tossed with pork, beef, special sauces, and hot peppers. While Brazilian food is served hot, it is not highly spiced. Peppers are optional, and usually provided on the side.

Unmistakably Brazilian are the colorful seafood dishes from the northeastern state of Bahia, where African cultural influences have produced a unique and tasty regional cuisine. Bahian restaurants are rare in Rio, but most seafood restaurants will serve a dish called *moqueca*, a fish fillet or shrimp cooked in a sauce of coconut and palm oil.

Brazilians love to eat, and the size of lunches and dinners in tropical Rio will surprise, if not shock, most first-time visitors. To compensate, breakfast consists of coffee and a slice of bread. Hotels include breakfast in their room rates, and the leading hotels all serve large, buffet-style breakfasts with fresh tropical fruits and juices plus eggs and bacon. But don't go looking for this type of breakfast on the street; it exists only for tourists.

Lunch is served from noon until 3 and is typically a full meal, although of late the hectic pace of Rio life has produced an invasion of fast-food outlets. McDonald's and a Brazilian competitor, Bob's, are the leading chains in the fast-food derby. The better downtown restaurants all serve excellent lunches for business people, as do the top hotels. Dinner is eaten late, rarely before 8 PM and often after 10 PM. If you arrive for dinner at 7, you may be the only diner in the restaurant. Popular restaurants will still be seating customers after midnight on weekends; the normal closing hour is 2 AM. Many restaurants are closed on Monday.

After a long apprenticeship, Brazilian wine is now coming into its own. While not yet at the level of Chilean and Argentine wines, Brazil's wines are quickly closing the gap, and some white wines, namely those by Forestier, are dry enough to please most diners. The reds tend to be unremarkable, with little to recommend one brand over another. Imported spirits carry heavy duties and are therefore far more expensive than they are at home. When ordering a drink, always specify whether you want domestic or imported liquor, and ask in advance what the prices are for each. Tap water in Rio is not reliable, so ask for bottled mineral water, with or without bubbles (*com* or *sem gás*).

Rio runs counter to the notion that hotel cooking is undistinguished. The majority of the city's finest restaurants are located in the leading hotels, many of them world-class in food, decor, and service. Like the rest of the city's top eateries, the better hotel restaurants show a decided prejudice toward French cooking, especially nouvelle cuisine or variants thereof. In second place is Italian food, leaning toward *nuova cucina*. Most of these restaurants are in the hands of a single master chef, whose creativity often produces original works of culinary art.

Many of the better restaurants offer a special fixed-price menu with chef's recommendations. In all instances, however, an à la carte menu is also available. Every restaurant includes a cover charge for the bread and other appetizers placed on the table, and a 10% service charge is added to the final bill. It is customary to leave an additional 5% tip.

Highly recommended restaurants are indicated by a star ★.

Category	**Cost***
Very Expensive	over $20
Expensive	$15–$20
Moderate	$8–$15
Inexpensive	under $8

**per person, excluding drinks, service tax (10%), and tip*

The following credit card abbreviations are used: AE, American Express; CB, Carte Blanche; DC, Diners Club; MC, MasterCard; and V, Visa.

Very Expensive

Brazilian/French ★ **Club Gourmet.** The gourmet in question is the restaurant's owner and master chef, José Hugo Celidonio, who has created a unique cuisine that includes the basics of Brazilian cooking but employs European (especially French) techniques. No one has yet named this style of cooking, but Celidonio has moved closer than any other Brazilian chef to a modern definition of his country's cuisine. He has turned away from the heavy elements of Brazilian fare, substituting instead light, colorful ingredi-

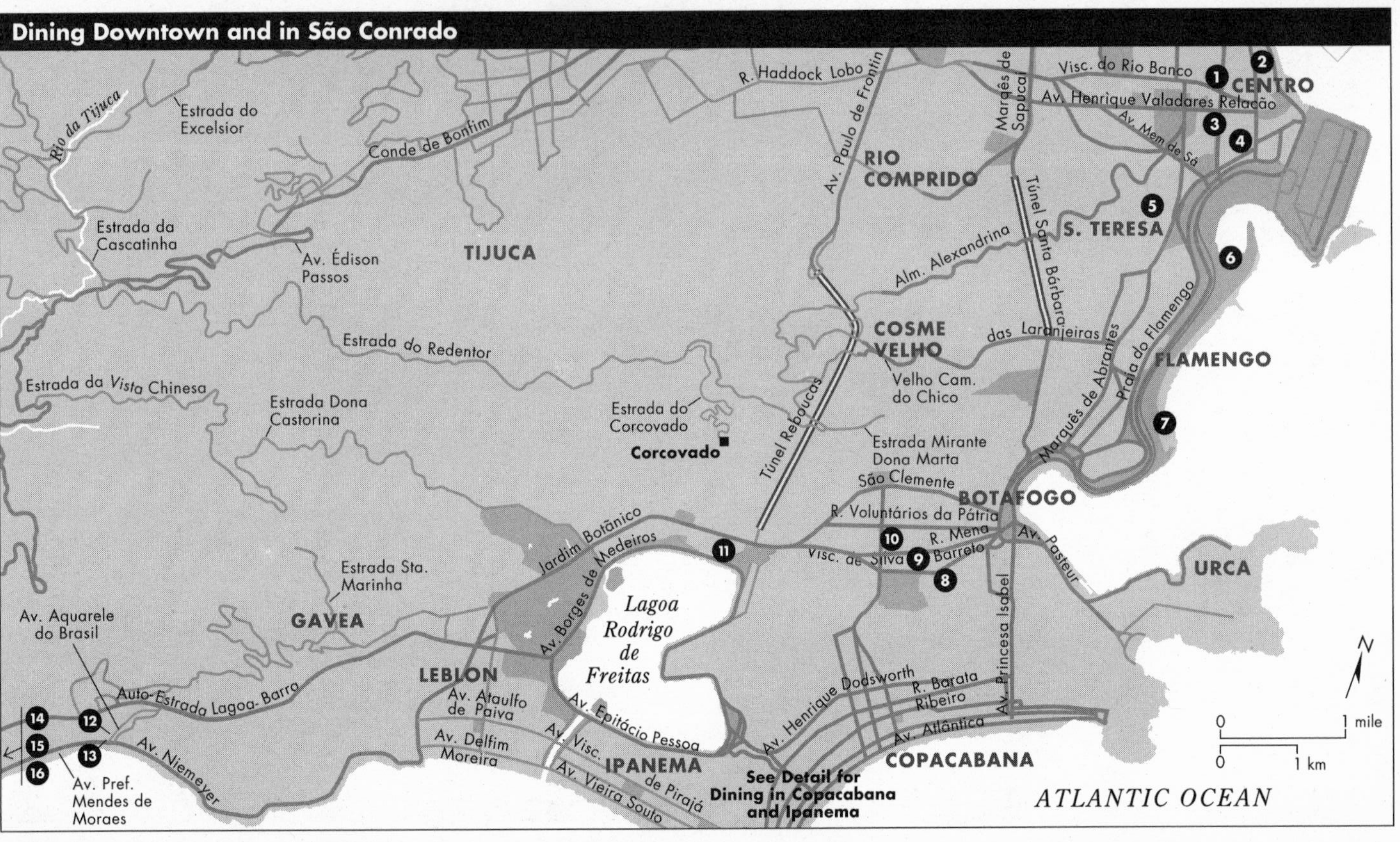
Dining Downtown and in São Conrado
CENTRO
Visc. do Rio Banco
Av. Henrique Valadares
Relação
Av. Mem de Sá
Marquês de Sapucaí
R. Haddock Lobo
Av. Paulo de Frontin
RIO COMPRIDO
Túnel Santa Bárbara
S. TERESA
Alm. Alexandrina
COSME VELHO
das Laranjeiras
Marquês de Abrantes
Praia do Flamengo
FLAMENGO
Velho Cam. do Chico
Túnel Rebouças
Estrada Mirante Dona Marta
São Clemente
BOTAFOGO
R. Voluntários da Pátria
R. Mena
Barreto
Visc. de Silva
Av. Pasteur
URCA
Av. Princesa Isabel
R. Barata Ribeiro
Av. Henrique Dodsworth
Av. Atlântica
COPACABANA
See Detail for Dining in Copacabana and Ipanema
ATLANTIC OCEAN
0
1 mile
0
1 km
N
Rio da Tijuca
Estrada do Excelsior
Conde de Bonfim
Estrada da Cascatinha
Av. Édison Passos
TIJUCA
Estrada do Redentor
Estrada da Vista Chinesa
Estrada Dona Castorina
Estrada do Corcovado
Corcovado
Jardim Botânico
Av. Borges de Medeiros
Lagoa Rodrigo de Freitas
Estrada Sta. Marinha
GAVEA
Av. Aquarele do Brasil
LEBLON
Av. Ataulfo de Paiva
Av. Epitácio Pessoa
Auto-Estrada Lagoa-Barra
Av. Delfim Moreira
Av. Visc. de Pirajá
IPANEMA
Av. Vieira Souto
Av. Niemeyer
Av. Pref. Mendes de Moraes
1
2
3
4
5
6
7
8
9
10
11
12
13
14
15
16

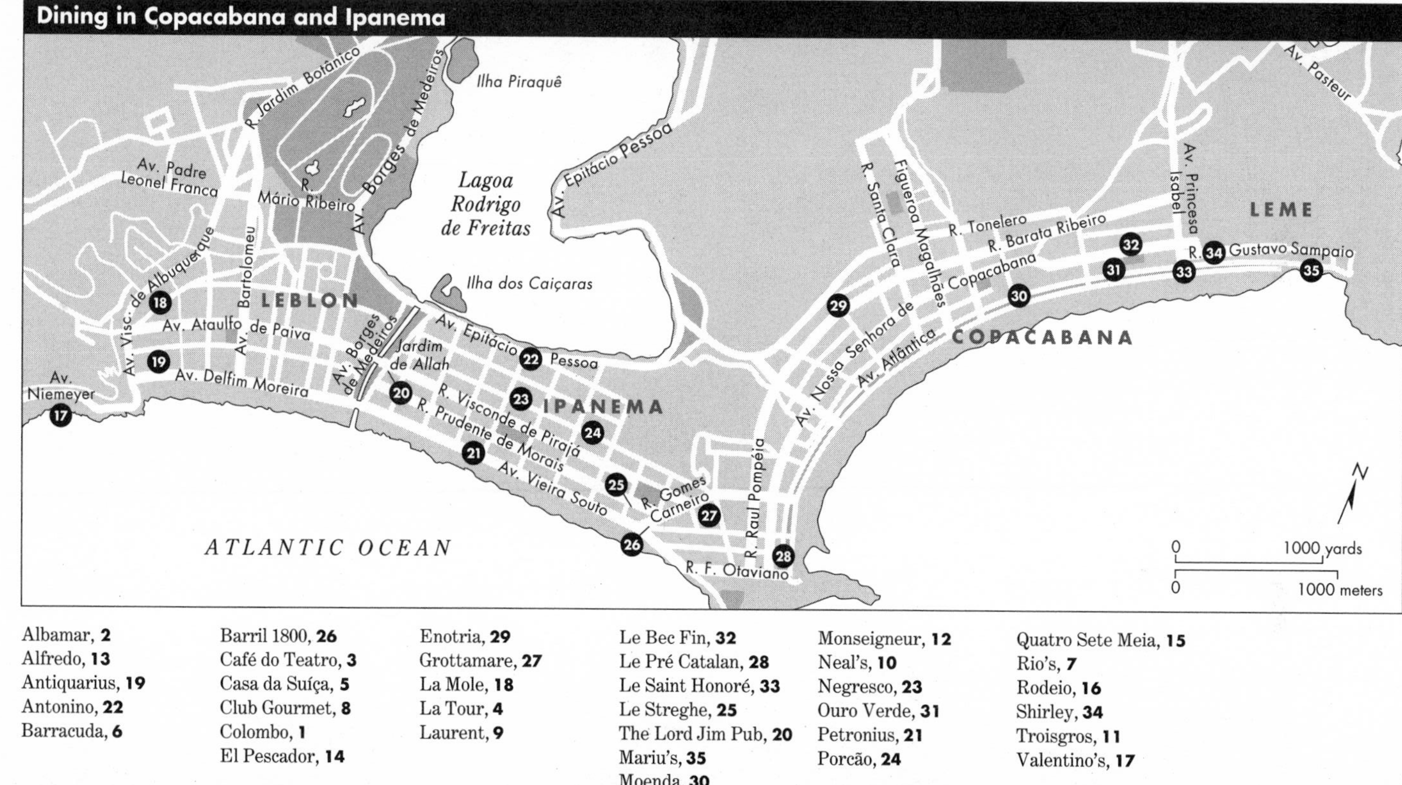

Albamar, **2**
Alfredo, **13**
Antiquarius, **19**
Antonino, **22**
Barracuda, **6**
Barril 1800, **26**
Café do Teatro, **3**
Casa da Suíça, **5**
Club Gourmet, **8**
Colombo, **1**
El Pescador, **14**
Enotria, **29**
Grottamare, **27**
La Mole, **18**
La Tour, **4**
Laurent, **9**
Le Bec Fin, **32**
Le Pré Catalan, **28**
Le Saint Honoré, **33**
Le Streghe, **25**
The Lord Jim Pub, **20**
Mariu's, **35**
Moenda, **30**
Monseigneur, **12**
Neal's, **10**
Negresco, **23**
Ouro Verde, **31**
Petronius, **21**
Porcão, **24**
Quatro Sete Meia, **15**
Rio's, **7**
Rodeio, **16**
Shirley, **34**
Troisgros, **11**
Valentino's, **17**

ents. The results can be as intriguing as honey-glazed duck breast served with an almond and prune *farofa* (a traditional Brazilian dish). A favorite dessert is the passion fruit crepes. Guests choose one item from each of four courses, paying a set price for the meal. The atmosphere is surprisingly relaxed and informal. The rustic bistro decor, with green-checkered tablecloths, is highlighted by copper cooking utensils suspended from the walls. Ask to see the wine cellar, the most complete in Rio. *Rua General Polidoro 186, Botafogo, tel. 021/295–3494. Reservations required. Dress: casual. No credit cards. Closed for lunch Sat. and dinner Sun.*

Continental **Rio's.** Above-average international cuisine and an unbeatable view of Guanabara Bay and Sugarloaf Mountain are a winning combination here. Located flush against the bay, this is one of the few places in town with a great vista even on rainy days. At night, the view by starlight is one of the most romantic in Rio. The restaurant sits at the edge of the near-downtown Flamengo Parkway, splendidly removed from the frantic pace of the city. Its plush interior adds to the escapist theme and attracts downtown business people who have made the establishment a favorite site for power lunches. The menu has both seafood and meat dishes, and famed flambé desserts. Arrive an hour before dinner to savor a drink at the intimate, luxurious bar, a popular rendezvous for "secret" romances. *Parque do Flamengo, Flamengo, tel. 021/551–1131. Reservations required. Dress: jacket and tie at lunch, neat but casual at dinner. AE, DC, MC, V.*

French **Laurent.** After serving as the head chef of the Le Saint Honoré for five years, Laurent Suaudeau set out on his own, and today this attractive colonial-style house on a side street in the Botafogo neighborhood is where he perfects his culinary creations. Laurent has gained international fame for the lightness of his sauces, many based on Brazilian fruits. One of his prize dishes is roast duck topped by *tucupi*, a spicy sauce from northern Brazil mixed with ginger and *jabuticaba* (a Brazilian berry). Decor here is eclectic and somewhat art deco, with Tiffany table lamps, tables covered with salmon-colored cloths, and lithographs of 18th-century French restaurants lining the walls. In back is a small garden, where you can dine beneath the stars. The ambience is formal: Laurent is a restaurant for those who take nouvelle cuisine seriously. *Rua Dona Mariana 209, Botafogo, tel. 021/266–3131. Reservations required. Dress: casual but sophisticated. AE, DC, MC. Closed Sun.*

★ **Le Pré Catalan.** Like other former castles of nouvelle cuisine, Le Pré Catalan of the Rio Palace hotel now has a menu divided between the modern and the traditional. Nothing has been lost in this transition, and the restaurant continues to be a must stop for aficionados of gracious French dining. Entering Le Pré Catalan is like being ushered into the salon of a Parisian millionaire; elegance is visible in every detail from table settings to furnishings to lighting. A *menu confiance* will guide you through two starters, sherbet, main course, and dessert. Although the menu changes periodically, it is certain to contain succulent meat dishes topped by light sauces, as well as such nouvelle cuisine classics as thin slices of duck breast with a sauce of honey and ginger. *Av. Atlântica 4240 (Rio Palace hotel), Copacabana, tel. 021/521–3232. Reservations advised. Dress: neat but casual. AE, DC, MC, V. No lunch on weekends.*

★ **Le Saint Honoré.** Le Saint Honoré spreads sumptuously across the 37th floor of the Meridien Hotel, offering diners not only excellent French cuisine but also an extraordinary view of Copacabana Beach and the ocean. You'll find candles and flowers atop the tables, soft pink tones, and dim lighting. The restaurant operates under the direction of French master chef Paul Bocuse, one of the creators of nouvelle cuisine. However, the restaurant now features a menu with more traditional French dishes alongside the nouvelle. In every case, the accent is on originality, with frequent use of Brazilian fruits and herbs to produce such gems as *les pièces du boucher marquées sauces gamay et béarnaise*, a fillet with both béarnaise and red-wine sauces. When he's in town, Bocuse himself goes to the street markets in search of ingredients. For lunch the restaurant has a special prix fixe menu, one of Rio's great dining bargains. *Av. Atlântica 1020 (Meridien Hotel), Copacabana, tel. 021/275–9922. Reservations required. Jacket and tie advised. AE, DC, MC, V. Closed Sun.*

★ **Monseigneur.** A pleasing mix of modern and traditional French cuisine is the calling card of this superb restaurant, one of five in the Inter-Continental Hotel and one of Rio's finest, thanks to Swiss chef Dominique Gapany. The decor matches the elegance of the meals—two striking lighted columns of translucent crystal dominate the center of the restaurant. Strolling violinists add a romantic touch. Guests should prepare themselves for a relaxed meal of smoked trout fillet served with spinach, mustard, and pepper, and delicious lemon crepes soufflés served for dessert. *Av. Prefeito Mendes de Morais 222 (Inter-Continental Hotel), São Conrado, tel. 021/322–2200. Reservations required. Dress: neat but casual. AE, DC, MC, V. Dinner only.*

Troisgros. For culinary adventure nothing can top the daily surprises that Claude Troisgros springs on his guests. On a visit to Rio, this distinguished French chef, scion of a family of famed chefs, fell in love with the city and its temptations, and today he routinely adds to the latter with his spectacular meals. With a petite menu prepared for the fortunate guests who fill his restaurant's 10 tables each evening, Troisgros maintains personal control over his establishment, basing his offerings on what is available at the market, which he visits daily. The result is a highly individualistic form of nouvelle cuisine, relying entirely on Brazilian ingredients. Every dish, whether a crab or lobster flan, or chicken, fish, or duck prepared with exotic Brazilian herbs and sauces, is pure pleasure, always exceptionally light. The dessert menu is headed by passion fruit mousse, a Troisgros classic that alone could make a trip to Rio memorable. The restaurant is in an appealing house hidden on an isolated street near the lagoon. *Rua Custódio Serrão 62, Jardim Botânico, tel. 021/226–4542. Reservations required. Dress: neat but casual. No credit cards. Dinner only; lunches can be arranged in advance for minimum of 10 persons.*

Italian

★ **Valentino's.** While the other leading hotels have concentrated on French cuisine, the Rio Sheraton has turned to Italy for its restaurant's inspiration. The emphasis here is on serious dining with creative dishes drawn from the nuova cucina of northern Italy. Chef Peter Weber offers a prix fixe menu as well as à la carte selections. Among the dishes that have earned enthusiastic praise are *fettuccine al maîtré*, with *porcini* mushrooms and veal fillet, and lobster tail in a truffle cream sauce. Piano music and subdued lighting add a touch of sophistication. *Av. Niemeyer 121 (Rio Sheraton Hotel), Vidigal, tel. 021/274–*

1122. Reservations required. Jacket and tie advised. AE, CB, DC, MC, V. No lunch.

Portuguese **Antiquarius.** Portuguese seafood is the specialty of this house, where you may purchase not only your meal but also the tables and chairs: All furnishings are antiques, and all are for sale. The decor changes constantly as objects are sold and replaced with new ones. For diners the result is usually delicious varieties of cod served amid Chinese lamps, Portuguese furniture, and paintings of colonial Brazil. The food often seems secondary to the setting and can be inconsistent. The setting, meanwhile, is always opulent and intriguing. *Rua Aristides Espinola 19, Leblon, tel. 021/294–1049. Reservations advised, especially for dinner. Dress: informal. No credit cards.*

Expensive

Churrascaria (Steak House) **Mariu's.** A convenient Copacabana beachfront location has made this the city's favored rodízio-style steak house among tourists. The decor is somewhat ostentatious, heavy on mirrors and white leather, but the cuts of meat are good and the varied accompaniments featured at rodízio restaurants are all here. However, proximity to the beach and hotels has its price: roughly twice that of other top churrascarias for the same all-you-can-eat meal. *Av. Atlântica 290, Copacabana, tel. 021/542–2393. No reservations. Dress: casual. AE, DC, MC, V.*

French **Le Bec Fin.** While the majority of Rio's French restaurants have gone modern, Le Bec Fin has maintained a menu of traditional dishes not unlike those with which it opened its doors in 1948. If you're a fan of traditional French cuisine, you'll find all of your favorites here—steak au poivre, steak Diane, plus a few house specialties, like fresh fish stuffed with smoked salmon and topped with hollandaise sauce. The pace at this intimate, nine-table restaurant is slow, with a clear attempt to evoke a bygone era of ease and style. *Av. Nossa Senhora de Copacabana 178, Copacabana, tel. 021/542–4097. Reservations required. Dress: casual. AE, DC, MC, V. Dinner only.*

★ **Ouro Verde.** As befits the restaurant of the Ouro Verde, one of Rio's most distinguished hotels, the cuisine here is classic, primarily French. The ample and varied menu has remained largely unchanged for two decades, a stabilizing presence in a city whose eateries tend to ride the latest trends from abroad. The decor is traditional and elegant, with soft, green hues, exquisite table settings, and Old World chandeliers. The waiters, who provide correct and courteous service, are the most proficient in Rio with flambé dishes. One gastronomic Everest served is the *filet Muscovite*, a chateaubriand with a caviar and vodka sauce that is set ablaze at your table. For the perfect ending to a carioca night, stop here for crepes suzette. *Av. Atlântica 4240 (Ouro Verde Hotel), Copacabana, tel. 021/542–1887. Reservations advised. Dress: informal. AE, DC, V.*

International **La Tour.** The essence of La Tour is La View, which is so good it seems a shame to put a restaurant here, especially this one. This revolving restaurant, set atop a downtown office building, offers a grand view, overlooking the downtown historical area, the bay, and virtually all of the city's leading landmarks. Fortunately, to appreciate this vantage point you don't have to stomach the food, which falls short of spotty—it is always bad. Step up to the bar and sip a drink while the restaurant revolves.

Rua Santa Luzia 651, Centro, tel. 021/240–5795. No reservations. Dress: casual. AE, DC, MC, V.

Italian ★

Alfredo. After a slow start this Rio branch of the renowned Roman eatery has now come into its own. The mainstay here is the pasta that made the original Alfredo world famous—fettuccine Alfredo. The waiters prepare it at your table, tossing the pasta with butter and grated Parmesan to form a rich sauce. The size of these servings will astonish any but the most fanatic pasta eaters. An ample cold buffet of antipasti can start off your meal, which, aside from fettuccine, may include traditional pastas such as ziti or linguine served with a variety of sauces. The restaurant is located in the Inter-Continental Hotel with a view of the pool area. *Av. Prefeito Mendes de Morais 222 (Inter-Continental Hotel), São Conrado, tel. 021/322–2200. Reservations advised. Dress: informal. AE, DC, MC, V.*

Enotria. This small (40-seat) and unpretentious restaurant is run by Italian immigrant Danio Braga, whose formidable knowledge of the cuisines of his native land comes to fore on each day's handwritten menu. The pasta and bread are homemade, and recipes are sometimes taken out of the pages of history—Braga is a dedicated researcher. Whatever he serves, you can be sure it is an authentic Italian dish, although you may have to inquire from which century. Braga is also a recognized wine expert and will be happy to recommend an accompaniment for any of his meals. Sofas and upholstered chairs give this two-story restaurant a cozy, homey feeling. *Rua Constante Ramos 115, Copacabana, tel. 021/237–6705. Reservations required. Dress: casual. No credit cards. Dinner only. Closed Sun.*

Le Streghe. This perennial contender for title of best Italian restaurant in Rio occupies the second floor of a stylish house in Ipanema. It has a relaxed yet sophisticated ambience; the generous and artistic use of tropical plants echoes the green color scheme throughout. The cuisine, as light and tasteful as the setting, is a mixture of traditional northern Italian cooking and nuova cucina. The pasta is homemade and includes gnocchi, spaghetti, *tagliatelle* (fettuccine), and tortellini. Among the house specialties are *grigliata di mare mista* (grilled seafood) and *agnolotti alla crema di tartufo* (pasta with truffle sauce). Downstairs is the Caligula disco, one of Rio's trendiest night spots. *Rua Prudente de Morais 129, Ipanema, tel. 021/287–1369. Reservations advised. Dress: neat but casual. No credit cards. Dinner only.*

Seafood ★

Petronius. Like the Caesar Park Hotel that houses it, this restaurant just keeps getting better. Although it overlooks the action-packed beachfront of Ipanema, the mood within is one of hushed elegance. Soft and intimate piano music, exquisite furnishings, a white marble floor, impeccable service, and white-gloved waiters make this far and away Rio's most sophisticated seafood restaurant. For sheer indulgence order the imperial seafood platter, a meal for two, with lobster, shrimp, shellfish, and three types of fish fillets, all grilled and served with herb butter. The soufflés are also excellent; try cod and crab. *Av. Vieira Souto 460 (Caesar Park Hotel), Ipanema, tel. 021/287–3122. Reservations advised. Dress: neat but casual. AE, DC, MC, V. Dinner only.*

Swiss

Casa da Suíça. This home of traditional Swiss cooking, located close to the Glória Hotel, near downtown, has been a longtime favorite with cariocas. A fondue heaven, it serves no less than eight types of fondue: four meat varieties, cheese, fish, shrimp, and an unforgettable chocolate fondue. Also popular are the flambé dishes, expertly torched at your table. *Rua Cândido Mendes 157, Glória, tel. 021/252–5182. Reservations advised. Dress: casual. No credit cards. No lunch Sat.*

Moderate

Brazilian ★

Moenda. For that rarity of rarities, a Rio restaurant specializing in Brazilian food, you can do no better than this time-honored eatery in the Hotel Trocadero. Here, while you enjoy the view of the Copacabana beachfront, waitresses in white turbans and long flowing dresses serve meals from Bahia. The emphasis is on seafood served with spicy sauces prepared with coconut and palm oil, tomatoes, peanuts, and okra. The really hot sauces are served separately so they can be mixed with the main dishes, although only if you are accustomed to hot peppers. Popular dishes are *vatapá* (a stew containing fish and shrimp), *moquecas* (fish or shrimp cooked in a delicious sauce of coconut and palm oil), *camarão a baiana* (shrimp cooked in tomatoes and coconut oil, similar to shrimp creole), and *caruru* (a shrimp-and-okra gumbo cooked in palm oil). On Saturday, the restaurant serves an authentic, delicious feijoada for lunch. Desserts are classically Brazilian and extremely heavy, making full use of coconut, egg yolks, and sugar. *Av. Atlântica 2064 (Trocadero hotel), Copacabana, tel. 021/257–1834. Reservations advised, especially on weekends. Dress: casual. AE, DC, MC, V.*

British ★

The Lord Jim Pub. Rio has attracted more than its share of colorful expatriates, from millionaire jewelers to runaway train robbers. For those hailing from Great Britain, home away from home is The Lord Jim Pub. With loving care proprietress Anne Phillips has created a carioca version of a London pub right down to the red call box at the front door. Steak-and-kidney pie, Yorkshire pudding, fish and chips, and appetizing curries await those who climb up a cast-iron spiral staircase to the pub's upper two floors. The cuisine is as determinedly British as the decor, although a few wholesome asides for Americans include barbecued ribs and T-bone steaks. A special attraction is the afternoon tea, served from 4 to 6:45 PM, with various types of teas, hot chocolate, muffins, shortbreads, tea sandwiches, cakes, waffles, jams, honey, marmalade, cookies, scones, and biscuits. The ground floor is reserved for throwing darts and downing beers. This is an excellent place to meet Rio's English-speaking residents. *Rua Paul Redfern 63, Ipanema, tel. 021/259–3047. Reservations required for afternoon tea. Dress: casual. No credit cards. Closed Mon.*

Churrascarias (Steak Houses) ★

Porcão. The quintessential Brazilian churrascaria, rodízio-style, Porcão (literally "big pig") is everything that its name implies. Waiters fly up and down between rows of wooden tables wielding giant skewers laden with sizzling barbecued beef, pork, and chicken. When they are not leaning over your plate ready to slice off another piece from their skewers, they are deftly providing heaping servings of salad, french fries, onion rings, hearts of palm, potato salad, and fried bananas. More than any of Rio's rodízio steak houses, this one captures the good humor of a slightly primitive form of eating. Also, unlike other churrascarias, no one here tries to push you out the door to make room for the next customer. You may stay as long as you like, to eat or simply to watch the "show." *Two locations: Rua Barão da Torre 218, Ipanema, tel. 021/521–0999; and Av. Armando Lombardi 591, Barra da Tijuca, tel. 021/399–3157. No reservations. Dress: casual. AE, DC, MC, V.*

Rodeio. While most tourists fall quickly and madly in love with rodízio steak houses, there is another more traditional churrascaria, where dishes are served à la carte rather than as an all-you-can-eat meal. Of these, Rodeio is the unchallenged leader, both in ambience and the quality of the beef served. As you enter the restaurant you pass by the grill, where succulent meats sizzle over charcoal. The decor is slightly rustic, with wine bottles lining the wood-paneled walls. Steaks and ribs are of the eye-opening, mouth-watering variety. While the accent is clearly on beef, the inventive chefs here have added a special attraction in the form of charbroiled hearts of palm, cooked in their bark and opened at your table. Located far from the hotels and beaches, this restaurant is next door to the sprawling Barra da Tijuca shopping center. *Av. Alvorada 2150, Barra da Tijuca, tel. 021/325–6163. Reservations advised. Dress: casual. AE, DC, MC.*

International

Café do Teatro. The international food, while palatable, is an afterthought at this extraordinary restaurant, which easily has the most unique restaurant decor in Rio. Taking center stage is the Assyrian motif, replete with columns and wall mosaics that look like something out of a Cecil B. DeMille epic. The bar resembles a sarcophagus, and two sculpted sphinxes flank the sunken dining area. Even if you have no interest in eating here, stop by for a drink and a look at this spectacle, located appropriately enough in the basement of the Municipal Theater. *Av. Rio Banco (basement of the Teatro Municipal), Centro, tel. 021/262–4164. Reservations advised. Dress: casual. Lunch only; closed weekends. AE, DC, V.*

Italian

Antonino. This venerable Rio restaurant owes its success as much to its location as to its cooking. Situated on the road that encircles the Rodrigo de Freitas Lagoon in Ipanema, diners with window tables have one of Rio's classic views: the lagoon with Corcovado and the city's other forested mountains surrounding it. Inside, 13 tables are set amid a simple decor of bookcases, mirrors, and plain white walls. Meals lean toward classical French, such as Medalhão Café de Paris, a filet Mignon served with a flavorful herb sauce. The food is good without being spectacular. Downstairs is one of Rio's most popular piano bars, an excellent spot to linger over a drink either before or after your meal. *Av. Epitácio Pessoa 1244, Ipanema, tel. 021/267–6791. Reservations required for window tables. Dress: casual. AE, DC, MC, V.*

Portuguese

Negresco. This cozy nine-table restaurant, with basic white walls contrasting the dark-wood furniture, is home to excellent Portuguese cuisine. Menu options include cod grilled with potatoes, onions, and olive oil, and *caldo verde,* a Portuguese potato-and-kale soup with sausage. The food and setting are just right for a quiet dinner for two, but be warned that Portuguese cooking is hearty, if not heavy, and is best avoided on a hot day. *Rua Barão da Torre 348, Ipanema, tel. 021/287–4842. Reservations required. Dress: casual. AE, DC, MC. Dinner only except Sat. Closed Mon.*

Seafood

Barracuda. Hidden away inside the Glória Marina, this intimate seafood restaurant is an excellent choice for a quiet dinner away from the rush of Copacabana and Ipanema. At lunchtime it is usually crowded with downtown executives, probably eating the restaurant's famed jumbo grilled shrimp served on a skewer. *Marina da Glória, Glória, tel. 021/265–4641. Reservations required for lunch. Dress: casual. AE, CB, DC, MC, V. Closes at 6 PM Sun.*

Grottamare. This seafood establishment is popular with tourists, who make up the majority of its customers during high season. Unfinished wood gives the downstairs a rustic air. Upstairs a large aquarium dominates the dining area; the Grottabar, with its leather chairs and green marble tables, is adjacent. The lobster, shrimp, and octopus are excellent, but the house specialty is fish, oven-baked with herbs, rosemary, olive oil, tomatoes, and potatoes. Grottamare sends out its own fishermen each day to come up with the day's catch. Pasta dishes are also served as accompaniment to the seafood. *Rua Gomes Carneiro 132, Ipanema, tel. 021/287–1596. Reservations required after 9 PM. Dress: casual. AE, DC, MC, V. Dinner only Mon.–Sat.; lunch and dinner Sun.*

★ **Quatro Sete Meia.** If you have ever dreamed of finding a seafood restaurant where you could flop down in shorts and sandals on a miserably hot day, grasp a refreshing drink, and stare off at the ocean waves lapping in front of you while attentive waiters prepare your afternoon feast, then this is the place for you. Internationally renowned, it is located one hour by car from Copacabana, at the end of a highway that offers stunning views of the coastline before plunging down a mountainside to the tranquil fishing village of Pedra de Guaratiba. (Getting here isn't easy for first-time visitors, but taxi drivers should know the way.) Simplicity is the soul of the village and the restaurant, whose name in Portuguese is its street number. There are only 11 tables available, five indoors and six in the garden at water's edge. The menu carries only seven options, divided between shrimp and fish dishes, but all are delicious and range from moquecas to grilled seafood to curries. The combination of setting, food, and the amiability of the owners, American expatriate Eugene Moss and his Brazilian partner, Bartolomeu Morais, makes for long, drowsy lunches. *Rua Barros de Alarcão 476, Pedra de Guaratiba, tel. 021/395–2716. Reservations required. Dress: casual. No credit cards. Lunch only.*

Spanish Seafood

El Pescador. Fishnets and castanets are the combination at this Spanish seafood restaurant, which tends to overwhelm with its special effects. This is one of those places that insists that you see your waiter grab a lobster out of a fish tank with the understanding that said lobster will shortly find its way to your plate. Until then, get ready for the flamenco dancers. Here, "mood and food" are the bywords, and your appreciation of the latter may be dependent on how well the former goes down. In fairness, though, the paella is Rio's finest, and the lobster, when it finally reaches your table, will not disappoint. Broiled and grilled cod are other house specialties, as are several grilled-beef selections that make this a true surf-and-turfer. *Praça São Conrado 20, São Conrado, tel. 021/322–0851. Reservations advised. Dress: casual. AE, DC, MC, V.*

Shirley. Spanish-seafood casseroles and soups are the draw at this traditional Copacabana restaurant. Try the *zarzuela*, a seafood soup, or *cazuela*, a fish fillet served with white wine sauce. Don't be turned off by the simple decor—nothing more than a few paintings hung on wood-paneled walls: The food is terrific. There is usually a waiting line, so step up to the bar for drinks and snacks while you wait. *Rua Gustavo Sampaio 610, Leme, tel. 021/275–1398. No reservations. Dress: casual. No credit cards.*

Inexpensive

American

Neal's. Rock videos and barbecued spareribs are the unusual (but successful) attractions at this Rio version of a New York bar and grill. Located in a two-story town house, this is an expatriate's delight. Posters from Broadway shows, midwestern quilts, and other Americana hang from the walls, and six television sets scattered around the restaurant blast out the latest in video clips from the states. The food, heavy on sandwiches, is good, and the hamburgers are the best in Rio. *Rua Sorocaba 695, Botafogo, tel. 021/286–0433. No reservations. Dress: casual. No credit cards. No lunch on weekends. Closed Mon.*

Cafés

Barril 1800. Snacks and cold draft beer are the most popular items at this beachside bar and restaurant, an Ipanema landmark and one of only three bars along the entire length of the Ipanema–Leblon beach. Now in its third decade, this laid-back swimsuit-and-sandals hangout has shown a remarkable ability to rejuvenate, moving along from one generation of golden Ipanema youth to the next: Today the motorcycles of the latest "in" crowd accumulate in front. But people-watching aside, the food is far better than you would expect. The menu ranges from the expected hamburger and french fries to seafood (try shrimp rolled inside balls of mozzarella) and steaks of prodigious size. Tables on the ground-floor terrace have the best view of the street and the beach beyond. *Av. Vieira Souto 110, Ipanema, tel. 021/227–2447. No reservations. Dress: casual. DC, MC, V.*

Colombo. At the turn of the century this was Rio's preeminent café, home to afternoon teas for high-society senhoras and a center of political intrigue and gossip. Those days have gone, but much of the Belle Époque atmosphere remains. Wall-length mirrors line the upstairs dining room, and piano music filters down to the first floor, where waiters twist through the crowd. Food here clearly loses out to ambience. The meals are adequate, although on the heavy side; portions will usually serve two. If you're downtown, stop in for a pastry and coffee on the ground floor or at the stand-up snack bar and absorb the atmosphere and history. Another branch is in Copacabana (Av. Nossa Senhora de Copacabana 860), but it is a mere half-century old and lacks the flavor of the original. *Rua Gonçalves Dias 32, Centro, tel. 021/232–2300. No reservations. Dress: casual. No credit cards. Lunch only. Closed Sun.*

Italian
★

La Mole. This popular chain of low-cost Italian restaurants is a good bet for that day when you are not interested in spending a great deal of money for lunch or dinner; these are "forget the romance and let's get down to basics" eateries. Yet for inexpensive prices (under $4 for a filet Mignon), the food is surprisingly good. Pasta is the main item and lasagna, fettuccine, and gnocchi dishes are all tasty. Because of the low prices and large servings, these restaurants are popular with middle-class carioca families, especially on weekends when their maids are off. *Four locations: Rua Dias Ferreira 147, Leblon, tel. 021/294–*

0699; Av. Nossa Senhora de Copacabana 552, Copacabana, tel. 021/235–3366; Praia de Botafogo 228, Botafogo, tel. 021/551–9499; Av. Armando Lombardi 175, Barra da Tijuca, tel. 021/399–0625. No reservations. Dress: casual. No credit cards.

Seafood **Albamar.** If you are downtown for lunch or an early dinner, try out this remnant from Rio's 1930s municipal market. The restaurant occupies the only remaining tower of the market, which provides sufficient atmosphere as well as a view of the surrounding bay and port area, always of interest. The specialty of the house is fresh fish—baked, fried, or broiled—accompanied by a variety of sauces, most of them wine-based. The fare is simple but generally good. At lunch the restaurant is packed. *Praça Marechal Ancora 184, Centro, tel. 021/240–8378. Reservations advised. Dress: casual. AE. Closed Sun.*

7 Lodging

Introduction

by Edwin Taylor

Life in Rio centers around the beach, and so it is in the beach neighborhoods that you'll find most of the hotels attractive to tourists. The largest concentration of hotels is in Copacabana and Ipanema. Copacabana hotels have the advantage of being close to the action but suffer from one of the neighborhood's least desirable characteristics, its noise. The decibel level in Copacabana must be the highest in the world, and there are few hotels in the neighborhood that escape it. Ipanema is better in this respect; hotels in São Conrado and Barra da Tijuca are the quietest, although somewhat removed from the center of things. There are at present no recommendable downtown hotels; those that exist are aging relics and most visitors will want to avoid them. For business people, the best choices are the handful of hotels in the near-downtown neighborhoods of Glória and Flamengo.

Beachfront hotels are the most expensive; hotels just a block or two from the water cost substantially less. Expect to pay a premium for a room with a view: Rooms overlooking either the beach or Rio's distinctive mountain backdrop will cost an average of $25 more per night.

Rio is not a home to hidden treasures—to small, unique hotels heavy on service and loaded with charm and atmosphere. Ambience has, on the whole, not been a major concern of Rio's hotel proprietors. Consequently, even the more luxurious hotels often have rooms that are clean, functional, well-equipped, but with little more character than a stateside Howard Johnson. Service in all hotels tends to be courteous and friendly but slightly haphazard, except in the top hotels.

Rio has many "motels," but be warned that they are not aimed at tourists. They attract couples looking for romance and privacy, and usually rent by the hour. With the exception of the Rio Sheraton and Inter-Continental, the big-time resort concept has not yet arrived in Rio, and even the amenities of these two hotels can't compare with the all-encompassing activities packages available in other tourism centers.

Air-conditioning, showers, and in-room TV are the norm in all hotels, regardless of price. All hotels include breakfast in the room rate, although the quality of these breakfasts ranges from a full buffet to a hard roll with butter. Almost all rooms come with minibars, small refrigerators stocked with bottled water, soft drinks, beer, and often snacks and liquor. Chambermaids keep track of what has been consumed, and the total is automatically added to your bill. Swimming pools, the kind you can actually swim in, are rarer in Rio than you might imagine. Be aware that a few hotels advertise pools that in reality are no more than wading pools.

Embratur, the Brazilian tourism board, gives all of the city's hotels a star rating from one to five. However, since the board is run by politicians, these ratings are often inaccurate and generally dismissed by the trade. There are five outstanding hotels in Rio that warrant the top five-star billing: the Rio Sheraton, Inter-Continental, Caesar Park, Rio Palace, and Meridien. A number of others fail to live up to this rating.

Room rates given in this guide are for high season (approximately December to April), although the days just prior to and during Carnival can see rates double, or even triple, according to what the traffic will bear. Remember that if you are traveling during Carnival or other peak periods it is important to make reservations as far in advance as possible. Rates are calculated at the official exchange rate.

Highly recommended lodgings in each price category are indicated by a star ★.

Category	Cost*
Very Expensive	over $140
Expensive	$80–$140
Moderate	$40–$80
Inexpensive	under $40

**All prices are for a standard double room for two, including 10% service charge.*

The following credit card abbreviations are used: AE, American Express; CB, Carte Blanche; DC, Diners Club; MC, MasterCard; and V, Visa.

Very Expensive

★ **Caesar Park.** Superior taste, style, and attention to detail are the trademarks of this beachfront hotel. Since its opening in 1978, it has established itself as a favorite of business travelers, celebrities, and heads of state who appreciate its impeccable service and overall emphasis on quality. The lobby has an impressive collection of art work, and the guest rooms are pleasingly decorated in soft tones of rose, beige, blue, and gray. The hotel boasts three excellent restaurants: the elegant Petronius; Mariko, one of Rio's top sushi bars; and the rooftop Tiberius. On weekends Petronius and Tiberius offer two traditional Brazilian meals, *feijoada* (black beans with pork and rice) on Saturdays and *cozido* (vegetable and pork stew) on Sundays, which are enormously popular with tourists. Executive services for business travelers are also provided. *Av. Vieira Souto 460, Ipanema, 22420, tel. 021/287-3122. 221 rooms and suites. Facilities: 3 restaurants, 3 bars, small pool, sauna, satellite TV. AE, DC, MC, V.*

Copacabana Palace. At one time this hotel was better known than Copacabana Beach itself. Built in 1923, the Copa was the first luxury hotel in South America and held this singular distinction for the next 30 years. Casino gambling brought the rich and adventurous, and renown soon brought the celebrities. With the passage of time (and the outlawing of gambling in 1946) the hotel slipped into a long, steady decline. In the 1980s, however, it invested heavily in restoring its lost allure, and today its ice cream–cake facade graces the Copacabana beachfront with a rejuvenated spirit. Inside, you'll find an airy, spacious feeling, largely created by high ceilings. A sense of unhurried elegance pervades, from the huge public areas to the

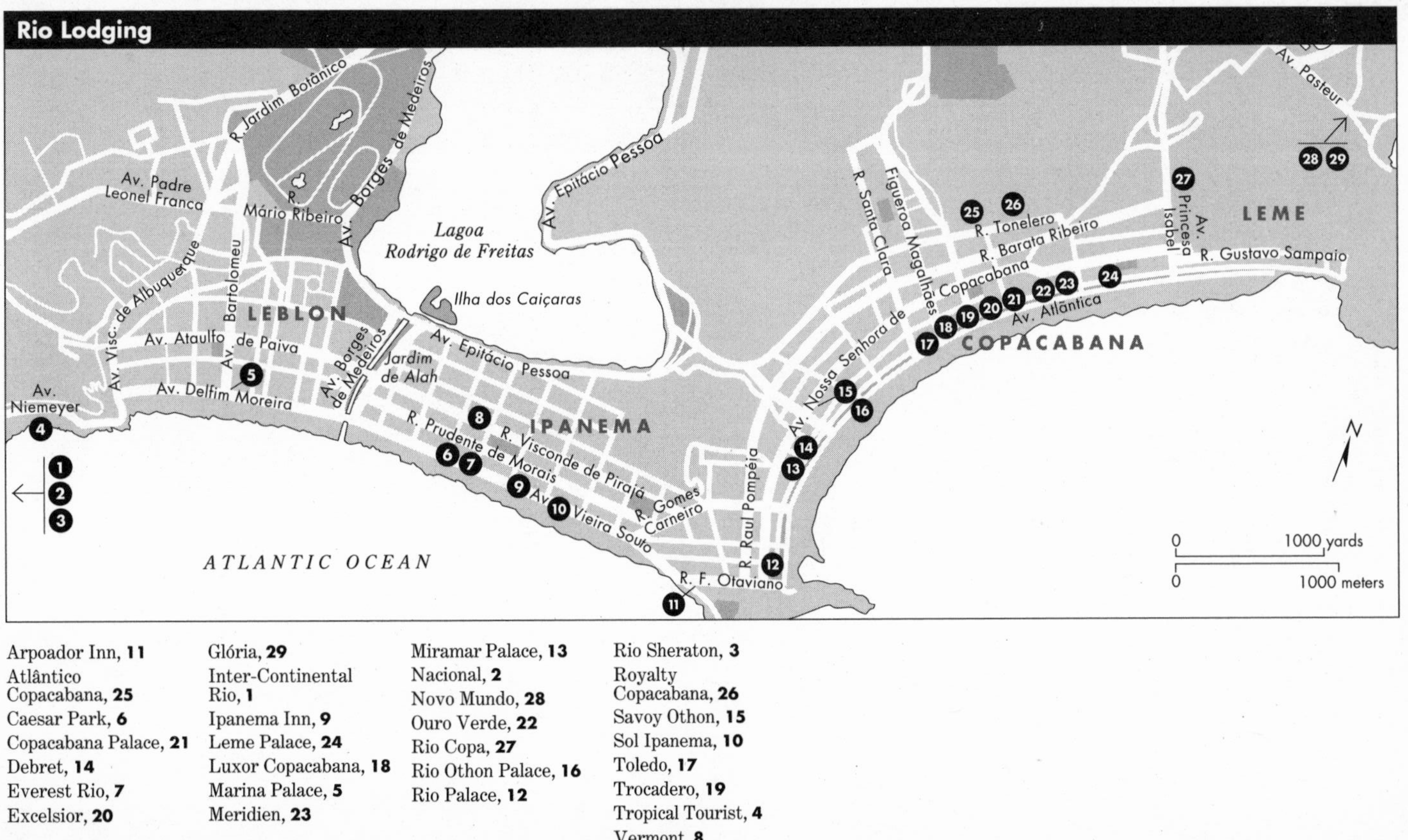

Arpoador Inn, **11**
Atlântico Copacabana, **25**
Caesar Park, **6**
Copacabana Palace, **21**
Debret, **14**
Everest Rio, **7**
Excelsior, **20**
Glória, **29**
Inter-Continental Rio, **1**
Ipanema Inn, **9**
Leme Palace, **24**
Luxor Copacabana, **18**
Marina Palace, **5**
Meridien, **23**
Miramar Palace, **13**
Nacional, **2**
Novo Mundo, **28**
Ouro Verde, **22**
Rio Copa, **27**
Rio Othon Palace, **16**
Rio Palace, **12**
Rio Sheraton, **3**
Royalty Copacabana, **26**
Savoy Othon, **15**
Sol Ipanema, **10**
Toledo, **17**
Trocadero, **19**
Tropical Tourist, **4**
Vermont, **8**

crystal-chandeliered meeting rooms to the long, wide corridors. The sizable guest rooms are individually decorated and have marble bathrooms and 1920s furniture. A place of honor is reserved for the pool, site of many memorable occurrences (like the day an admiring fan pulled off the top of Jayne Mansfield's bikini!). The complex consists of the main building and a setback annex facing the pool and beach. To capture the hotel's full flavor stay in the main building. *Av. Atlântica 1702, Copacabana, 22021, tel. 021/255–7070. 122 rooms, 102 suites. Facilities: 2 restaurants, 2 bars, large pool, sauna, theater. AE, DC, MC, V.*

Glória. The grande dame of Rio's hotels, this classic was built in 1922 at a time when the waters of Guanabara Bay lapped at its doorstep. Time and landfills, however, have pushed the bay back and left the hotel high and dry. Frequent renovations and its convenience for business travelers (it's a five-minute taxi ride from downtown) have helped it retain its popularity. Public areas come in an eclectic mixture of colonial Brazilian and turn-of-the-century European styles, and suites are packed with antique furniture. The hotel responded well to its transition to catering to business people, and it provides ample convention and meeting facilities. For tourists it has also added most of the amenities of a resort hotel, as its space has allowed. Its major liability is its distance from the beaches, which forces guests to rely on taxis for transportation. *Rua do Russel 632, Glória, 22210, tel. 021/205–7272. 600 rooms, 33 suites. Facilities: 4 restaurants, 3 bars, 2 pools, sauna, exercise room. AE, DC, MC, V.*

★ **Inter-Continental Rio.** This Rio member of the respected Inter-Continental chain is one of only two resort hotels in the city. It is located in the extraordinarily beautiful São Conrado Beach neighborhood right next door to the Gávea Golf and Country Club (a plus for anyone interested in golfing in course-deficient Rio). Standing alone on its own slice of beachfront, the hotel gives one a pleasant feeling of isolation from the rest of the world. At the swim-up bar in the main pool you can grab a cool drink, stretch out your legs, and gaze up at palm trees, jungle-covered mountains, and the hot Brazilian sun. The hotel's pool is a center of expatriate life in Rio. Relaxation is the main theme here, and every effort is made to make guests feel as at ease as possible. The atmosphere is laid-back, from the lobby, crossed by barefoot bathers in swimwear, to the comfortable rooms and public areas. Guest rooms are decorated with dark furnishings and color schemes ranging from wine to green, and each has an original tapestry done by a Brazilian artist. The focal point of every room is its view: Each has a balcony overlooking the ocean. The hotel is especially popular with families, who appreciate its ample space, large public areas, and wide range of sports and social activities, many of which are aimed at children. At night the place comes alive with a number of dining and entertainment options, including the respected Monseigneur French restaurant and one of Rio's trendiest piano bars. *Av. Prefeito Mendes de Morais 222, São Conrado, 22600, tel. 021/322–2200. 483 rooms and suites. Facilities: 5 restaurants, piano bar/nightclub, disco, 2 bars, 3 pools, lighted tennis courts, sauna, fully equipped exercise center, shopping arcade, satellite TV. AE, DC, MC, V.*

Marina Palace. For reasons known only to management, room rates here were recently raised to more than $200 a night, making this the most expensive hotel in Rio. If it were also the best this would be acceptable. But while the hotel is certainly good, it doesn't come close to being one of the city's finest. What it does have is the Leblon beachfront (one of Rio's most coveted strips of real estate), and a corner location that gives all rooms sea views. Decor has received special attention here, but with mixed results. Each floor has a different color scheme, the emphasis primarily bright orange, yellow, or green. This tropical explosion unfortunately tends to clash with the ornate, custom-made furniture in the rooms. *Av. Delfim Moreira 630, Leblon, 22441, tel. 021/259–5212. 120 rooms, 40 suites. Facilities: restaurant, 2 bars, pool, satellite TV. AE, DC, V.*

★ **Meridien.** Rising 37 stories into the sky, the Meridien establishes itself as a formidable presence at the beginning of Copacabana Beach. Completed in 1975, this member of the French Meridien chain was one of the prime movers in the 1970s renovation of Rio's hotel scene, and it has since then solidified its position as one of the city's top hotels. Service is efficient and the rooms, although smaller than the norm, are tastefully decorated in pastel tones with dark wood furniture. Unfortunately the hotel suffers from a lack of character in both look and feel, but guests are easily consoled by its prime beachfront location. The Le Saint Honoré restaurant crowns the hotel's 37th floor and routinely tops Rio's lists of leading restaurants (*see* Chapter 6). Of the top Copacabana hotels the Meridien is the closest to downtown, which may be the reason it has attracted so many business travelers; it recently added a complete executive center for its business guests. *Av. Atlântica 1020, Copacabana, 22012, tel. 021/275–9922. 443 rooms, 53 suites. Facilities: 3 restaurants, bar, pool, sauna, satellite TV. AE, DC, MC, V.*

Rio Othon Palace. The flagship of the Othon chain, Brazil's largest hotel group, this modern hotel has become a Copacabana landmark since it opened its doors in 1975. Its 30 stories tower over the surrounding 12- to 15-story buildings, making it a reference point and a natural gathering place as well. Beachfront activity, night and day, seems to gravitate to the area in front of the hotel. Potted palms and wood paneling give a warm, cozy touch to public areas. The comfortable-size rooms are tastefully decorated in warm woods and a blue-and-brown color scheme. The high point, literally, of the hotel is its rooftop pool/bar and sun deck, offering the best view in Copacabana of the neighborhood's distinctive black-and-white sidewalk mosaic. At night the magic of the rooftop setting is enhanced by live samba and bossa nova music at the Skylab Bar. Secretarial services are available for business travelers. *Av. Atlântica 3264, Copacabana, 22070, tel. 021/255–8812. 554 rooms, 30 suites. Facilities: 2 restaurants, 2 bars, nightclub, pool, health club, sauna, satellite TV. AE, DC, MC, V.*

★ **Rio Palace.** This is recognized as the best hotel on Copacabana Beach—a case in studied elegance, from the marbled lobby to the antique Brazilian furnishings and colonial artwork that decorate the public areas and rooms. These luxurious touches were present when the hotel opened in 1979, and since then its owners have added more practical attractions as well. The recently opened Imperial Club, aimed at the business traveler, offers services from bilingual secretaries to fax and telex. New in 1988 was a complete fitness center, with an exercise room and weight-lifting facilities. For nightlife, the hotel has one of the city's finest French restaurants, Le Pré Catalan; the Horse's Neck piano bar; and the Palace Club, a private disco open to guests. The building's H-shape design gives all rooms views of either the sea or the mountains—or both. *Av. Atlântica 4240, Copacabana, 22070, tel. 021/521–3232. 418 rooms and suites. Facilities: 2 restaurants, tea room, 2 bars, nightclub, 2 pools, fitness center, sauna, executive center, satellite TV. AE, DC, MC, V.*

★ **Rio Sheraton.** Built so that it dominates Vidigal Beach, located between Ipanema and São Conrado, this hotel enjoys the distinction of being the only one in Rio with a private beach. In recent years Sheraton has poured more than $15 million into remodeling the hotel, with the result that today it is the chain's showcase in South America. The bright, spacious new lobby (one of the largest in Rio) is an eye-grabber, with its bronze columns, beige marble floor, and mirrored walls and ceiling. Guest rooms are decorated in soft, soothing colors and all offer beach views. In addition to the beach, guests can take advantage of lighted tennis courts, three pools, and a complete fitness center. Business guests have access to a special executive-services program. At night the hotel is home to international cuisine at Valentino's restaurant (a favorite with Rio high society), and to the lively beat of Brazilian music at the One Twenty One Lounge, one of the city's hottest night spots. Its resort character makes this hotel a hit with families, groups, and business people with time to spare. *Av. Niemeyer 121, Vidigal, 22450, tel. 021/274–1122. 617 rooms, 22 suites. Facilities: 4 restaurants, bar/nightclub, bar, 3 pools, lighted tennis courts, sauna, fitness center, shops. AE, DC, MC, V.*

Expensive

★ **Everest Rio.** The only thing that prevents this 1975 hotel from being among the most popular in Rio is its location—not directly on the beach. Offering impeccable service and one of Rio's finest rooftop views (a postcard shot of Corcovado and the lagoon), it is a favorite with business travelers and those who know the ins and outs of Rio's hotels. Rooms are simply decorated in white, green, and brown with light wood furniture. Back rooms offer sea views, and front rooms above the 14th floor look out on Corcovado and the lagoon. Although it is a block away from Ipanema Beach, the hotel is still in the heart of the neighborhood's premier shopping and dining area. *Rua Prudente de Morais 1117, Ipanema, 22420, tel. 021/287–8282. 159 rooms, 10 suites, one presidential suite. Facilities: restaurant, bar, small rooftop pool. AE, DC, MC, V.*

★ **Leme Palace.** Leme, the extension of Copacabana Beach that lies closest to Sugarloaf, is an oasis of calm in the midst of frantically paced Copacabana, and this hotel, the first of the Othon properties in Rio, reflects this. Large rooms and a quiet beachfront location have made it the hotel of choice with frequent Rio visitors. Built in 1964, it was partially remodeled in 1987 and 1988 but still retains its original subdued, conservative air. Brown and beige tones dominate public areas, guest rooms are colorful, and bathrooms are bright and modern. *Av. Atlântica 656, Leme, 22010, tel. 021/275–8080. 168 rooms, 26 suites. Facilities: restaurant, bar. AE, DC, MC, V.*

Nacional. This soaring glass tower on São Conrado Beach has everything to guarantee success: a terrific beachfront location, a daring architectural design by Brazil's most famous architect, Oscar Niemeyer, and a major convention facility with a 1,600-seat auditorium. Unfortunately, the hotel, built in 1971, had, until recently, been plagued by mismanagement. Poor service, disorganization, and an overall sloppy approach to maintenance (there were even two fires in the 1980s) had sadly become its trademarks. On a more positive note, new management took over in 1988, and it is hoped that the hotel will now live up to its potential. The rooms are large, decorated in chic wine and gray with white wood furniture, and have panoramic sea and mountain views through the building's famous all-glass facade. This plus its resort-style amenities and improved management should ensure the hotel's future. *Av. Niemeyer 769, São Conrado, 22000, tel. 021/322–1000. 510 rooms, 27 suites. Facilities: 2 restaurants, 3 bars, disco/nightclub, auditorium, large swimming pool, 3 lighted tennis courts. AE, DC, MC, V.*

★ **Ouro Verde.** One of only a handful of Rio hotels aimed at the "discriminating traveler," this has been a preferred lodging for visiting business people for three decades. The hotel is famed for its efficient, personalized service. Tasteful Brazilian colonial decor and dark wood furniture are right in step with the hotel's emphasis on quality and graciousness. All front rooms face the beach, and back rooms from the sixth to 12th floors have a view of Corcovado. Among other distinctions, this is the only beachfront hotel in Copacabana with a reading room for its guests. Indeed, the sensation upon entering the hotel is that business suits might be more appropriate here than swimsuits. Sound serious? It is, but it isn't stuffy, and visitors looking for sun and fun in Rio need not feel put off. A lively alfresco bar plus one of Rio's finest restaurants, the namesake Ouro Verde, attract patrons into the morning hours. Make reservations well in advance as the hotel has a long list of faithful customers. *Av. Atlântica 1456, Copacabana, 22041, tel. 021/542–1887. 61 rooms, 5 suites. Facilities: restaurant, bar, reading room. AE, DC, MC, V.*

Moderate

★ **Arpoador Inn.** This pocket-sized hotel occupies one of Rio's more privileged locations, a stretch of beach known as Arpoador at the Copacabana end of Ipanema. Here surfers ride the waves and pedestrians rule the roadway—a traffic-free street that gives the hotel's guests direct access to the beach. Simple but comfortable, the hotel is reasonably priced considering the location. The real treat, however, awaits early risers and late-afternoon romantics: In the morning hours fishermen cast their nets into the waters of Arpoador, while at sunset the view from the rocks that mark the end of the beach is considered one of the most beautiful in Rio. Both sights are visible from the hotel's back rooms. Avoid the front rooms, which face a noisy street. *Rua Francisco Otaviano 177, Ipanema, 22080, tel. 021/247–6090. 46 rooms, 2 suites. Facilities: restaurant, bar. AE, MC, V.*

Atlântico Copacabana. One of Rio's newer hotels, this was built in 1986. The large lobby with its marble walls, red carpeting, black leather furniture, and mirrors will look modern to some, pretentious to others. Guest rooms are slightly larger than the average for Rio hotels. Suites have saunas and whirlpools, and the Executive Suite comes with a private pool. The Atlântico is located four blocks from the beach in a residential area. *Rua Sigueira Campos 90, Copacabana, 20000, tel. 021/257–1880. 97* *rooms, 18 suites. Facilities: restaurant, 3 bars, small rooftop pool, sauna. AE, DC, MC, V.*

Debret. This former apartment building was converted to a hotel in 1972 and has scored points for combining a beachfront location with moderate prices. The decor pays tribute to Brazil's colonial past, with baroque statues in the lobby and prints depicting colonial scenes and dark, heavy wood furniture decorating the rooms. The hotel has a loyal following among diplomats and business people. *Av. Atlântica 3564, Copacabana, 22041, tel. 021/521–3332. 90 rooms, 10 suites. Facilities: restaurant, bar, satellite TV. AE, DC, MC, V.*

Excelsior. More than any of its contemporaries, this 1950s hotel has retained its original style and flavor. The result is a Copacabana beachfront hotel with surprising touches of refinement, such as a marble lobby with leather-upholstered sofas, and closets paneled in rich *jacarandá* (Brazilian redwood). All rooms were remodeled in 1988 and given a much-needed update of new curtains and carpets. The Excelsior is a good choice for those seeking an alternative to Rio's many impersonal high rises. *Av. Atlântica 1800, Copacabana, 22000, tel. 021/257–1950. 175 rooms, 13 suites. Facilities: restaurant, bar. AE, DC, MC, V.*

★ **Ipanema Inn.** This small, no-frills hotel was built in 1977 for tourists who want to stay in Ipanema but have no interest in paying the high prices of a beachfront hotel. To that end, it has been a complete success. Just a half block from the beach, it is convenient not only for sun and water worshipers but also for those seeking to explore Ipanema's varied nightlife: Top restaurants and bars are within walking distance of the hotel. The pastel-colored rooms are functional and clean, if reminiscent of those found in American motels. But if you are looking for no more than a place to change your clothes and sleep, this is a good choice. *Rua Maria Quitéria 27, Ipanema, 22410, tel. 021/287–6092. 56 rooms. Facilities: bar. AE, MC, V.*

Luxor Copacabana. This modern beachfront hotel fits into the general category of vertical motel. Though the rooms are comfortable and clean, there is nothing particularly distinguishing about them. Similarly, service is professional but not remarkable. This hotel will give you value for your money but will fade quickly from your memory as do so many modern, characterless hotels. *Av. Atlântica 2554, Copacabana, 20000, tel. 021/257–1940. 119 rooms, 4 suites. Facilities: restaurant. AE, DC, MC, V.*

★ **Miramar Palace.** This 38-year-old establishment, one of Rio's veteran hotels, was entirely remodeled in 1986. The happy result is a beachfront venue with a satisfying mix of the old and the new. The rooms, among the largest in Rio's hotels, have a blue, green, or beige color scheme and light-colored furniture. The public areas are dominated by classic touches, from the Carrara marble floor of the lobby to the spectacular glass chandeliers that light the two restaurants. For many years the hotel was famous for its rooftop bar which, until the 1970s, was the only one overlooking Copacabana Beach. Although it no longer holds this distinction, the hotel's 16th-floor bar is still notable for its unobstructed view of the entire sweep of Copacabana; after 6 PM live Brazilian music adds a special touch of romance to the view. *Av. Atlântica 3668, Copacabana, 22010, tel. 021/287–6348. 133 rooms, 11 suites. Facilities: restaurant, coffee shop, tea room, 2 bars. AE, DC, MC, V.*

Rio Copa. The basic intent of this hotel, located three blocks from the beach on a busy thoroughfare, is to serve business people who want to stay in Copacabana but still have easy access to downtown. Unfortunately, the Copa has been fighting noise and pollution since it opened in 1978. To the management's credit, extra soundproofing has been added to the rooms, but guests may still feel assaulted by car horns and exhaust fumes when they walk out the front door. The comfortable guest rooms underwent a complete renovation in 1988, and the rather somber-looking public areas are scheduled for renovation in the near future. Front rooms overlook the street and are the noisiest. *Av. Princesa Isabel 370, Copacabana, 22011, tel. 021/275–6644. 88 rooms, 22 suites. Facilities: restaurant, bar, satellite TV. AE, DC, MC, V.*

Royalty Copacabana. Opened in 1987, this hotel has made a superb first impression due to a host of amenities, including an exercise room, sauna, and satellite TV, usually found only in the big beachfront hotels. Its moderate price has made it one of the best bargains in Rio and has caught the attention of business travelers who want to escape the hectic pace of the beachfront Avenida Atlântica. The hotel's location, three blocks from the beach, is convenient for beach goers yet removed enough to satisfy those looking for peace and quiet—a rarity in Copacabana. The back rooms from the third floor up are the quietest, and all have mountain views; front rooms have sea views. The decor is the norm for Rio—pastels in the rooms and a few comfortable armchairs and plants in the lobby. *Rua Tonelero 154, Copacabana, 22030, tel. 021/235–5699. 130 rooms, 13 suites. Facilities: restaurant, bar, small rooftop pool, exercise room, sauna, satellite TV. AE, DC, MC, V.*

Savoy Othon. This hotel, opened in 1970 and located two blocks from the beach, is considered one of the best of the Brazilian Othon chain. It escapes the usual characterlessness of these hotels, although some might think the British theme is overdone: Britons will feel either embarrassed or right at home in this carioca salute to the union jack. Tartan plaids on everything from bedspreads to the walls and ceiling of the restaurant, royal blue carpeting throughout, and touches like framed fox-hunting prints make it clear that the owners were serious when they named their hotel Savoy. Since it is located on one of Copacabana's noisier streets, guests are advised to avoid the front rooms that face the street, in particular those on lower floors. *Av. Nossa Senhora de Copacabana 995, Copacabana, 22060, tel. 021/257–8052. 130 rooms, 23 suites. Facilities: restaurant, coffee shop, bar. AE, DC, MC, V.*

Sol Ipanema. Another of Rio's 1970 crop of tall, slender hotels, this one anchors the eastern end of Ipanema Beach. Guest rooms have motel-style beige carpets and drapes and light-colored furniture. The front rooms have panoramic views of the beachfront, while the back rooms, from the eighth floor up, have views of the lagoon and Corcovado. The functional but undistinguished lobby has a bar and a sitting room furnished with dark turn-of-the-century furniture. *Av. Vieira Souto 320, Ipanema, 22420, tel. 021/267–0095. 66 rooms, 12 suites. Facilities: restaurant, bar, small rooftop pool, satellite TV. AE, DC, MC, V.*

Trocadero. Colonial Brazil is the motif of this 1958 Copacabana beachfront veteran. The theme is expressed with decorative Portuguese mosaic tiles and classic jacarandá furniture in the public rooms. Service is reliable, the rooms are ample and comfortable, and the hotel's L shape and corner location give all rooms some sea view. A key attraction is the Moenda restaurant, where waitresses clad in the turbans and white flowing skirts of Bahia serve up some of the finest Brazilian cuisine in Rio. *Av. Atlântica 2064, Copacabana, 22077, tel. 021/257–1834. 108 rooms, 12 suites. Facilities: restaurant, 2 bars. AE, DC, MC, V.*

Inexpensive

Novo Mundo. This aging eminence has clearly seen better days. Built in 1948, it looks more like a 1940s department store than a hotel. Due to its near-downtown location in the Flamengo neighborhood, it tends to attract Brazilian business people on a low travel budget, and it has also become a favorite with young adventurers making their way through South America on a shoestring. The wallpaper and furnishings in guest rooms and public areas are showing their age, but the management claims a major renovation is being planned. In the meantime, its only virtues are its proximity to downtown and the view, from the front rooms, of Guanabara Bay, Flamengo Park, and Sugarloaf. *Praia do Flamengo 20, Flamengo, 22210, tel. 021/225–7366. 194 rooms, 10 suites. Facilities: restaurant, bar. AE, DC, MC.*

Toledo. This unpretentious hotel goes the extra mile to make the best of what it has. There are few amenities, but service is friendly and efficient. The public areas are surprisingly plush, with a marble entryway to the lobby and comfortable brown leather armchairs. Room decor is simple but tasteful, with brown or blue carpets and dark wood furniture. Its main plus is its location on a quiet back street of Copacabana, one block from the beach. The back rooms from the ninth to the 14th floors have sea views. *Rua Domingos Ferreira 71, Copacabana, 22050, tel. 021/257–1990. 87 rooms, 8 suites. Facilities: coffee shop, bar. DC, MC, V.*

★ **Tropical Tourist.** Although the Barra da Tijuca beach is Rio's longest, it has yet to experience a hotel construction boom. This was one of the first lodgings to appear on the beachfront in 1970, and remains one of only a handful of Barra Beach hotels. Space is not a problem in the Barra, and this is reflected in the hotel's large rooms decorated in colonial style with dark wood furniture. The hotel has taken advantage of its nearness to the ocean—only a few yards away across a two-lane street—with a glass-enclosed lobby and large picture windows in the rooms. If you are looking for a good hotel on the beach at a low price, this one can't be beat. What keeps the price down is the hotel's distance from the other beaches and downtown—the same hotel in Copacabana or Ipanema would charge twice as much. *Av. Sernambetiba 500, Barra da Tijuca, 22600, tel. 021/399–0660. 86 rooms, 1 suite. Facilities: restaurant, bar, coffee shop. DC, MC, V.*

Vermont. Newly renovated, this hotel is clean, reliable, and situated just two blocks from the beach—a good choice for budget travelers. The rooms, simply decorated, have new beige wallpaper, matching carpet, and light-colored furniture. The hotel's only drawback is its location on the main commercial street of Ipanema, which means incessant noise during the day, although it tends to quiet down at night after the shops close. Those interested in shopping, however, may appreciate being in the heart of this world-class shopping district of boutiques, jewelry stores, and street fairs. *Rua Visconde de Pirajá 254,*

Ipanema, 22410, tel. 021/521–0057. 54 rooms. Facilities: bar. No credit cards.

Apart-Hotels

In recent years several excellent residence hotels have been built in the city. Called *apart-hotels,* they are concentrated in Ipanema and the Barra da Tijuca and are a good bargain, especially if you are staying for 30 days or more. They come with fully equipped kitchens and offer daily maid service. Many of those in the Barra are on the beach, and several are part of condominiums with access to swimming pools and tennis courts. Rates are moderate, normally under $80 a day even at high season. Among the better residence hotels are **Barramares Flat** (Av. Sernambetiba 3300, Barra da Tijuca, 22630, tel. 021/399–5656), with beachfront, pool, and tennis; **Marapendi Flat Service** (Av. Sernambetiba 5706, Barra da Tijuca, 22630, tel. 021/233–3636), with beachfront and a pool; **Leblon Flat Service** (Rua Prof. Antonio Maria Teixeira 33, Leblon, 22440, tel. 021/274–7222); **Rio Ipanema** (Rua Visconde de Pirajá 66, Ipanema, 22410, tel. 021/233–3636); and **Copacabana Hotel Residência** (Rua Barata Ribeiro 222, Copacabana, 22050, tel. 021/235–1828).

8 The Arts and Nightlife

The Arts

by Dwight V. Gast

In recent years Rio de Janeiro's role as Brazil's cultural capital has been diminished—since the country's politics moved to Brasília, and its money (along with the contemporary culture it buys) to São Paulo. But what has remained in Rio—an elegant counterpoint to the city's legendary hedonism—is a conservatism that has nurtured the traditional performing arts.

That tradition is best exemplified by the **Teatro Municipal.** Its construction was begun in 1905 during the early days of the Republic, and it was based on the Paris Opera House, complete with its own set of allegorical statues representing the arts. With its marble, bronze, mosaic, and ceramic fittings, it was the most luxurious and expensive structure ever built in Brazil. Opened in 1909, the Teatro Municipal has been the city's main venue for dance, opera, and theater ever since. Events are scheduled year-round, although the season officially runs from April to December. Though the theater may have been modeled on Mother Europe, and indeed hosts a number of prestigious foreign guest artists (the Bolshoi Ballet performed there a few seasons back), it has its own ballet and opera companies and two orchestras, all of which concentrate on Brazilian works.

There are many other performing-arts options in Rio, which include theater, music, dance, and film. Consistently high-quality events are mounted by such cultural foundations as Funarte, Funarj, Fundação Roberto Marinho, and Fundação Calouste Gulbenkian. To find out what they and other organizations are presenting during your visit, pick up a copy of the bilingual *Este Mês no Rio/This Month in Rio* or similar publications available at most hotels. Also check the entertainment sections of the Portuguese-language newspapers *Jornal do Brasil* or *O Globo* (which are generally easy to understand even for those who don't speak Portuguese).

Tickets, which are inexpensive by international standards, may be purchased at the theater or concert hall box offices, though for many events they are available at **Agência dos Teatros (ACET),** offices at Rio Sul shopping center (tel. 021/542–4477), Largo da Carioca 1, Centro (tel. 021/542–4477), and at Praça Nossa Senhora da Paz, Ipanema (tel. 021/287–5698).

Dress is informal but upscale at most cultural events in Rio, though the conservative carioca upper crust still likes to dress up for the Teatro Municipal. No matter what you wear, though, remember not to put on valuable jewelry and to carry minimal cash. The safest and most reliable form of transportation is hotel-furnished cars and drivers; taxis are also available at most cultural destinations.

Dance

In addition to the Teatro Municipal's own ballet company and the international ballet festival held in the theater during April and May, dance in Rio takes many other forms. Local and visiting companies perform classical and modern dance at the following locations and others. Check local listings under "Dança" for up-to-date information.

Casa Laura Alvim (Av. Vieira Souto 176, Ipanema, tel. 021/227–2444).
Teatro João Caetano (Praça Tiradentes, Centro, tel. 021/221–0305).
Teatro Municipal (Praça Floriano, Centro, tel. 021/210–2463).
Teatro Nacional (Hotel Nacional, Av. Niemeyer 769, São Conrado, tel. 021/322–1000).
Teatro Nelson Rodrigues (Av. Chile 230, Centro, tel. 021/212–5695).
Teatro Villa Lobos (Av. Princesa Isabel 430, Leme, tel. 021/275–6695).

Film

Rio recently began hosting its own international film festival, **FestRio** (contact Rua Paissandu 362, Flamengo, tel. 021/285–7649 for information), centered in the Hotel Nacional each November. All year long, original-language films are screened in small art houses called *cineclubes*, or state-of-the-art movie theaters, although Cinelândia, the area where many of Rio's theaters are concentrated, is dangerous at night. For information about art houses, contact the **Federação dos Cineclubes** (Av. Graça Aranha 416, Centro, tel. 021/242–6683). The following are the most comfortable first-run movie theaters; check local listings under "Cinema" for current programs. All movies are shown in their original language with Portuguese subtitles.

Art Casa Shopping I, II, & III (Casa Shopping, Barra da Tijuca, tel. 021/325–0746).
Art Fashion Mall I, II, III, & IV (São Conrado Fashion Mall, São Conrado, tel. 021/322–1258).
Barra I, II, & III (Barra Shopping, Barra da Tijuca, tel. 021/325–6487).
Condor Copacabana (Rua Figueredo Magalhães 286, Copacabana, tel. 021/255–2610).
Largo do Machado I & II (Largo do Machado 29, Flamengo, tel. 021/205–6842).
Mêtro Boavista (Rua do Passeio 62, Centro, tel. 021/240–1291).
Ricamar (Av. Nossa Senhora de Copacabana 360, Copacabana, tel. 021/237–9932).
Roxy (Av. Nossa Senhora de Copacabana 945, Copacabana, tel. 021/236–6245).
São Luiz I & II (Rua do Catete 307, Catete, tel. 021/285–2296).
Veneza (Av. Pasteur 184, Botafogo, tel. 021/295–8349).

Music

While the proliferation of Brazilian popular music (known in Portuguese as *música popular brasileira*, or MPB) may overshadow classical music (called *música erudita*) in the city, Rio has a number of orchestras. The Orquestra Sinfônica Brasileira and the Orquestra do Teatro Municipal are the most prominent. The following are the most patronized, most reliable places to hear classical music in Rio. For current information check the "Música Erudita" listings in local periodicals.

Casa Laura Alvim (Av. Vieira Souto 176, Ipanema, tel. 021/227–2444) focuses on experimental Brazilian theater.
Sala Cecilia Meireles (Largo da Lapa 47, Centro, tel. 021/232–9714) is a center for classical music.
Teatro Dulcina (Rua Alcindo Guanabara 17, Centro, tel. 021/240–4879) is a small theater which features classical opera and concerts.
Teatro João Caetano (Praça Tiradentes, Centro, tel. 021/221–0305) offers variety shows featuring comedy, music, and dance nightly.
Teatro Municipal (Praça Floriano, Centro, tel. 021/210–2463) presents a variety of arts—ballet, concerts, and theater, to name a few.
Teatro Paço Imperial (Praça XV, Centro, tel. 021/222–0174), like the Teatro Municipal, features a varied schedule of theatrical, musical, and dance performances.

Opera

The **Teatro Municipal**'s (Praça Floriano, Centro, tel. 021/210–2463) opera company puts on superb productions and often attracts international divas as guest artists. Also try the **Teatro João Caetano** (Praça Tiradentes, Centro, tel. 021/221–0305), and check listings under "Opera" in local periodicals.

Theater

As the success of Brazilian film and television abroad has shown, acting is one of the liveliest arts in Brazil, and the theater is no exception. Rio's theaters provide an excellent opportunity for visitors to extend their knowledge of Portuguese as well as to watch performances by Brazilian actors they may know from their work in film and television. The following theaters are among the most active in the city, but there are dozens more, so check local listings under "Teatro" for current programs.

Teatro Cândido Mendes (Rua Joana Angélica 63, Ipanema, tel. 021/267–9882).
Teatro Copacabana Palace (Av. Nossa Senhora de Copacabana 327, Copacabana, tel. 021/255–7070).
Teatro Ipanema (Rua Prudente de Morais 824, Ipanema, tel. 021/247–9794).
Teatro João Caetano (Praça Tiradentes, Centro, tel. 021/221–0305).
Teatro Municipal (Praça Floriano, Centro, tel. 021/210–2463).
Teatro Villa Lobos (Av. Princesa Isabel 430, Leme, tel. 021/275–6695).

Nightlife

Lively night spots like the one where Fred Astaire and Ginger Rogers danced the carioca in *Flying Down to Rio* have long faded from Hollywood films, but in the movie's namesake city the tradition is alive and kicking—not to mention drinking, dancing, and singing. Apart from Rio's beaches, the city's biggest year-round draw for natives and visitors alike is its nightlife, which, like Carnival, captures the essence of the exuberant carioca spirit.

Rio's nightlife options range from samba shows so shamelessly aimed at the tourist that the locals disparagingly call them gringo shows, to sultry dance halls called *forrós,* which began in Brazil's northeast during World War II when American GIs stationed at refueling stops opened up their clubs "for all." Musically, you'll find night spots featuring the sounds of big band, rock, and everything in between. One of the happiest mediums is *música popular brasileira,* or MPB, which translates as Brazilian popular music but is the generic term for current Brazilian sounds ranging from pop to jazz. It is the music you'll hear most often in Rio's bars and lounges, and after an evening spent listening to its easy rhythms you'll understand why.

Since many places vary their programs throughout the week, check the bilingual *Este Mês no Rio/This Month in Rio* or other such publications available at many hotels, as well as listings in the Portuguese-language newspapers *Jornal do Brasil* and *O Globo,* for specific times and types of music available.

Unless otherwise noted below, nightlife in Rio usually starts around midnight and goes on until the wee hours. As in most cities, weekdays are slower than weekends, especially for drinking or dancing, but the perennial tourist shows and special appearances by well-known musicians generally guarantee plenty of company during the week as well.

Most establishments ask a cover charge of a few dollars, which may or may not include drinks, and many offer either complete meals or appetizers, called *petiscos* or *salgadinhos.* Note that drinks made with imported liquor are disproportionately expensive. Local beer, wine, or domestically produced alcohols (called *nacionais),* like the sugarcane alcohol *cachaça* or vodka, are a much better value.

Rio's relaxed atmosphere is reflected in casual dress requirements at most bars and clubs. Clothes are informal but not sloppy, since cariocas pride themselves on their flair for fashion. Be aware that some clubs—mostly nightclubs—still do not admit single patrons. If you're making a go of it alone, have your hotel call beforehand to make sure you'll be allowed in.

Whether or not you're a night owl at home, you'd be wise to be one in Rio. Nowhere else in the world will you find such a variety of high-quality entertainment for so little money.

Finally, a word to the wise night owl: Remember the usual caveats about carrying small amounts of cash and taking taxis to and from your destination—or destinations, since you're likely to end up making quite a night of it. And, as always, leave valuable jewelry at home. Be particularly alert when venturing away from heavily traveled areas.

Bars and Lounges

Out-of-towners and cariocas alike meet for drinks or dinner at Rio's bars and lounges, where late in the evening combos play MPB or jazz. The music is usually low-key, and if the musicians aren't famous they're dependably competent. These establishments often ask a nominal cover of a few dollars in the form of either a drink minimum or music charge, and, as opposed to nightclubs, usually admit single patrons with no fuss. Don't overlook the hotel bars and lounges, which are often as popular with locals as they are with hotel guests.

Alô-Alô (Rua Barão da Torre 368, Ipanema, tel. 021/521–1460) is one of the city's most upscale bar/restaurants. Owner Ricardo Amaral is an international socialite and draws a chic crowd to the plush banquettes of his lounge, as well as to his *churrascaria* restaurant, Sal e Pimenta, upstairs.

Biblo's Bar (Av. Epitácio Pessoa 1484, Lagoa, tel. 021/521–2645), with its magnificent nighttime views of Corcovado, houses a discotheque and is attached to the French restaurant Rive Gauche. The biggest draw here, however, is its piano bar, popular with young professionals, which offers a varied program of jazz and MPB in an intimate candlelit setting.

Chico's Bar (Av. Epitácio Pessoa 1560, Lagoa, tel. 021/287–3514), owned by Rio night-spot entrepreneur Chico Recarey (Asa Branca, Scala, Un, Deux, Trois), often attracts musicians from his other establishments and elsewhere to this quiet night spot to jam after playing their regular gigs. Both the bar and the adjoining restaurant, Castelo da Lagoa, are big with affluent cariocas, both singles and couples.

Horse's Neck (Av. Atlântica 4270, Copacabana, tel. 021/521–3232) is an option for guests at the Rio Palace hotel, where it is located, or anyone who wants to admire the sweeping crescent of Copacabana. It is often filled with Americans and other visitors.

Jazzmania (Av. Rainha Elizabeth 769, Ipanema, tel. 021/227–2447) is Rio's number-one jazz club and the only place in town that offers jazz exclusively. Both Brazilian and international artists are featured, and the common denominator of the appreciative crowd is that they are all jazz maniacs.

Le Rond-Point (Av. Atlântica 1020, Copacabana, tel. 021/275–9922), with its red-leather banquettes just off the lobby of the Meridien hotel, gets a mixed crowd, including French tourists listening to *le jazz hot*, Brazilian-style, and locals from the local red-light district outside.

Mistura Fina (Rua Garcia D'Avila 15, Ipanema, tel. 021/259–9394), which also houses a restaurant and outdoor café tables, is a popular meeting place for Rio's well-to-do young, especially on weekends. A guitarist or pianist is featured until 10 PM, after which a livelier band takes over until 2 AM.

One Twenty One Lounge (Av. Niemeyer 121, Vidigal, tel. 021/274–1122) is among the most pleasant of the city's hotel lounges, and a convenient choice for guests at the somewhat isolated Rio Sheraton hotel. Besides visitors, the crowd usually has a number of affluent locals. Adjacent is the Italian restaurant Valentino's (*see* Chapter 6).

O Viro de Ipiranga (Rua Ipiranga 54, Laranjeiras, tel. 021/225–ive setting of a restored 18th-century building. This neighborhood, near Botafogo, is a pleasant residential one. Have your hotel check what's scheduled during your stay, since the options are some of the most varied and unusual you'll find in Rio.

People (Av. Bartolomeu Mitre 370, Leblon, tel. 021/294–0547) has a musical-instrument decor that belies its status as the most popular place in the city for listening to MPB and meeting people. Cariocas dress up for an evening here. A recently opened downstairs floor, done in a new-wave style, attracts a younger, more casual crowd.

Skylab Bar (Av. Atlântica 3264, Copacabana, tel. 021/255–8812), true to its name, occupies the top floor of the Rio Othon Palace hotel, with views of the ocean and hills on either side. This casual, small, indoor-outdoor bar sports a tropical decor and is located next to the hotel pool. It is quite popular with hotel guests, among whom are many Americans, who come for the view, drinks, and live music. This laid-back atmosphere is perfect for viewing the sunset after a day at the beach.

Cabaret

Variety is the byword of the cabaret scene in Rio, which provides visual and sensual stimulation to suit all tastes. The most extravagant of the lot are the so-called samba shows, Las Vegas–type revues whose tawny, bare-breasted beauties called *mulatas* are the most spectacular of Rio's cabaret artistes. Other types of cabaret entertainment are not so tame, including old-fashioned striptease and live sex.

Concha Verde (Pão de Açucar, Morro da Urca, tel. 021/541–3737) is the place to see a genuine samba school perform outside of Carnival season in a cabaret setting. Every Monday night (and occasionally on Thursdays), the Beija-Flor school, directed by Joãozinho Trinta, puts on an elaborately costumed show for tourists in this green concrete amphitheater on Morro da Urca, the mountain midway between the mainland and Sugarloaf. The club is reached by cable car, and the glittering nocturnal views of the city alone are worth the trip. A video presentation about Beija Flor begins at about 9 PM; the live show follows. Many sightseeing agencies, including Gray Line (Av. Niemeyer 121, São Conrado, tel. 021/274–7146), arrange escorted evenings here.

Frank's (Av. Princesa Isabel 185, Copacabana, tel. 021/275–9398) is one of the most established of many dark little clubs devoted to burlesque, striptease, and sex shows along Avenida Princesa Isabel near the Meridien hotel. The burlesque part of the show is in Portuguese, but the rest of the entertainment doesn't require a dictionary. Since the club is located in the heart of Rio's red-light district, expect to find working girls (and men dressed as such) inside and out of this club and the others in the vicinity.

Oba-Oba (Rua Humaitá 110, Botafogo, tel. 021/286–9848) is a private-house-turned-club where Oswaldo Sargentelli, known locally as Mr. Samba, emcees one of Rio's two remaining grand-scale samba shows. Brazilian themes are interspersed with snippets of patter and popular songs from tourists' native lands. The club's so-so menu is not recommended, but spectators go gaga for its famed mulatas, whose invitations to dance are eagerly taken up at the end of the show. Gray Line (Av. Niemeyer 121, São Conrado, tel. 021/274–7146) and other companies arrange escorted evenings here.

Plataforma I (Rua Adalberto Ferreira 32, Leblon, tel. 021/274–4022) holds the older and more spectacular of Rio's two samba shows, with elaborate costumes and a greater variety of Brazilian musical numbers. There are two performances each evening at 9 PM and at midnight. Although the show is strictly for tourists, the churrascaria restaurant downstairs is a popular hangout for Brazilian television personalities. Gray Line (Av. Niemeyer 121, São Conrado, tel. 021/274–7146) and other companies arrange escorted evenings here.

Teatro Alaska (Galeria Alaska, Copacabana, tel. 021/247–9842) puts on a tired transvestite show in its slightly seedy space in Galeria Alaska, a block-long arcade in Copacabana running from Avenida Nossa Senhora de Copacabana 1241 to Avenida

Atlântica 3806, parallel to Rua Francisco Sa. The passageway is the main drag of Rio's gay and lesbian scene, and since the homosexuals who go there look for money as often as love, the going gets somewhat rough at times, despite the police station at the Avenida Nossa Senhora de Copacabana end of the arcade.

Dance Clubs

In addition to discos, there are a number of places in Rio that offer uniquely Brazilian rhythms for dancing to live music. Samba clubs specialize in the beat of the country's best-known dance. *Gafieiras* are old-fashioned ballroom dance halls, usually patronized by an equally old-fashioned clientele. *Forrós* are much funkier, and feature the rhythms of Brazil's northeast. Ask your hotel to check and see if any of the clubs are holding special evenings of *lambada*—the latest dance craze to hit Brazil. Banned by President Getúlio Vargas when it first became popular in the 1930s, this sensual contact dance has recently resurfaced in São Paulo and is now beginning to make the rounds of Rio's dance halls.

Asa Branca is Chico Recarey's large and glamorous nightclub, where the decor combines modern, geometric designs with old-fashioned fixtures. Big bands, as well as gafieira and popular Brazilian musicians, keep the crowd moving about the dance floor until the wee hours. *Av. Mem de Sá 17, Lapa, tel. 021/252–0966. Closed Mon. and Tues.*

Carinhoso (Rua Visconde de Pirajá 22, Ipanema, tel. 021/287–3579) is an elegantly appointed place for dining on international cuisine amidst bright floral patterns and mirrored walls, or dancing to the beat of Brazilian or international music.

Elite is an unpretentious gafieira in a tough part of town (take a taxi here). Once inside and up the rickety stairs, however, you'll find an oasis for respectable if not necessarily affluent couples—usually middle-aged—who take their ballroom dancing seriously. It's done beneath the watchful eyes of saints' images, set in shrines and surrounded by colored lights, that adorn the walls. Both live and taped music are featured. If you'd like to learn the dances, a sign advertises afternoon classes taught by a certain Pé de Vento, which translates roughly as "feet of wind." *Rua Frei Caneca 4, Centro, tel. 021/232–3217. Closed Mon.–Thurs.*

Estudantina, like Elite, is another upstairs gafieira in the same part of town, and is also visited most safely by reserving a taxi or hotel car in advance rather than risking the streets. Ballroom dancing, usually to a live band, is the draw here. *Praça Tiradentes 79, Centro, tel. 021/232–1149. Closed Sun.–Wed.*

Forró Forrado has all the decorative charm of a high school gymnasium but attracts carioca intellectuals and nordestinos with a changing program of forró, rock, and lambada. *Rua do Catete 235, Catete, tel. 021/245–0524. Closed Mon.–Thurs.*

Sôbre as Ondas is "on the waves" overlooking Copacabana Beach with an expansive view of the ocean from its outdoor balconies. Here you can dance to live music, usually MPB or samba, and dine at the Terraço Atlântico restaurant downstairs. *Av. Atlântica 3432, Copacabana, tel. 021/287–6144. Closed Sat. and Sun.*

Un, Deux, Trois, another of Chico Recarey's many night spots, provides perhaps the most upscale ambience in Rio. A sophisticated decor of light browns and greens, plush furnishings, and soft lighting make this an ideal place for a romantic evening. There is an excellent restaurant downstairs and an intimate supper club upstairs, where Brazilian musicians play behind a small dance floor. *Av. Pasteur 520, Botafogo, tel. 021/541–3737. Closed Sun.*

Vogue (Rua Cupertino Durão 173, Leblon, tel. 021/274–8196), in addition to dancing, has a busy bar/restaurant/*karaokê* club (*see* Karaokê, below) that keeps its chic young patrons busy.

Discos

The most familiar dance options for most visitors will be Rio's discotheques (*danceterias* in Portuguese)—complete with flashing lights, loud music, and exclusive memberships. Staying at one of Rio's better hotels automatically guarantees admission to the most selective places; ask the concierge to call ahead for you. Otherwise, try to arrange to go with a member.

Biblo's Bar (Av. Epitácio Pessoa 1484, Lagoa, tel. 021/521–2645), which also houses a piano bar, is one of Rio's most active places for live music and disco dancing, and is especially popular with singles.

Caligula (Rua Prudente de Morais 129, Ipanema, tel. 021/287–1369), along with Hippopotamus, is Rio's current "in" disco. It is decorated in the glamorous decadence of the late Roman Empire, with both live and taped music providing the entertainment. Upstairs is Le Streghe, an excellent Italian restaurant. Dressing up is in order for a visit here.

Help (Av. Atlântica 3432, Copacabana, tel. 021/521–1296) is Rio's largest and noisiest disco. It attracts a huge, mixed crowd of tourists, single men, and single women, many looking to offer some "help" of their own, for a price.

Hippopotamus (Rua Barão da Torre 354, Ipanema, tel. 021/247–0351), another of Ricardo Amaral's enterprises, is the most exclusive and expensive of Rio's discos, requiring membership (available to guests of the better hotels) and a stiff cover (about $30 per person) to get in. Inside you'll find comfortable sofas and chairs covered in bright fabrics, tropical plants scattered about, and an interior garden. The disco is often closed for private parties, so be sure to call beforehand to check. Reservations are necessary, and not held past 11:30 PM.

Mistura Fina (Estrada da Barra da Tijuca 1636, Barra da Tijuca, tel. 021/399–3460) in Barra is larger than its counterpart in Ipanema (*see* Bars and Lounges, above), with a huge dance floor populated by teenyboppers from Rio's more affluent families. There is also an outdoor café.

Palace Club is the Rio Palace hotel's members-only disco. Membership is open to the hotel's guests (the Rio Palace is a favorite with Americans) and includes a large number of locals. The style is varied, and revelers can be seen sporting everything from tuxedos to jeans. *Av. Atlântica 4240, Copacabana, tel. 021/521–3232. Closed Mon.*

Studio C, in the basement of the Rio Othon Palace hotel, is another private disco, again accessible to guests of the Othon or other first-class hotels. It attracts a young, informal crowd, largely locals and visitors in their twenties. *Av. Atlântica 3264, Copacabana, tel. 021/521–5522. Closed Sun.*

Zoom (Largo de São Conrado 20, São Conrado, tel. 021/322–4179), a glitzy holding in Chico Recarey's entertainment empire, is one of Rio's flashiest discos. Its elaborate light show, six bars, and casual atmosphere attract a young crowd, usually couples.

Karaokê

One recent trend in the otherwise remarkably untrendy Rio nightlife scene is karaokê, which gets its name from the Japanese word for "empty stage." On a good night, however, the stage doesn't stay empty for long since patrons themselves soon fill it, providing the entertainment by singing songs from song sheets handed out with the dinner menu, a practice that originated in São Paulo's Japanese community long before the general public caught on to it. Music is supplied by backup tapes or, occasionally, live bands. Since the karaokê trend reached its peak a couple of years ago, clubs don't always offer it on a regular basis. Have your hotel check that it's scheduled beforehand if you feel the urge to make a spectacle of yourself, or watch others do so.

Canja (Av. Ataulfo de Paiva 375, Leblon, tel. 021/511–0484) attracts more Brazilians (though even they are now mostly tourists) than other karaokê clubs due to the presence of Ivon Curi, a popular Brazilian singer who expansively emcees the evening's proceedings in this tiny, lively space.
Limelight (Rua Ministro Viveiros de Castro 93B, Copacabana, tel. 021/542–3596), a Japanese-style bar, has a selection of some 3,000 tapes to choose from, and seemingly as many varieties of tourists as well.
Manga Rosa (Rua 19 de Fevereiro 94, Botafogo, tel. 021/266–4996) alternates karaokê with prose and poetry readings and gramophone music on various nights of the week on its upstairs level. There is also a piano bar downstairs.
Mikado (Rua Ministro Viveiros de Castro 127, Copacabana, tel. 021/541–7597), as its name implies, is decorated Japanese-style and usually gets an appropriately subdued but sophisticated mix of locals and out-of-towners.
Vogue (Rua Cupertino Durão 173, Leblon, tel. 021/274–8196) is the fanciest and busiest of the clubs that offer karaokê, and has dining and dancing besides.

Nightclubs

The live music in Rio's nightclubs ranges from large house bands evocative of Fred and Ginger's era to current stars of Brazilian jazz and MPB. For the best tables, try to reserve in advance; otherwise, arrive a little earlier than show time (generally around 11 PM). The following nightclubs serve food, but since their main attraction is usually music, it's best to eat elsewhere earlier if you're looking for serious dining. Remember that many clubs have a policy of admitting couples only; singles should have their hotel check to make sure they'll be admitted.

Asa Branca is considered by many to be a dance hall, but owner Chico Recarey made certain from the beginning that his hall would be the most glamorous in Rio, and he invited his pal King Juan Carlos of Spain to the opening. The house band plays until show time, when a major Brazilian talent usually takes over. *Av. Mem de Sá 17, Lapa, tel. 021/252–0966. Closed Mon. and Tues.*

Canecão (Av. Venceslau Braz 215, Botafogo, tel. 021/295–3044), near the Rio Sul shopping center, is the city's largest nightclub. It can seat nearly 2,500 people at the tiny tables in its cavernous space, making it the logical place for some of the biggest names on the international music scene to hold their concerts. The food here, provided by local catering queen Maria Tereza Weiss, is quite above average; sample it before the show if you're interested, since service is suspended during the performance.

Circo Voador (Arcos da Lapa, Lapa, tel. 021/265–2555) presents top MPB artists in a circus-tent setting, and after the concert you can stay and dance. There is limited seating, so be sure to reserve in advance or you may wind up sitting on the dance floor.

Noites Carioca (Morro da Urca, Pão de Açucar, tel. 021/541–3737), a club on Urca Mountain, between the mainland and Sugarloaf (and with the predictable but nonetheless breathtaking views), features Brazilian singing stars. Among those who have performed here recently are Chico Buarque de Hollanda, Milton Nascimento, and Gaetano Veloso.

Scala (Av. Afrânio de Melo Franco 292, Leblon, tel. 021/239–4448), entertainment entrepreneur Chico Recarey's flagship nightclub, recently changed its exclusively "gringo show" offerings to include well-known Brazilian musicians. Its twin spaces, I and II, are Rio's most elegantly decorated and attract a mixture of tourists and local fans of the featured performers.

Rock Clubs and Video Bars

The 1985 Rock in Rio festival finally put the city on the map as far as international rock music is concerned, and as derivative and occasionally outdated as the Hollywood Rock festival held in January may be, Rio gets fresh energy from it annually. The rest of the year Rio's rockers (who in spite of their cultivated chalk-white complexions recently refer to themselves, in English, as "darks" because of their preference for somber clothing) content themselves with a few clubs presenting MTV and other rock videos and the occasional new-wave band.

Crepúsculo de Cubatão (Rua Barata Ribeiro 543, Copacabana, tel. 021/235–2045), owned by British train robber Ronald Biggs, who has become something of a celebrity in Brazil, is the main hangout of the New-Wave crowd, known as "darks" in Rio. Here you'll barely see them amidst the moldly videos which decorate this smoky, dark room.

Esiste Um Lugar (Estrada das Furnas 3001, Barra da Tijuca, tel. 021/399–4588) holds evenings devoted to Beatles music and—believe it or not—American country-and-western music in a dark, intimate setting filled with swinging benches suspended from the ceiling.

Neal's (Rua Sorocaba 695, Botafogo, tel. 021/266–6577), Rio's longest established rock-video bar, attracts Americans and would-be Americans to a comfortable American setting with American food to watch American videos (*see* Chapter 6).

Robin Hood Pub (Av. Edson Passos 517, Alto de Boa Vista, tel. 021/268–9266) is an expansive theme-club complex, reminiscent of an English street, with dancing and videos. A game room features darts, dominoes, backgammon, and chess. Make sure you arrange for transportation back to your hotel, since taxi drivers don't like to venture this far out.

For Singles

Besides such gathering places as **Chico's Bar** or **Biblo's Bar** and other discos, plain but pleasant bars called *choperias* attract an unattached crowd. Some of the most popular are near the beaches, especially in Ipanema, and begin filling up when the crowd starts to shift inland off the sands; they also get lively again late at night. An ice-cold *chope*, or Brazilian draft beer, is the order of the day; fresh-squeezed fruit juices can also hit the spot. The drinks can usually be accompanied by petiscos if further sustenance is required.

Alberico's (Av. Vieira Souto 236, Ipanema, tel. 021/267–3793) is a choperia packed on weekends, especially the tables facing the Ipanema Beach.

Amarelinho (Praça Floriano 55B, Lapa, tel. 021/240–8434), located in the movie-theater district called Cinelândia near the Teatro Municipal, with its huge yellow awning and tiny tables, is reminiscent of a Parisian-style café, and in fact is one of Rio's oldest bohemian haunts. It is worth a visit during the daytime or in the late afternoon, when nearby office workers stop by for a chope. Avoid it after dark, since despite the presence of a sleepy police booth the area's nightlife consists largely of lowlife.

Barril 1800 (Av. Vieira Souto 110, Ipanema, tel. 021/227–2447) is another of Ipanema's unpretentious and popular beachfront choperias and a convenient meeting place before an evening at the nearby club Jazzmania (*see* Bars and Lounges, above).

Garôta de Ipanema (Rua Vinicius de Morais 49, Ipanema, tel. 021/267–8787) is where Vinicius de Morais, author of "The Girl from Ipanema," used to sit and longingly watch the song's heroine head for the beach. In homage the street has now been named for the songwriter and the bar for his song, and the longing looks continue in the best carioca tradition.

The Lord Jim Pub (Rua Paul Redfern 63, Ipanema, tel. 021/259–3047), as you might guess, is run by an Englishwoman and attracts a lively crowd of English-speakers, both native and otherwise. Chope is served in proper beer mugs (tea and Irish coffee are also available), and if drinks turn to dinner there is a full menu of pub-style specialties (*see* Chapter 6).

Lucas (Av. Atlântica 3744, Copacabana, tel. 021/247–1606), an unassuming but active choperia, ranks as Copacabana's most popular beachfront gathering spot. Draft beer has been served at this café and restaurant for more than 40 years.

9 Excursions

Introduction

by Dwight V. Gast

Visitors to Rio should realize that their exploration of this beautiful and exciting city does not have to be contained by city limits. Just a short journey away, you'll find mountains, valleys, islands thick with tropical forests, miles of unpolluted beaches, and lovingly maintained historical and architectural sites. The Serras (mountain ranges) above Rio, the Costa do Sol (Sun Coast) stretching to the east of the city, and the Costa Verde (Green Coast) curving westward to São Paulo are no secret to the residents of Rio, many of whom keep second homes in these areas.

Essential Information

Guided Tours

Though the independent traveler can easily tour the areas mentioned below by car or public transportation, the following companies can arrange guided visits. Agencies located in the towns themselves are listed in their respective sections.

Gimeza Turismo (Av. Ataulfo de Paiva 226, Leblon, 22440 Rio de Janeiro, RJ, tel. 021/294–7345).
South American Turismo (Av. Nossa Senhora de Copacabana 788, Copacabana, 22055 Rio de Janeiro, RJ, tel. 021/235–1490).
Walpax Viagens e Turismo (Rua Visconde de Pirajá 547, Ipanema, 22410 Rio de Janeiro, RJ, tel. 021/511–1242).

Dining

The area around Rio offers some of the most varied dining in Brazil, ranging from fine international cuisine to the traditional Brazilian *churrascaria* (barbecue). In the Serras, the European background of many of the area's residents led to a demand for the assortment of dining choices now found in the region: French, German, Swiss, and Russian cuisine, often accompanied by locally brewed beer.

Seafood, prepared in a variety of ways, naturally plays a main role in the coastal cuisine. *Peixe de capote* (fish cooked in lemon juice) is a specialty of the Costa do Sol; *peixe azul-marinho* (fish cooked with unripened bananas) is more often associated with the Costa Verde. Búzios, on the Costa do Sol, is known as one of the country's gastronomic capitals. Paratí, on the Costa Verde, Brazil's *cachaça* (sugarcane alcohol) capital, is the place for a *caipirinha* or a *batida*, two local cocktails.

The following price categories are used for restaurants throughout this chapter:

Category	Cost*
Expensive	over $20
Moderate	$10–$20
Inexpensive	under $10

**per person without service or drinks*

The following credit card abbreviations are used: AE, American Express; CB, Carte Blanche; DC, Diners Club; MC, MasterCard; and V, Visa.

Lodging

Accommodations outside Rio range from elegant island resorts to simple *pousadas* (inns) in colonial towns like Paratí. For all, reservations are recommended, especially from December to March and in the month of June. The following price categories are used throughout this chapter:

Category	Cost*
Very Expensive	over $120
Expensive	$90–$120
Moderate	$50–$90
Inexpensive	under $50

**double room, including full breakfast; add 10% service tax*

The following credit card abbreviations are used: AE, American Express; CB, Carte Blanche; DC, Diners Club; MC, MasterCard; and V, Visa.

The Serras

In 1832 English explorer Richard Burton said of the Serras, "It is no small matter to find within five hours of Rio de Janeiro a spot where appetite is European, where exercise may be taken freely, and where you enjoy the luxury of sitting in a dry skin." The same can still be said of this region, and modern transportation makes it even more accessible today. Once the summer home of Dom Pedro II and his court, the Serras, northeast of Rio, are still frequented by cariocas who come to enjoy the area's relatively cool climate, unspoiled natural beauty, and European culture. A car is helpful for exploring the great expanse of the **Parque Naçional da Serra dos Orgãos** (Organ Pipe Mountains National Park), although public transportation does reach both Petrópolis and Teresópolis, two of the more interesting towns in the Serras.

Tourist Information

Petrópolis **Petrotur** (Av. Barão do Amazonas 98, Centro, tel. 024/242–1466).

Teresópolis **Informações Turisticas** (Praça Olimpica, Centro, tel. 021/742–3352), **Terminal Tancredo Neves** (Saida pelo Rio de Janeiro, Alto Soberbo, tel. 021/742–2422).

Getting Around

By Car Take Federal Highway BR-040 (Estrada de Petrópolis) north from Rio to Petrópolis, or BR-116 north from Rio to Teresópolis. The two towns are linked by BR-486, which runs through the Parque Naçional da Serra dos Orgãos.

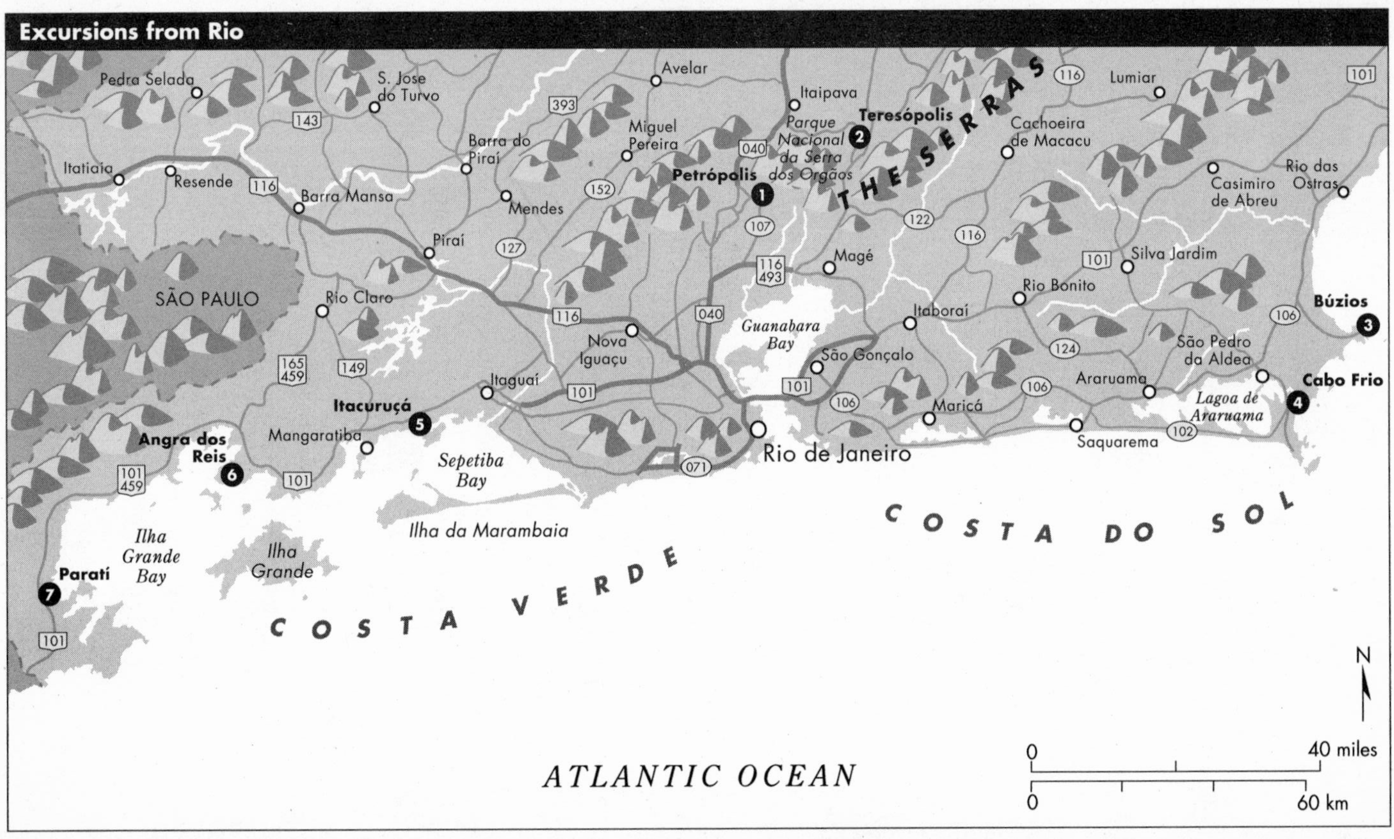
Excursions from Rio
Pedra Selada
S. Jose do Turvo
Avelar
Itaipava
Teresópolis
THE SERRAS
Lumiar
Cachoeira de Macacu
Miguel Pereira
Barra do Piraí
Parque Nacional da Serra dos Orgãos
Petrópolis
Itatiaia
Resende
Barra Mansa
Mendes
Casimiro de Abreu
Rio das Ostras
Piraí
Magé
Silva Jardim
SÃO PAULO
Rio Claro
Rio Bonito
Búzios
Nova Iguaçu
Guanabara Bay
Itaboraí
São Gonçalo
São Pedro da Aldea
Itaguaí
Araruama
Cabo Frio
Itacuruçá
Maricá
Lagoa de Araruama
Angra dos Reis
Mangaratiba
Saquarema
Rio de Janeiro
Sepetiba Bay
Ilha da Marambaia
COSTA DO SOL
Ilha Grande Bay
Ilha Grande
Paratí
COSTA VERDE
ATLANTIC OCEAN
N
0
40 miles
0
60 km
1
2
3
4
5
6
7
101
116
393
143
040
152
107
122
127
116 493
165 459
149
106
124
101 459
071
102

By Bus The **Unica Bus Company** provides bus service to Petrópolis from the following Rio de Janeiro stations: Rodoviária Novo Rio (Av. Francisco Bicalho 1, tel. 021/291–5151) and Rodoviária Menezes Cortes, known locally as "Castelo" (entrances at Rua São Jose, Primeiro de Março, Rua a Quitanda, and Av. Erasmo Braga, tel. 021/242–5414). Petrópolis's bus station is located at Rua Doutor Porciuncula 75 (tel. 024/243–1703). The **Viacão Teresópolis Bus Company** also provides service from these Rio stations to Teresópolis's bus station, located at Rua Primeiro de Maio 100 (tel. 021/742–3352). There is also service connecting Petrópolis with Teresópolis.

❶ Tour 1: Exploring Petrópolis

On the way to Petrópolis, about 4 miles outside of town, is the **Quitandinha Clube,** a large and luxurious complex built in 1944 in a Norman style, using heavy wood beams and stone, to house a fashionable casino. Gambling was outlawed in Brazil two years later, and Quitandinha was converted to a country club. Visitors can stroll the well-groomed grounds.

The main attraction in Petrópolis itself is the **Museo Imperial** (Imperial Museum), located in the center of town. Originally built as a summer palace for Emperor Dom Pedro II, the museum is full of royal memorabilia, including Dom Pedro's imperial crown, encrusted with 639 diamonds and 77 pearls, and the royal cradle, an ornate, gilded basket in the shape of a shell. When you enter the museum, you'll be given felt slippers to wear while you amble through the building on the polished wood floors amid period furniture and paintings. The heirs of Dom Pedro still occupy two mansions in town, one of which is across the street from the museum. *Museo Imperial, Rua da Imperatriz 220, Centro, tel. 024/242–7012. Nominal fee. Open Wed.–Sun., noon–5:30.*

The other principal attraction in Petrópolis is the neo-Gothic **Cathedral de São Pedro de Alcântara** on the Avenida Tiradentes, where Dom Pedro II, Empress Doña Teresa Cristina, and Princesa Isabel are entombed. Continuing along Avenida 13 de Maio, a five-minute walk from the center of town, you will find another remnant of royalty, the **Paláçio de Cristal** (Crystal Palace). Sent from France in 1884 by Count d'Eu, Dom Pedro II's son-in-law, the cast-iron and glass building was used originally to house agricultural and horticultural exhibitions, and was later converted into a ballroom. Princesa Isabel danced at a ball held here to celebrate the emancipation of the slaves on April 1, 1888. *Paláçio de Cristal, Praça da Confluencia, Rua Alfredo Pacha. Admission free. Open Tues.–Sun., 9–5.*

Down Avenida Alfredo Pacha and Avenida Roberto Silveira from the Paláçio de Cristal is **Casa de Santos Dumont,** the summer home of Brazil's Father of Aviation. In Brazil it is believed that Dumont, not America's Wright Brothers, was the first to fly. The tiny man built this vacation cabin scaled-down to his own size, so to many taller visitors it looks like a dollhouse; it now has displays of his inventions, documents, and other memorabilia. *Rua do Encanto 124. Open Tues.–Sun. 9–5.*

You might want to take Rua João Pessoa from the Casa de Santos Dumont to Rua Teresa, where a number of shops sell inexpensive *malhas* (cotton jerseys), which are produced in local industry.

Some 20 kilometers (12 miles) from Petrópolis on the road to Rio de Janeiro is the **Museu Ferreira da Cunha,** a collection of 16,000 weapons and historical instruments of torture housed in a replica of a medieval castle. *Rua Fernandes Vieira 390, tel. 024/242–6546; reservations in Rio, 021/273–9948. Nominal admission fee. Open Sat. and Sun. 9–5 by appointment only.*

Dining **Adega dos Frades.** Nineteen kilometers (12 miles) from downtown Petrópolis, this restaurant offers a sophisticated international menu with a strong Portuguese flavor. Chicken in red wine sauce, rabbit with a mustard and bacon sauce, and baked duck served with pasta are recommended dishes. *Estrada União-Industria 11421, Itaipava, no phone. Reservations not necessary. Dress: informal. AE, MC, V. Closed Mon. Moderate–Expensive.*

Majórica. The two rooms in this simple, cozy churrascaria have pine wood paneling, Spanish paintings on the walls, and an informal atmosphere. *Rua do Imperador 754, tel. 024/242–2498. Reservations not necessary. Dress: informal. AE, DC, MC, V. Moderate.*

Maloca. This restaurant is another centrally located churrascaria specializing in rodízio-style dining. The atmosphere is romantic, and the building looks like a bungalow, with lots of woodwork inside. *Rua Washington Luiz 600, tel. 024/242–3262. Reservations not necessary. Dress: informal. DC, MC, V. Moderate.*

One for the Road. This restaurant, 12 kilometers (7 miles) from downtown Petrópolis, offers some of the area's most inventive international cuisine in a cozy pub-style setting complete with fireplace. Dishes to try include a green salad with mustard vinaigrette accompanied by toast with melted goat cheese; salmon crepes with caviar and vodka sauce; roast beef with brandy, orange, and green pepper sauce; and chicken breast served with a passion fruit sauce. Leave room for the delicious desserts. *Rua Agostinho Goulão 169, Correias, no phone. Reservations not necessary. Dress: informal. Closed Mon. and Thurs. Moderate.*

Parrô do Valentim. This place, located 18 kilometers (11 miles) from downtown Petrópolis, draws large crowds for its Portuguese menu. Grilled foods are the specialty here, and pork and sardines are popular options. Other dishes include rabbit in wine sauce, eel paella, fish, and cream pastries for dessert. There's also a very good selection of wines. *Estrada União-Industria 10289, Itaipava, tel. 024/222–1281. Reservations not necessary. Dress: informal. Closed Mon. AE, MC, V. Moderate.*

Lodging **Casa do Sol.** A private residence that was converted to a hotel nine years ago, the Casa do Sol has lovely views of the surrounding countryside and lounges for visitors to relax in. Located 6 kilometers (3.7 miles) from downtown Petrópolis on the road to Rio, the hotel retains a homey feeling. *Saida Rio, Quitandinha, tel. 024/243–5062. 6 apartments, 6 suites, with private bath. Facilities: restaurant, swimming pools, game room, conference room, sauna, soccer field, tennis court, volleyball court, playground. AE, DC. Moderate.*

Margaridas. Located amid peaceful gardens and park-like grounds three minutes from downtown Petrópolis, this 20-

year-old, two-story hotel has a lounge with a fireplace, and wicker and leather furniture. Guest rooms are spacious and have wall-to-wall carpeting. There are four bungalows available. *Rua Bispo Don José Pereira Alves 235, Colina di Fatima, tel. 024/242–4686. 12 rooms, 4 cottages with private bath. Facilities: parking, swimming pool, ping-pong. No credit cards. Moderate.*

La Belle. This tiny inn, located 10 kilometers (6 miles) from Petrópolis, is a converted private residence with seven cozy guest rooms. The rooms are decorated in light colors and have exposed brick walls and floral-patterned curtains. Its restaurant, La Belle Menuiere, offers the area's best classic French cuisine. *Estrada União-Industria 2153, tel. 024/221–1084. 7 rooms with private bath. Facilities: parking. No credit cards. Inexpensive.*

❷ Tour 2: Exploring Teresópolis

Named for Empress Teresa Cristina (who kept a summer residence here), Teresópolis, which is 91 kilometers (56 miles) northeast of Rio, is now known for its summer homes, country clubs, and its proximity to the Parque Naçional da Serra dos Orgãos—a national park with mountains, distinctive rock formations, and spectacular scenery. Though the downtown area is relatively undistinguished, there are several sights in outlying areas that make a trip to Teresópolis worthwhile. A visit here may be combined with a visit to Petrópolis on the same day by car or bus or on guided tour.

For a panoramic overview of Teresópolis and the nearby countryside, follow Avenida Feliciano Sodre from the center of town to the top of **Colina dos Mirantes** hill. Also accessible from town are the **Amores waterfalls** and an adjoining public bathing resort, which lie beyond Praça Nilo Pecanha, and the **Imbú waterfalls,** located off the Estrada para Petrópolis. If you feel up to a challenging hike, you can visit these places on foot, but you will definitely need a car or taxi for Teresópolis's most notable sight, the **Parque Naçional da Serra dos Orgãos** (tel. 021/742–0266).

The park encompasses 11,000 hectares (27,170 acres) of forest, streams, waterfalls, and mountains. Visitors can take advantage of the camping and picnicking grounds, as well as the great number of hiking trails. Observers of flora and fauna will note the many species of tropical bird that inhabit the park and the numerous varieties of exotic orchid. Also located inside the park is the **Museu Von Matius,** a natural history museum. *Estrada para Niteroi, tel. 021/742–0266. Open daily 8–5.*

The park is best known for its rocky terrain. Climb to the top of the Mirante do Soberno, where, on a clear day, you can see as far as Guanabara Bay and the Costa do Sol's Cabo Frio. Mountain climbers will appreciate the park's other notable rock formations, including the *Dedo de Deus* (Finger of God), the *Dedo de Nossa Senhora* (Finger of Our Lady), the *Nariz do Frade* (Friar's Nose), and the *Agulha do Diabo* (Devil's Needle). The park's highest peak, *Pedra do Silo* (Rock of the Bell), is 2,263 meters (7,422 feet) high and may be climbed via footpath in about four hours.

Dining

Dona Irene. Excellent Russian cuisine is featured at this four-table restaurant. Owner Dona Irene, an 86-year-old immigrant from Siberia, will personally discuss with you her prix-fixe menu and explain the dishes she's been serving for 21 years. Appetizers include borscht, stuffed green peppers, and pâté; a tasty entrée is the eggplant and fish soufflé. *Rua Yeda 730, Barro Tijuca, tel. 021/742–2901. Reservations necessary. Dress: informal. No dinner Sun.; closed Mon. and Tues. No credit cards. Inexpensive.*

Lodging

Rosa dos Ventos. This three-year-old luxury resort, located on a farm 27 kilometers (16.8 miles) from Teresópolis, is patterned after a Swiss chalet. A wide range of activities are provided for its upper-crust clientele. Guest rooms are in a rustic style and emphasize the use of woodwork. Five room categories are offered, from standard to deluxe suite. *Estrada Teresópolis-Nova Friburgo, tel. 021/742–8833. 31 rooms with private bath. Facilities: parking, restaurant, swimming pool, video and game rooms, wine cellar, shopping, beauty salon, sauna, tennis court, horseback riding, lake, woods. Children under 14 not allowed. No credit cards. Expensive.*

São Moritz. Located 36 kilometers (22.4 miles) from Teresópolis on a landscaped estate, the São Moritz offers a range of activities similar to those offered at the Rosa dos Ventos. *Estrada Teresópolis-Nova Friburgo, Distreito de Vieira, tel. 021/742–4360 (reservations in Rio de Janeiro, 021/239–4445). 32 rooms with private bath. Facilities: parking, restaurant, swimming pools, game room, health facilities, sauna, soccer field, tennis courts, volleyball courts, bicycling, horseback riding, lake, paddleboats, playground, children's activities on weekends. AE, DC, MC, V. Expensive.*

Caxanga. This seven-story hotel set on spacious grounds with lovely views of the surrounding countryside is used primarily for conventions. Guest rooms are located on the three upper floors. The hotel's lounge has a fireplace, and the cafeteria turns into a bar at night. There are three categories of guest rooms: standard, special, and deluxe. *Rua Caxanga 68, Alto, tel. 021/742–1042 (reservations in Rio, 021/255–6721). 84 rooms with private bath. Facilities: parking, restaurant, swimming pools, game room, sauna, volleyball court, basketball court, tennis courts. DC, MC, V. Moderate.*

Costa do Sol

Since it was discovered by the international jet-set crowd in the 1960s, the Costa do Sol (Sun Coast) has been Rio's Côte d'Azur—a chic, tropical hot spot where handsome playboys and glamorous women congregate to see and be seen. Despite its celebrity status and its improved accessibility, the Costa do Sol retains an aura of native simplicity. Búzios is the sophisticated focal point of the Costa do Sol and a must for visitors in the area.

The Costa do Sol is easily reached by bus or taxi, but a car is necessary to explore its beautiful terrain properly. A car can also come in handy for beach hopping, one of the prime pursuits on the Sun Coast.

Tourist Information

Informações Turisticas (Rua Raul Veiga 709, Cabo Frio, tel. 024/643–1689).

Guided Tours

Ekoda Turismo (Rua Mexico 11, Room 1502, tel. 021/262–5420, 262–5237; or Búzios, Rua Manuel Turbinio de Faria 293, loja 3, tel. 024/623–1490) offers tours of Búzios from Rio de Janeiro. The company provides transport to and from Cabo Frio, as well as Jeep tours of Búzios, rides to the beaches, boat tours, and water-sports equipment.

Getting Around

By Plane **Costair Taxi Aereo** (reservations in Rio, tel. 021/220–9052; in Búzios, tel. 024/623–1303) flies directly to the Ilha Rasa airfield from Santos Dumont airport in Rio.

Companhia Votec (reservations in Rio, tel. 021/325–9044) also flies out of Santos Dumont airport to the Salinas Perinas airfield, located 18 kilometers (11 miles) from Cabo Frio.

By Car Take State Highway RJ-106 for a spectacular drive through the mountains and a mango grove. Exit for Cabo Frio on RJ-140, just before São Pedro da Aldeia; from Cabo Frio a dirt road leads to Búzios. The other route to Cabo Frio, Federal Highway BR-101 (the Cabo Frio turnoff is RJ-124 at Rio Bonito), is newer but more heavily trafficked and less scenic.

By Bus A company called **1001** (pronounced mil e oom) provides bus service from the Rodoviária Novo Rio terminal (Av. Francisco Bicalho 1, tel. 021/291–5151) in Rio de Janeiro to the Cabo Frio bus station (Av. Profesora Julia Kubitschek, tel. 024/643–1521). You can change in Cabo Frio for local bus service or a taxi to Búzios. There is also bus service from Niterói and Petrópolis.

By Taxi Taxis and private cars arranged by your hotel can take you to Búzios, Cabo Frio, or elsewhere on the Costa do Sol.

By Boat You can hire a boat with a crew to take you to Búzios. The Escola de Vela at the Marina da Glória rents everything from racing sailboats to *saveiros* (fishing boats), schooners, and large motorboats for fishing expeditions. Call 024/205–8646 and ask for Francisco Fragoso, who speaks English.

❸ Tour 1: Exploring Búzios

Búzios is the kind of place people intend to go to just for a visit. But there are many tales of folks who go home, repack their bags, quit their "nine-to-fives," and return to Búzios to stay—so many that you begin to believe those transplants who tell you that *Búzios* (Shells) is enchanted.

Whether or not the magic is real, the colony of Argentinians and Europeans who have transformed this peninsula from a sleepy fishing village to a chic enclave of multiling al professionals have devoted considerable talents and energies to their new home. Technically, Búzios is a small peninsula at the eastern end of the Costa do Sol, but cariocas also use the name to refer to the village of Armacao dos Búzios, 191 kilometers (118 miles) north of Rio (about 3½ hours by land or 30 minutes by air).

Twenty-five years ago, the fine restaurants, homey but plush pousadas, chic shops, and unique architectural style that place Búzios in the same league as St. Tropez or Mykonos didn't exist. Fishermen and their families were the only residents of Búzios before Brigitte Bardot appeared with her Brazilian boyfriend of the moment in 1964.

It was a fateful visit for Búzios, which was never the same again. With international paparazzi crawling about snapping pictures of "B.B." in the buff, someone was bound to notice the raw beauty of the cape's 23 beaches, each one offering a vista lovelier than the last. Búzios's destiny was sealed when *Paris Match* published the photos and made the town instantly and internationally famous. A French colony formed in Búzios, then a British colony grew. The peso was strong back then, and many Argentinians bought land. Those who came early were searching for relaxation and peace. People built private homes. More pousadas opened. Growth was gradual; until 1980, there were only three public phones in town, with numbers 1, 2, and 3. Those days, however, are gone.

Size has completely transformed Búzios. A permanent population of 12,000 swells to 50,000 in high season. Fancy boutiques line the small grid of the Centro district, replacing the Bohemian feel of old. New restaurants seem to be opening all the time, and Jose Hugo Celidonio, the well-known dining expert, now believes that there are three great restaurant towns in Brazil: São Paulo, Rio, and Búzios, in that order. An airstrip helps to bring in an increasing number of Búzios-bewitched visitors. Huge vacation complexes are being constructed. The boom has changed Búzios in a few, fleeting years from a solitary, unspoiled beach town to a sophisticated international watering hole.

Having a car is a great help in Búzios, since aside from the shops and restaurants concentrated along Rua das Pedras in the downtown area, the principal sights are the 23 beaches, which are accessible only by bumpy dirt roads. The beaches range from the village atmosphere of the broad strand of Armacao (which has an active nightlife scene), in the downtown area near stores and restaurants, to the isolated privacy of the tiny, horseshoe-shape Ferradurinha Cove.

Dining

Adamastor. This restaurant, located on the beach, specializes in seafood. Dishes include steamed lobster, octopus in white wine sauce, garlic shrimp, and numerous fish selections. *Rua José Bento Ribiro Dantas 712, tel. 024/623–1162. Reservations necessary. Dress: informal. No credit cards. Closed Tues. and Aug. Moderate.*

Au Cheval Blanc. First-class French and Swiss cuisine is served in a seaside setting at this restaurant. Escargot and grilled seafood, including lobster and fish, are specialties. The bar and dining room have become the unofficial meeting place for weary refugees from the city, who check in first with owner Paul Blancpain for a warm welcome, followed by a few relaxing drinks and dinner. You can eat either on the terrace overlooking the bobbing boats in the small harbor of Praia da Armaçáo, or indoors in casual ease with soft music playing in the background. *Rua José Bento Ribiro Dantas 181, tel. 024/623–1445.*

Reservations necessary. Dress: informal. No credit cards. No lunch weekdays and May–Dec. Moderate.

Satiricon. An excellent Italian restaurant featuring fish and seafood specialties, with a big selection of grilled fresh fish and shrimp, fried squid, and rock lobsters (at the high end of the menu's price scale at about $24). The *spaghetti frutos do mar* (spaghetti with seafood) comes perfectly cooked, loaded with mussels, squid, shrimp, scallops, and a tantalizing fresh herb sauce, in portions big enough to share. If you're not careful, you might fill up on the *couvert* (an array of appetizers, including cabbage salad, white bean salad, al dente eggplant and green peppers with garlic, marinated mussels, and fish in lemony sauce). *Rua José Bento Ribiro Dantas 412, tel. 024/623–1595. Reservations not necessary. Dress: informal. AE, DC, MC, V. Moderate.*

La Streghe Búzios. This is the original version of the restaurant affiliated with the Caligula disco in Rio. Decorated in the elegantly rustic style that has come to epitomize Búzios, the beachside restaurant offers a menu with a healthy balance between classic northern Italian cooking and *nuova cucina* (nouvelle cuisine). Appetizers range from the delicate *Cappelle di Funghia alla Griglia* (grilled mushrooms) to the hearty *Carpaccio al Parmigiano* (sliced raw beef covered with Parmesan cheese). The pasta is all homemade, and you can choose from gnocchi, spaghetti, tagliatelle, and tortellini in a variety of sauces. Veal, in dishes such as Saltimbocco and Scaloppine di Vitella al Limone, is a specialty here. For dessert, try *Pera delle Streghe* (pear cooked in white wine, filled with vanilla ice cream, and topped with peach, guava, or strawberry sauce, depending on the season). *Rua José Bento Ribiro Dantas 201, no phone. Reservations necessary (must be made in person). Dress: informal. AE. No lunch weekdays. Closed Mon. and Aug. Moderate.*

Lodging

Nas Rochas Club. The most sumptuous vacation complex in Búzios, this self-contained luxury resort is located on its own little island. The tropical decor in the guest rooms utilizes bamboo furniture, bright print bedspreads and curtains, and stone floors. Especially popular with couples, Nas Rochas succeeds in upholding its image as an elite hideaway for the privileged few. Transportation to other islands and beaches is provided by the hotel's schooner. *Ilha Rasa, Búzios, tel. 024/623–1303; reservations in Rio, 021/253–0001. 70 rooms with private bath. Facilities: parking, swimming pool, track, game room, beauty salon, boutiques, disco, tennis, archery, scuba, snorkeling, boating, schooners, windsurfing, social activities, medical facilities. AE, DC, MC, V. Very Expensive.*

Pousada Casas Brancas. Situated on a rise overlooking the serene waters of Praia da Armaçáo, this inn is Búzios at its best. Guests here can look forward to airy oceanfront rooms with terraces, comfortable living rooms for friendly gatherings, and a large veranda by the swimming pool where a complimentary breakfast is served. The excellent frigo bars (hotel room refrigerators) are stocked with pâté, cheese, soft drinks, fruit juices, chocolate bars, cookies, crackers, mints, milk, beer, chilled white wine, and mineral waters. *Morro Humaitá 712, Búzios, tel. 024/623–1458 (for reservations write Cx.P. 56, Cabo Frio 28900, RJ, 2 wks in advance). 18 rooms with private bath. Facilities: swimming pool, bar, restaurant. AE, CB, DC, MC, V. Very expensive.*

Pousada dos Búzios. This simple hotel, centrally located on the beach, is decorated with woodwork and a variety of furniture styles. The Pousada dos Búzios is popular with families. *Rua José Bento Ribiro Dantas 21, tel. 024/623–1155; reservations in Rio, 021/274–6608. 7 rooms with private bath. Facilities: swimming pool. AE. Inexpensive.*

4 Tour 2: Exploring Cabo Frio

Breezy Cabo Frio (Cape Cold) is the coolest spot on the Sun Coast, 168 kilometers (104 miles) east of Rio de Janeiro (about 3 hours by car). Discovered by the Portuguese in 1503, the area became the object of a power struggle between them and the French and Dutch, before becoming permanently Portuguese in 1615. Once an important center for timber and agriculture, the people of Cabo Frio eventually turned to the sea to make a living through fishing and salt extraction. Today the town boasts an unpretentious colony of sculptors, and its extensive beaches support a sizable summer community of cariocas. Though beautiful, ecological abuse threatens the future of these beaches. A day trip to unassuming Cabo Frio can be combined with a visit to the more upscale Búzios.

Most of Cabo Frio's historic monuments are churches, but since many of these are closed to visitors, you may opt to head for the beach with the rest of the crowd. One exception is **Matriz de Nossa Senhora da Assunção,** a richly decorated church in the downtown area. The church was built in 1616 and restored in 1966. *Praça Porto Rocha. Open during mass only, weekdays 6:30 AM and 7:30 PM, Sat. 7:30 PM, Sun. 7 AM, 9 AM, and 6:30 PM.*

While downtown you can also do some shopping for pottery and straw and leather goods—Cabo Frio is especially noted for its leather sandals. Usually held on weekends, the flea market and crafts fair on Rua Jonas Garcia is also open on weekdays during tourist season.

Though somewhat run down, the original French fort, **Fort São Mateus** (Praia do Forte), just outside of town, is open to the public daily 10–5:30. Nearby is the popular and centrally located **Praia do Forte** beach. Another popular beach worth visiting is the **Praia do Pero,** which is located outside of town but is accessible by the bus that leaves from the Convento dos Anjos.

Lodging

Acapulco. Located on the Dunas beach (the hotel is surrounded by sand dunes), with magnificent views of the sea, this casual hotel caters to families. The rustic, L-shape building is decorated with heavy wood furniture and lots of plants, and guest rooms are furnished in soothing white and beige. *Rua 14, lote E, tel. 024/643–0202. 64 rooms with private bath. Facilities: restaurant, 3 pools, playground, sauna, volleyball court, parking, game room, sauna, soccer court. AE, DC. Moderate.*

Pousada Portoveleiro. This hotel, with a great location in front of two channels just 6 kilometers (3.7 miles) north of Cabo Frio in Ogiva, is popular with families and honeymooners. All guest rooms face the water and are decorated in a rustic colonial style with cool white walls and ceramic tiles on the floors. *Av. dos Espadartes 129, Caminho Verde, Ogiva, 28900, tel. 024/643–3081; reservations in Rio, tel. 021/231–0944. 24 rooms with private bath. Facilities: restaurant, bar, 2 pools, sauna, water sports. AE, DC, MC, V. Moderate.*

Costa Verde

The Costa Verde (Green Coast), Rio's south shore, curves around Sepetiba and Ilha Grande bays and stretches westward toward São Paulo. As in Cabo Frio in the north, excessive development of this coastline threatens ecological ruin within the next few years. Ecologists warn that the fish in Sepetiba Bay are gradually becoming extinct, and soon the waters here will be as polluted by traffic and sewage as in any city beach.

Fortunately for visitors in the immediate future, paradise is not yet lost. Thirty-six islands are scattered throughout Sepetiba Bay, and scores more extend down the coast between Angra dos Reis and Paratí, two colonial towns in Costa Verde with an abundance of historical wealth.

The coastal drive from Rio is filled with magnificent views of the two bays on one side and mountains covered with tropical forests, banana plantations, and waterfalls on the other. Although the most convenient way to explore this coast is in a car, there is regular bus service available to the Costa Verde areas. Also, long fishing boats called saveiros and other water craft can provide transportation to and among the many islands in the bay.

You can get a taste of the islands in just one day by taking a short bus ride to Itacuruçá, transferring to a saveiro for a cruise out to sea, then stopping at one of the islands with hotel and restaurant facilities for an afternoon of relaxation on the beach.

Tourist Information

Angra dos Reis **Informações Turisticas** (Largo da Lapa, tel. 024/365–1175).

Paratí **Informações Turisticas** (Av. Roberto da Silveira, Praça Macedo Soares, tel. 024/371–1631).

Guided Tours

A number of tour operators run a **Tour das Ilhas Tropicals,** and it's a good value for people with time restrictions. Book the trip through your hotel or travel agent. A bus will pick you up between 8 and 9 AM at your hotel and drop you off there at the end of the day.

The following agencies offer schooner tours of Sepetiba Bay from Itacuruçá:

Itacuruçá Turismo (Av. Raphael Levy Miranda 439, tel. 021/780–1710; reservations in Rio, 021/259–2599).
Passamar (Rua Evelina 37, tel. 021/780–1776; reservations in Rio, 021/236–4136).
Saverios Tour (Praça Macilio Dias 2, tel. 021/780–1003; reservations in Rio, 021/287–5796). The oldest of the operators, Saverios offers a day trip, including lunch, with stops at Jaguanum, dos Martins, and Itacuruçá islands.
Sepetiba Turismo (Praça Padre Luiz Quatropani 40, tel. 021/780–1959; reservations in Rio, 021/235–2893 or 021/235–2889) has tours with stops at Jaguanum Island for lunch and a swim.

The following agencies provide schooner tours of Angra dos Reis and the bay of Ilha Grande. A buffet lunch on one of the islands is included:

Mar de Angra (Travessa Santa Luzia 35, tel. 024/365–1350).

Tropical Angra Tur (Cais de Santa Luzia 231, tel. 024/365–0402).

Getting Around

By Car Federal Highway BR-101 west from Rio passes through Itacuruçá, Angra dos Reis, and Paratí.

By Bus The **Eval Bus Company** provides service from Rodoviária Novo Rio bus terminal in Rio (Av. Francisco Bicalho 1, tel. 021/291–5151) to the Itacuruçá bus stop (Ponto de Onibus, Praca Nilo Pecanha, no phone), the Angra dos Reis bus station (Largo da Lapa, tel. 024/365–1280), and the Paratí bus station (Av. Roberto da Silveira, tel. 024/371–1196). Eval also provides service to Angra dos Reis from Niterói; the **Colitur Bus Company** provides connections between Paratí and Angra dos Reis.

5 Tour 1: Exploring Itacuruçá

Itacuruçá, 82 kilometers (51 miles) west of Rio de Janeiro, is known to cariocas for its numerous yacht clubs and luxury accommodations.

Itacuruçá is primarily a departure point for excursions in its section of the bay; there is little to see in the town itself. **Igreja de Santana** (Praça Padre Luiz Quatropani) is the town's church, dating from 1840. The beach, **Praia de Itacuruçá,** is a pleasant place for a stroll before taking a schooner tour of Ilha, Itacuruçá, Jaguanum, Martins, and other islands in the bay.

6 Tour 2: Exploring Angra dos Reis

Today Angra dos Reis (Bay of Kings) is known principally for its wild, beautiful beaches and the hundreds of islands off its coast, but during the 17th century the "Vila dos Reis Magos da Ilha Grande" was a haven for pirates and one of the most important ports of Brazil. By 1749 there were 15 sugar mills and 91 related factories, evidence of a substantial agricultural, commercial, and industrial base. Angra's stagnation began after the completion of a railroad connecting Rio and São Paulo, which depleted the shipping trade. The emancipation of the slaves in the late 1800s led to the floundering of Angra's manpower-intensive economy. The town turned to fishing and faded into obscurity.

The tables turned in the early 1970s when the Rio-Santos Highway opened, linking Angra to Brazil's two population centers and opening the area to tourism. The city itself is 151 kilometers (94 miles) west of Rio, about a three-hour drive.

Angra contains a mixture of colonial and industrial architecture from its days as a port and sugar-processing center. The city is alive with boating, fishing, and water-related activities, especially around Carnival, when it becomes a floating celebration. The *Festas Juninas* (June Festivals) are marked by folk music, dance competitions, and a great party. Beginning at the tourist information office, just off the town dock, walk to Rua do Comércio 206, where a nameless artisan's shop sells local clay and wood crafts. Farther along that same street you'll notice the **Capela de Santa Luzia** (open 8–11 AM), a chapel dating from 1632.

At the end of Rua do Comércio is a 16th-century convent, the **Convento de Nossa Senhora do Carmo,** and an adjacent 17th-century church of the same name (Rua Doutor Coutinho at the corner of Rua Frei Inacio; open weekdays 7–8 PM, Sun. 6–9 AM and 5–6 PM). Continuing along Rua da Conceição, you'll pass the 17th-century church, **Igreja Matriz de Nossa Senhora da Conceição,** at Praça General Silvestre Travassos. Up the hill from here, on Morro de Santo Antonio, is Angra's most impressive historical monument, the **Convento de São Bernardo de Sena** (open Tues.–Sun. 8–11:30 AM and 1–5 PM), an 18th-century monastery built on the site of the original 17th-century monastery.

Back at the port, the Conerj company on the Lapa quay (Cais da Lapa) offers ferry service (Mon., Wed., and Fri. at 4 PM) to **Ilha Grande,** the bay's main attraction. Ilha Grande offers simple accommodations and camping—you're almost sure to find your own private beach. Be sure to register with the police in the village of Abraão if you're spending time on the island.

Dining

Chez Dominique. Located in the Hotel do Frade, this restaurant offers seafood specialties with a French touch. A pleasant outdoor deck overlooks a canal. *BR-101, Km 123 (Estrada para Ubatuba), tel. 024/365–1212. Reservations not necessary. Dress: informal. AE, DC, MC, V. Moderate.*

Lodging

Club Med-Rio das Pedras. This new, colonial-style Club Med village is nestled between the mountains and the bay on a crescent-shape stretch of beach. Guests are accommodated in air-conditioned bungalows furnished with twin beds. The facilities and activities are extensive, with an emphasis on land and water sports, including soccer, tennis (nine tennis courts lit at night), and bay excursions. The Mini Club program provides plenty of activities for children ages 6 to 10. *Estrado Rio Santos, Km55, Mangaratiba, tel. 800/CLUB MED for reservations. 325 rooms with private bath. Facilities: tennis courts, squash courts, fitness center, sailing, windsurfing, waterskiing, pool, soccer, volleyball, basketball, handball. AE, CB, DC, MC, V. Very Expensive.*

Portogalo. Located on a cliff overlooking Ilha Grande Bay, the Portogalo provides one of the most breathtaking views on the Costa Verde. The public spaces are inviting and the comfortable guest rooms feature exposed brick walls, wall-to-wall carpeting, and bright floral-patterned bedspreads and curtains. Open-air lifts, similar to ski lifts, carry guests down to the beach, where there are cottages, a marina, and an excellent buffet-style restaurant. Day-long bay cruises departing from the hotel are available. The hotel provides air-conditioned coach transportation for guests traveling from Rio. *BR-101, Km 71, Itapinhoacanga, tel. 024/365–1022; reservations in Rio, 021/267–7375. 100 rooms with private bath. Facilities: parking, restaurant, swimming pool, sauna, tennis courts, soccer field, windsurfing. AE, DC, MC, V. Very Expensive.*

Hotel do Frade. Situated on a semiprivate beach between Angra and Paratí, the Hotel do Frade is an ideal retreat for families, featuring plenty of activities for children in a safe, supervised environment. This fully equipped luxury resort offers a wide range of activities, including horseback riding and golfing on a tournament-size 18-hole course. Guest rooms and public areas reflect the hotel's tropical setting in bright print fabrics and wood furniture. For a delightful dining experience try Chez Dominique, an excellent French restaurant located at the hotel. *BR-101, Km 123 (Estrada para Ubatuba), tel. 024/365–1212; reservations in Rio, 021/267–7375. 134 rooms with private bath. Facilities: parking, restaurant, game room, boutique, sauna, tennis, soccer court, golf, horseback riding, bicycling, boating, snorkeling, scuba, playground. AE, DC, MC, V. Expensive.*

7 Tour 3: Exploring Paratí

The city of Paratí, 241 kilometers (149 miles) outside of Rio, was originally a prominent shipping town involved in the trade and transport of precious stones and metals, slaves, tobacco, and a number of other commodities.

When the construction of a more direct route to Rio caused a drastic decrease in the shipping business, the residents of Paratí turned to the manufacturing of *cachaça* (sugarcane alcohol) to support themselves. While connoisseurs still consider Paratí's cachaça to be the best in the country, the emancipation of the slaves in 1888 crippled the sugarcane industry, condemning Paratí to a state of gradual decay.

In 1954 the construction of a new road ended Paratí's isolation. The tranquil beauty and historic flavor of this lovely town were discovered, and Paratí experienced a revival. Today, it is well known for its *Festa do Divino* and frequent folkloric events.

Considered one of the world's richest reserves of 18th-century architecture, Paratí contains a charming historic center—a collection of whitewashed buildings with tiled roofs and brightly painted wood doors and shutters, neatly aligned along cobblestoned streets. No traffic, except for the occasional horse cart, is allowed here. The six square blocks of this historic section are recognized as a national monument in Brazil and have been placed on UNESCO's World Heritage List. As you walk through these quiet streets, you can hear birds singing and the clang of the old iron city gate closing as it did at nightfall during colonial times. At the waterfront, stroll to the end of the pier, then turn around for a priceless view of the past.

Enter the historic section of the city from the tourist office on Avenida Roberto da Silveira, where bamboo, straw, and wood crafts are on sale. Following the same street, which becomes Rua Maria Jacome de Mello, turn left on Rua da Patitiba, and follow it until you reach Beco do Proposito, where you'll see the **Capela da Generosa,** a chapel near the Pereque-Acu River. From here the Travessa do Gragoata leads past a row of *sobrados* (two-story structures characteristic of 19th-century Brazilian architecture) to the **Igreja Matriz Nossa Senhora dos Remedios,** an unfinished 18th-century church that was supposed to serve the city's white middle-class families (each social stratum had its own separate church in Colonial Brazil). Continue along the river to where it meets the bay at the **Igreja das Dores,** a church built in 1800 for the city's aristocrats. Follow Rua Fresca three blocks ahead and turn right on Rua Doutor

Samuel Costa. Where it intersects with Rua Tenente Francisco Antônio four blocks ahead, you'll find the **Igreja do Rosario,** a church erected in 1735 for the city's slaves. Turn left on Rua Tenente Francisco Antônio and walk two blocks to Rua Maria Jacome de Melo.

Here you will see one of Paratí's most beautiful buildings, the **Sobrado dos Bonecos.** From the sobrado, Rua Santa Rita leads to **Igreja de Santa Rita,** the oldest church in Paratí, built in 1722 for the city's mulattos. Next to it is the **Museu de Arte Sacra** (tel. 024/371–1620; open Tues.–Sun. 9–5), the city's museum of sacred art. Rua Santa Rita then leads toward the bay to the Mercado vegetable market. Out on the water beyond the market you can watch the town's fishermen transporting the day's catch.

A kilometer (half mile) along the Praia do Pontal beach is **Forte Defensor Perpetuo** (Morro da Vila Velha, tel. 024/371–1165), a 1703 fort that provides visitors with a magnificent view of the surroundings.

Dining **Fazenda Murycana.** This casual restaurant offers basic Brazilian cuisine on a 17th-century colonial farm located outside of town. The restaurant has a simple, rustic decor with tile floors and stone and wood walls. It is considered one of the best places to sample *aguardente* (sugarcane liquor). Specialties of the house include *feijoada* (black bean and pork dish), roast pork, chicken with chicken blood sauce, and fish fillet with shrimp sauce. *Estrada para Cunha, tel. 024/371–1153. Reservations not necessary. Dress: informal. No dinner. No credit cards. Inexpensive.*

Hiltinho. Located on the main square close to Igreja da Matriz, this well-preserved former colonial house offers diners a simple, cozy environment. The interior is pleasant, with 15 tables, fresh flowers, and ceramic tile floors. The restaurant offers a number of delicious seafood dishes, the specialty of the house. *Rua Marechal Doedoro 233, tel. 024/371–1432. Reservations not necessary. Dress: informal. No credit cards. Inexpensive.*

Santa Rita. This simple restaurant was originally the first hotel in town. Modified now and decorated with antique furniture, knickknacks, and a colonial facade, Santa Rita has 15 tables and a cheery family environment. Be sure to try the seafood and the feijoada. *Rua Santa Rita 2, tel. 024/371–1206. Reservations not necessary. Dress: informal. No credit cards. Inexpensive.*

Lodging **Frade Pousada Paratí.** This cozy, simple little inn is housed in one of Paratí's many colonial buildings. Rooms are decorated in a colonial style with brightly painted wood furniture that contrasts the plain, whitewashed walls. The dining room has large windows that look out on the town's quiet streets. There is also a private tropical garden. The hotel provides air-conditioned coach transportation for guests arriving from Rio de Janeiro. *Rua do Comercio 1, tel. 024/371–1205; reservations in Rio, 021/267–7375. 44 rooms with private bath. Facilities: parking, restaurant, swimming pool. AE, DC, MC, V. Moderate.*

Index

Personal Itinerary

Departure *Date*

Time

Transportation

Arrival *Date* *Time*

Departure *Date* *Time*

Transportation

Accommodations

Arrival *Date* *Time*

Departure *Date* *Time*

Transportation

Accommodations

Arrival *Date* *Time*

Departure *Date* *Time*

Transportation

Accommodations

Personal Itinerary

Arrival *Date* *Time*

Departure *Date* *Time*

Transportation

Accommodations

Arrival *Date* *Time*

Departure *Date* *Time*

Transportation

Accommodations

Arrival *Date* *Time*

Departure *Date* *Time*

Transportation

Accommodations

Arrival *Date* *Time*

Departure *Date* *Time*

Transportation

Accommodations

Personal Itinerary

Arrival *Date* *Time*

Departure *Date* *Time*

Transportation

Accommodations

Arrival *Date* *Time*

Departure *Date* *Time*

Transportation

Accommodations

Arrival *Date* *Time*

Departure *Date* *Time*

Transportation

Accommodations

Arrival *Date* *Time*

Departure *Date* *Time*

Transportation

Accommodations

Addresses

Name

Address

Telephone

Name

Address

Telephone

Name

Address

Telephone

Name

Address

Telephone

Name

Address

Telephone

Name

Address

Telephone

Name

Address

Telephone

Name

Address

Telephone

Name

Address

Telephone

Name

Address

Telephone

Name

Address

Telephone

Name

Address

Telephone

Name

Address

Telephone

Name

Address

Telephone

Name

Address

Telephone

Name

Address

Telephone

Addresses

Name

Address

Telephone

Name

Address

Telephone

Name

Address

Telephone

Name

Address

Telephone

Name

Address

Telephone

Name

Address

Telephone

Name

Address

Telephone

Name

Address

Telephone

Name

Address

Telephone

Name

Address

Telephone

Name

Address

Telephone

Name

Address

Telephone

Name

Address

Telephone

Name

Address

Telephone

Name

Address

Telephone

Name

Address

Telephone

Notes

Notes

Notes

Notes

Fodor's Travel Guides

U.S. Guides

Alaska
Arizona
Atlantic City & the New Jersey Shore
Boston
California
Cape Cod
Carolinas & the Georgia Coast
The Chesapeake Region
Chicago
Colorado
Dallas & Fort Worth
Disney World & the Orlando Area
Florida
Hawaii
Houston & Galveston
Las Vegas
Los Angeles, Orange County, Palm Springs
Maui
Miami, Fort Lauderdale, Palm Beach
Michigan, Wisconsin, Minnesota
New England
New Mexico
New Orleans
New Orleans (Pocket Guide)
New York City
New York City (Pocket Guide)
New York State
Pacific North Coast
Philadelphia
The Rockies
San Diego
San Francisco
San Francisco (Pocket Guide)
The South
Texas
USA
Virgin Islands
Virginia
Waikiki
Washington, DC
Williamsburg

Foreign Guides

Acapulco
Amsterdam
Australia, New Zealand, The South Pacific
Austria
Bahamas
Bahamas (Pocket Guide)
Baja & the Pacific Coast Resorts
Barbados
Beijing, Guangzhou & Shanghai
Belgium & Luxembourg
Bermuda
Brazil
Britain (Great Travel Values)
Budget Europe
Canada
Canada (Great Travel Values)
Canada's Atlantic Provinces
Cancun, Cozumel, Yucatan Peninsula
Caribbean
Caribbean (Great Travel Values)
Central America
Eastern Europe
Egypt
Europe
Europe's Great Cities
Florence & Venice
France
France (Great Travel Values)
Germany
Germany (Great Travel Values)
Great Britain
Greece
The Himalayan Countries
Holland
Hong Kong
Hungary
India, including Nepal
Ireland
Israel
Italy
Italy (Great Travel Values)
Jamaica
Japan
Japan (Great Travel Values)
Jordan & the Holy Land
Kenya, Tanzania, the Seychelles
Korea
Lisbon
Loire Valley
London
London (Great Travel Values)
London (Pocket Guide)
Madrid & Barcelona
Mexico
Mexico City
Montreal & Quebec City
Munich
New Zealand
North Africa
Paris
Paris (Pocket Guide)
People's Republic of China
Portugal
Rio de Janeiro
The Riviera (Fun on)
Rome
Saint Martin & Sint Maarten
Scandinavia
Scandinavian Cities
Scotland
Singapore
South America
South Pacific
Southeast Asia
Soviet Union
Spain
Spain (Great Travel Values)
Sweden
Switzerland
Sydney
Tokyo
Toronto
Turkey
Vienna
Yugoslavia

Special-Interest Guides

Health & Fitness Vacations
Royalty Watching
Selected Hotels of Europe
Selected Resorts and Hotels of the U.S.
Shopping in Europe
Skiing in North America
Sunday in New York

Help us evaluate hotels and restaurants for the next edition of this guide, and we will send you a free issue of Fodor's newsletter, TravelSense.

Title of this guide:

1 **Hotel ❑** **Restaurant ❑** *(check one)*

Name

Number/Street

City/State/Country

Comments

2 **Hotel ❑** **Restaurant ❑** *(check one)*

Name

Number/Street

City/State/Country

Comments

3 **Hotel ❑** **Restaurant ❑** *(check one)*

Name

Number/Street

City/State/Country

Comments

General Comments

Please complete for a free copy of TravelSense

Name

Number/Street

City/State/Zip